EARLY ENGLISH STAGES

1300 to 1660

Volume Four Requiem and an Epilogue

EARLY ENGLISH STAGES 1300 to 1660
By
Glynne Wickham

Volume One 1300 to 1576

Volume Two 1576 to 1660, Part I

Volume Two 1576 to 1660, Part II

Volume Three Plays and their Makers to 1576

Volume Four Requiem and an Epilogue

EARLY ENGLISH STAGES

1300 to 1660

Volume Four Requiem and an Epilogue

by

GLYNNE WICKHAM

London and New York

First published 2002
by Routledge
11 New Fetter Lane, London EC4P 4EE

Simultaneously published in the USA and Canada
by Routledge
29 West 35th Street, New York, NY 10001

Routledge is an imprint of the Taylor & Francis Group

© 2002 Glynne Wickham

Typeset by RefineCatch Limited, Bungay, Suffolk
Printed and bound in Great Britain by
TJI Digital, Padstow, Cornwall

British Library Cataloguing in Publication Data
A catalogue record for this book is available from the British Library

Library of Congress Cataloging in Publication Data
A catalog record for this book has been requested

ISBN 0–415–19782–1 (set)
ISBN 0–415–20304–X (volume 4)

Disclaimers

The publishers have made every effort to contact authors/copyright
holders of works reprinted in *Early English Stages 1300 to 1660*.
This has not been possible in every case, however, and we
would welcome correspondence from those individuals/
companies whom we have been unable to trace.

References within each chapter are as they appeared in the
original complete work.

Frontispiece The Ruins of Tintern Abbey, near Monmouth.

For

my grandchildren

LAURA, ALICE and MELISSA WICKHAM;

ORLANDO, FLORA and PERDITA PARTNER;

and

HAMISH, ISOBEL and ISLA WICKHAM

PREFACE

IN preparing this fourth and final volume of *Early English Stages*, my principal concern has been to supply readers of the preceding volumes with the one aspect of their contents that has thus far been almost wholly neglected. This is an overview of the re-birth of drama within Christian society in Western Europe late in the tenth century AD; its subsequent development into ever-widening educative and pleasurable productions throughout the next six centuries, followed by a sudden eclipse which in England was provoked by a constitutional crisis that culminated in the outbreak of a Civil War in 1642 which brought all acting, both in London and the provinces, to an end for nearly twenty years.

In attempting to repair this omission within the pages of this volume, my task has thus been to try first to disentangle the explicitly dramaturgical and theatrical skeins of the narrative from those shifts of direction in the external religious, political, economic and social pressures operating upon them century by century, and then to relate them to each other again in a coherent, if inevitably simplified, form. To correct possible imbalances resulting from this process, I have chosen (in many instances within the text itself) to refer readers back to those pages or illustrations in the earlier volumes that serve to amplify with firm, factual evidence what may seem here to be offered as mere assertions.

This volume is accordingly divided into three distinct parts. Book I, 'The Forging of Dramatic Art in Christian Europe and its Theatrical Representation, *c.* 975–1530', covers all forms of drama and its realisation in performance (both religious and secular) that were brought into being under the aegis of the Roman Catholic Church, and supplemented by the landed aristocracy in rural districts and by the civic authorities in the cities and large market towns during what can be undisputedly described as the Middle Ages—i.e. between *c.* 975 and the accession of the House of Tudor to the English throne in 1485.

It thus starts with a survey of the relationship between those seasonal festivals habitually observed in pre-Christian times as adapted for licensed celebration within the Christian Calendar, and the recourse taken to dramatic and theatrical means of externalising their significance in order to explain this to illiterate audiences: or, in words more frequently used at that time, the exposition of 'earnest' (Christian doctrine) through recourse to 'game' or 'play' which, during the eleventh and twelfth centuries, came to be regarded as legitimising play-acting both to reinforce faith and to serve as a major force in the education of an illiterate laity.

This is then followed in Chapters 2 and 3 by an examination of the ecclesiastical and secular festivals used for these purposes. From there, it extends outwards in Chapters 4 and 5 to a more detailed study of the conditions under which the preponderantly anonymous medieval play-makers, actors and theatrical craftsmen were employed, and through which they developed their skills in meeting the rapidly expanding demands made upon them through the thirteenth, fourteenth and fifteenth centuries.

Book II—'Change and Innovation'—adopts the same method but to different ends. The first of these is to take notice of the startlingly new perspectives opened up between 1470 and 1530 by the invention of printing and gunpowder; by the discoveries of maritime explorers; by the revolution in approaches to education begun by the introduction of the study of Greek and classical Latin into English schools, universities and law-schools; and by the emergence of militant forms of national self-consciousness in the palaces of continental Europe.

The second was an attack, fuelled by a rising tide of anti-clericism, on the Pope's authority to govern the Church that was to fracture the universality of Roman Catholic doctrine as previously accepted in Germany, Switzerland, France and England irreparably, and to bring monastic life to an end.

Both of these changes were radical enough to force Tudor play-makers, actors and audiences alike to come to terms with them in ways that were at best unfamiliar to them and at worst could involve arrest, fines or imprisonment, and possible loss of life.

Among the most important of these changes was the rapid acceleration in the numbers of small groups of actors privately maintained as household servants by members of the nobility and landed gentry who were licensed by their masters, when not required for household duties, to travel beyond the borders of their own Counties and present their repertoire of short plays wherever they could find audiences willing to pay to see and hear them, especially in London; the appearance at schools like Eton and St. Paul's of boys as actors in plays by Roman authors; and the adaptation of Moral Interludes to include subject-matter of overtly political and religious polemic.

Subsuming all of these changes, however, and others like them, was the wholesale politicisation of virtually all forms of drama—religious and secular—that accompanied the Reformation of the government of the Church in England between 1531 and 1536, followed by the dissolution of the Monasteries between 1536 and 1540: for this obliged King Henry VIII and all his Tudor successors to introduce stage-censorship (to replace that formerly exercised by the Vatican in Rome and its clerical agents in England) implemented by recourse to Parliamentary Statutes over all plays prior to both performance and subsequent publication: and that, in its turn, led on to the making of latter-day martyrs out of those play-makers and actors proved guilty of ignoring these regulations between 1540 and 1559.

All these matters are treated in the order in which they arose in Chapters 6 and 7, and place question marks over the supposed replacement of 'medieval' methods of both play-construction and emblematic visual realisation of them by 'renaissance' alternatives when set in the context of a reversion to Roman Catholic observances of all ecclesiastical Calendar holidays between 1553 and 1558 which brought with it a licensed resumption of performances of religious plays created to celebrate the Feast of Corpus Christi and the lives and deeds of patron saints and martyrs. All such question marks, however, inevitably returned into the foreground of the political arena five years later when Mary I was succeeded by her Protestant half-sister, Elizabeth I, in 1559. This became evident at once when the Papal Nuncio presented his credentials to his new Sovereign: speaking in his most polished Italianate Latin he was answered by Elizabeth in Greek.

Chapter 8 thus sets out to supply its readers with an explanation for the extension of the reprieve already granted to performances of overtly religious plays for a further ten years, and to provide them with the reasons that provoked the final decision to suppress them during the 1570s. It seeks also to direct readers' attention towards the paradox implicit in the fact that within the same years that York, Chester, Wakefield, Coventry and Carlisle were being stripped by the Privy Council (through its agents in the North of England) of their right to organise, finance and stage productions of their own repertoires of religious plays, licences were being granted simultaneously to professional actors and property developers in London to erect at least three custom-built public playhouses and one private theatre for the regular performance of plays on weekdays.

While we may properly regard this as the datum-point marking transition from one form of theatrical activity regarded by the State as legitimate to another, we would perhaps be closer to the truth were we to regard it as a transfiguration; for apart from the subject-matter of those plays commissioned by the commercially-motivated actor-managers of the new playhouses, the methods of play-construction and theatrical representation used by the poets, actors and craftsmen whom they employed remained as firmly rooted in the precedents established within those same medieval religious plays that were being forcibly suppressed as they ever were before. It is my contention that this was dictated principally by a commercially-driven desire to retain both the homogeneity and loyalty of those audiences for whom play-going had already become and still remained a favourite recreational activity at prices they could still afford to pay.

The Epilogue that concludes the final volume is directed towards three residual aspects of what may legitimately be described as 'medieval drama and theatre' which might otherwise be ignored or overlooked.

First, its qualitative as opposed to its strictly chronological zenith: for this, as I continue to maintain here as in the earlier volumes of *Early English Stages*, is to be found neither in 1485 nor in 1530, but within that canon of plays which received their first performance within Shakespeare's working lifetime as actor, poet and play-maker.

Next, its swift disintegration and final collapse under the twin pressures of commercial exigency allied to social élitism on the one hand, and increasing Puritan hostility to the continuance of play-acting in Britain between approximately 1612 and 1642.

Thirdly, it exists to remind readers of the slow, but steadily more active renewal of interest in all aspects of Gothic art, architecture and literature that accompanied German romanticism late in the eighteenth century which was to attain its musical, dramatic and theatrical fulfilment during the latter half of the twentieth century when realised through the use of original instruments and 'open stages'.

Once freed from the tyranny exercised in theatres throughout the eighteenth and nineteenth centuries by the proscenium arch, and by the consequent lifting of the restrictions it had placed upon dramatists by obliging them to pursue pictorial realism in scenic representation (and as cinematic motion-pictures moved into their ascendance during the first decade of the twentieth century), so play-makers, actors and their audiences began to recover the freedom to exercise their imaginations that had been their shared prerogative throughout the Middle Ages. It thus again became possible, through recourse to poetic images and allusions in the scripting of plays, and to emblematic methods of staging them, to abstract the 'earnest' underpinning the recreational appeal of theatre-going measured in terms of 'game and play'. What was still lacking was that 'sense of occasion' which had proved to be so attractive to medieval audiences; but even that has begun to resurrect itself within the fast-growing number and locations of Festivals devoted to literature, music and drama. Many of these have continued to win sufficient popular support to have become annual events—like Corpus Christi plays during the fourteenth and fifteenth centuries before them—of which those at Aldeburgh, Cheltenham, Bath, Hay-on-Wye, Malvern, Leeds and Edinburgh can now be cited as outstanding and enduring examples.

ACKNOWLEDGEMENTS

I HAVE first to thank the University of Bristol for the award of the Senior Research Fellowship that has been renewed annually throughout the years that it has taken me to assemble this fourth and final volume of *Early English Stages,* and has thus enabled me to complete the task which I began on joining the staff of this University as a Probationary Junior Fellow in its newly established Department of Drama in 1948.

I have also to thank Professor Herbert Berry at the University of Saskatchewan and Professor William Ingram at the University of Michigan who, as friends, colleagues and co-editors of *English Professional Theatre, 1530–1660* for the Cambridge University Press's series *Theatre in Europe: a documentary history,* have provided me with many of the source materials referred to in Chapter 8 of this book.

I must likewise thank Professor Alexandra Johnston at the University of Toronto for her tireless energy and exemplary scholarship in both launching and overseeing (with invaluable financial assistance from the Canada Council) the twelve volumes thus far published of *Records of Early English Drama:* for she, and their respective volume editors, have between them greatly extended the factual evidence that has suddenly become available to students of medieval drama and theatre throughout England during the past twenty years, and which has assisted me in the preparation of Chapters 4 to 7 of this book.

To Dr. Oliver Neville and Professor Martin White, I am indebted for the time and courtesy extended to me in reading early drafts of one chapter or another in this book, and for drawing my attention to evidence that I had overlooked, and for making suggestions that resulted in the removal of ambiguities or errors that might otherwise have still been present in the text.

In this respect, I must extend especial thanks to the Rt. Rev. Peter Firth for his painstaking assistance in navigating a passage through the treacherous rocks and rapids that await historians who choose to chart a course through the turbulent waters of those political and theological changes in English social and cultural life occasioned by the Reformation, and that were, in their turn, to

ACKNOWLEDGEMENTS

affect playmakers, actors and audiences alike between 1530 and 1580.

Finally, I would like to thank Frances Parkes, Paula White and Natalie Foster at Routledge for the constant encouragement and support that I have received in bringing this book to its conclusion in its new format of five volumes within four.

Publisher's acknowledgements

The Publishers would like to thank the following for permission to reprint their material:

CADW: Welsh Historic Monuments, 'The ruins of Tintern Abbey, near Monmouth, as they appear today'. Crown Copyright.

St. George Orthodox Information Service, 'Ikon of St. Alban, Protomartyr of Britain; The Brotherhood of St. Seraphim of Savor, Burgundy, Suffolk'.

St. Deiniol's Library and R. J. L. Smith and Associates, 'The miracle of the transforming of water into wine at the wedding feast in Cana, Galilee'. Photograph by R. J. L. Smith of Much Wenlock.

Bob Trubshaw, '"The Green Man"; a recurring figure in English Literature, folklore and church carvings, here seen as a roof-boss in Warmington church, Cambridgeshire'. © Bob Trubshaw.

J. Salmon Ltd., 'The Guildhall, Much Wenlock, Shropshire, as built in 1540', © Copyright J. Salmon Ltd., Sevenoaks, England.

Öffentliche Kunstsammlung Basel, Kunstmuseum, 'Hans Baldung Grien *Death and a Woman*, early 16th century (accession nr. 19)'. Photograph, Öffentliche Kunstsammlung Basel, Martin Bühler.

Steve Venton, 'The replica of John Cabot's ship, *Matthew*, leaving Bristol on its maiden voyage to St. John's, Newfoundland, May 3rd 1997'. © Steve Venton. E-mail: Steve.venton@bigfoot.com.

The National Portrait Gallery, 'Cardinal Tomas Wolsey by an unknown artist, c. 1520'.

English Heritage Photo Library, 'Reconstruction of the Chapter House at Wenlock Priory by Peter Urmston as it appeared before the dissolution of the monasteries, 1536–38'. © English Heritage Photo Library.

ACKNOWLEDGEMENTS

The British Library, 'Queen Elizabeth I's entry into the City of London, January 1559'.

C. Walter Hodges, 'Reconstructions of the Rose Playhouse in Southwark'.

The Keeper of the Theatre Collection, University of Bristol, 'The Globe Playhouse by William Poel'.

Phaidon Press, 'Vieux Colombier, Paris as renovated by Copeau for the Compagnie de Quinze, 1919', from *A History of the Theatre* by Glynne Wickham, 1992, 2nd Edition.

University of Bristol Theatre Collection, Department of Drama, 19 Park Row, Bristol, BS8 1UP, 'The Drama Studio in the Wills Memorial Building at Bristol University, opened in 1957'.

The publishers have made every effort to contact authors/ copyright holders of works reprinted in *Early English Stages 1300 to 1660: Requiem and an Epilogue*. This has not been possible in every case, however, and we would welcome correspondence from those individuals/companies we have been unable to trace.

CONTENTS

CONTENTS

ILLUSTRATIONS

PLATES

xix

ILLUSTRATIONS

ABBREVIATIONS
CUE TITLES, SYMBOLS, ETC.

CLRO	City of London Record Office
EES	Glynne Wickham, *Early English Stages*: Vol. I, 1959 (reprinted 1963); Vol. II (Pt. 1), 1963; Vol. II (Pt. 2) 1972; Vol. III 1981; Vol. IV, 2002.
ES	Sir Edmund Chambers, *The Elizabethan Stage*, 4 vols., 1923.
English Professional Theatre	Theatre in Europe: a documentary history, *English Professional Theatre, 1530–1660*, ed. Glynne Wickham, with William Ingram and Herbert Berry, CUP, 2001.
Kahrl, Lincolnshire	*Records of Plays and Players in Lincolnshire, 1300–1585*, ed. Stanley J. Kahrl, Malone Society *Collections VIII*, 1969 (1974).
Mackie	J. D. Mackie, *The Early Tudors*, OUP, 1952.
Medieval Stage	Sir Edmund Chambers, *The Mediaeval Theatre*, 2 vols., OUP, 1904.
MSC	Malone Society, *Collections*.
PRO	Public Record Office, London.
REED	*Records of Early English Drama*, Toronto University Press 1979:
	Chester, ed. Lawrence Clopper, 1979.
	Coventry, ed. R. W. Ingram, 1981.
	Herefordshire and Worcestershire, ed. David N. Zausener, 1990.
	Shropshire, ed. Alan B. Somerset, 1994.
	York, ed. Alexandra Johnston and Margaret Rogerson, 2 vols, 1979.

BOOK ONE

Drama and Occasion

The Forging of Dramatic Art and its Theatrical
Representation in Christian Europe, 975–1530

I

CALENDAR FESTIVALS
AND THE LEGITIMACY OF
PLAY-ACTING

F OR Tudor and early Stuart governments, no question occasioned greater problems respecting theatrical performances
than that of their legitimacy.

This question, like some sleeping volcano, had lain virtually
dormant (with only minor tremors to disturb it) for some five hundred years; but, in the wake of the Lutheran, Anglican and Calvinist
religious Reformation between 1525 and 1540, it erupted again
with a violence that obliged both Church and State to engage in a
radical reappraisal of all previously accepted ground-rules governing the legitimacy of both acting and stage-plays throughout Christendom. It would then take a full hundred years for this reappraisal
to work itself out and for new sets of ground-rules acceptable to
rulers both of Church and State, as well as to actors, play-makers
and theatre managers, to be agreed upon to replace those used
before the Reformation.

Within the old ground-rules that had applied from the early
years of the fourteenth century, legitimacy had been accorded to
dramatic performances as welcome holiday activities that served
both educative and devotional purposes in celebrating the principal
festivals of the Catholic Church year. Starting with the twelve-day
feast of Christmas, the year—as measured in ritual time—moved on
to the three-day feast of Shrovetide (or *Carnevale*) which preceded
the forty-day period of fasting (occasioned by winter food shortages
and commonly known as Lent) to the great forty-day spring festival
of Eastertide. That, in its turn, was followed by those of Ascension
Day and Pentecost (or Whitsuntide) to which, from the start of the
fourteenth century onwards, the Feast of Corpus Christi had been

added in honour of the Holy Trinity. Further festivals, like Lammas (lit., loaf-mass, or Harvest Thanksgiving: 1st August) marked by public holidays, fairs (like those of St. Bartholomew and St. Giles) and other seasonal festivities followed through the autumn to round off the ritual year. Other days were dedicated to commemoration of the Apostles, Saints and Martyrs and allotted throughout the whole year until Advent when the ritual cycle started again.[1]

Given the closeness of this association between the Calendar Festivals of the Catholic Church and the celebration of them with theatrical performances, it had come to be taken for granted by the start of the sixteenth century that acting was an activity permitted and practised, if only on an occasional and thus amateur basis. As such it was also one that could be pursued universally in cities, towns and other communities large enough to sustain them, both in terms of potential performers and spectators, and of financing the costs of production.

The words 'other communities' served to extend these concepts, however, during the course of the fifteenth century from large monastic foundations to universities; and from the Court itself, to baronial households licensed by the Crown to maintain a company of actors. Such licences even stretched to the wealthiest civic Livery Companies of merchant-traders—a context that inevitably invited the introduction of less strictly devotional and those more secularly entertaining aspects of script-writing that were considered appropriate both to the occasion celebrated and within the local environment where the celebration took place.

Such was the case then when Martin Luther, the first of the Protestant Reformers in Northern Europe, chose to challenge the fabric of Roman Catholic religious doctrine and practice from 1525 onwards. Almost immediately therefore the licence thitherto extended to theatrical performances by Popes, Cardinals, Abbots and parish priests loyal to Rome came to be questioned as products of idolatrous and superstitious celebrations imposed upon the major events of Christian history as recorded in Hebrew and Greek versions of the Old and New Testaments, and as expounded by the founding fathers of the Christian faith. All such objectionable accretions were then simply lumped together as works of the Anti-Christ housed in the Vatican and there compounded with deliberate obfuscation of biblical truth by translation into Latin.

In England, this questioning could only become the more rigorous and vexatious following King Henry VIII's decision to take responsibility for the leadership of the Church out of Papal hands into his own. No sooner had this happened, however, than it started to become clear that the leaders of Church and State within the newly established Anglican regime would be seeking to defend both divergent viewpoints and vested interests when debating what reforms were to follow.

Where Churchmen were concerned, the sectarian divide between loyal Catholics and zealous Protestants lifted questions pertaining both to heretical opinion and propagandist advantage to the top of their respective agendas. The Court, on the other hand—and with it the judiciary—was more interested in preserving civil order by timely police action as the impact of reform began to be felt throughout the nation: the Court, moreover, was anxious to protect its own privileges (and those of the landed gentry) where the maintenance of private companies of actors as household servants was concerned to provide domestic entertainment on festive occasions.

So simple a division of interest, however, could not last for long as the Crown, supported by its own officials, strove to establish its newly-born supremacy and, as the most loyal and courageous defenders of the old ecclesiastical regime fought back, to preserve as much of their former control over its own powers of appointment and jurisdiction as they could.[2] And in such circumstances, dramatic art, whether viewed as a predominantly amateur and community activity or as a nascent, professional undertaking seeking to establish itself on a more regular basis, could not hope to escape from the implications of its rebirth within Christendom as a lively child of Roman Catholicism. Clearly hallmarked by the birth (or rebirth) within the Latin liturgical ceremonies (the Proper to the Mass) at Calendar Festivals during the eleventh and twelfth centuries, it had then been encouraged to extend its parameters into the animation of both biblical history and Christian moral exegesis presented in English (instead of in Latin) to educate illiterate audiences following the introduction of the Feast of Corpus Christi into the festive calendar in 1313. Thus the licence accorded to both play-making and play-acting prior to 1530 offered itself to the 'reformers' as a prime target for immediate scrutiny with a view to severe restriction, curtailment or outright suppression.

In the event, alarm bells began ringing throughout the land almost at once. The first documented evidence we still possess to record this change of direction comes from the town of Ipswich in 1531: ominously prophetic in both the wording and tone, it simply states 'Corpus Christi play for ever laid aside'.[3] The following year, the Town Clerk of Chester decided to take the precautionary step of deleting all references to papal authority over the behaviour, during performances, of audiences attending that city's three-day Cycle of Mystery plays in his annual Proclamation advertising this popular Whitsuntide event in 1532.[4] Three years later, we find a civil servant in London, Sir Richard Morrison, urging Henry VIII to turn the tables on Roman Catholics by recommending the commissioning of plays denouncing the Pope and all aspects of Roman Catholic sacramental practice to replace those habitually performed on Catholic Holy Days.[5] A year later, we find that the Lord Chancellor, Thomas Cromwell, has already done just that in securing the services of a turncoat Carmelite monk, John Bale, not only to provide him with a sequence of such plays but to form a company of actors to present them. This he continued to do for the next four years until Cromwell himself was arrested and executed for high treason and Bale found himself obliged to seek refuge in Lutheran Frankfurt as an exile.[6] Even in retrospect, anyone who cares to read those of Bale's plays which still survive in print today will swiftly acknowledge that this form of 'alternative comedy' could only be regarded as blasphemous by staunch Catholics at that time and as no less likely to incite jealous Protestants to expose their opponents to ridicule and to more violent abuse.[7]

The nature of this abuse can be judged by the rioting which occurred in York *c.* 1536/7, causing Henry VIII to write to the Justices in that city to arrest and imprison all papists known or suspected to have responded by writing or performing in plays, branding the reformers as heretics.[8]

It was in these same years that, hardly surprisingly, the King (in consort with his Privy Council) reached the conclusion that if the desired reforms to all ecclesiastical practice within the new Anglican community were to proceed without risk of outright rebellion, their next step must be to dissolve the countless Roman Catholic monastic foundations throughout the country—whether Augustine, Benedictine, Carmelite, Cistercian, Dominican, Franciscan, Marian or Ursuline—since these remained the powerhouses of resistance to reform. Legislation to this effect was thus set in place between 1536 and 1539 with measures added to sequester the lands attached to them and their accompanying rentals into the hands of the Crown.[9] With that done, these lands (together with many of the buildings) could then be leased out again as rewards to the Crown's most reliable and influential supporters in the cause of reform. 'Cronyism' has a long history!

6

Thus within a decade following Henry VIII's schism with Rome, the writing had been clearly spelt out on the wall for all play-makers, actors and promoters of histrionic entertainments as leisure recreations which, up till then, had been taken for granted as normal accompaniments to all Calendar Holydays. In short, from 1540 onwards all future performances of religious plays at Calendar Festivals—whether in cities, towns or villages—had been placed under threat of discontinuance, as had many of the Calendar Festivals themselves. Within another decade such speculation had been translated into fact, with the risks implicit for actors and play-makers alike in striving to preserve the *status quo* even more plainly spelt out than they had been in 1540.

The most alarming of these followed within a year with the arrest, imprisonment and conviction of three priests for writing and performing plays judged to be heretical in content. All three of them were burned at the stake in or near Salisbury in 1541, thus becoming worthy of record in Foxe's *Book of Martyrs*.[10]

The attack moved next to the University of Cambridge where a Lutheran play of German origin, *Pammachius* (translated into English by John Bale), was performed at Christ's College in 1545, apparently with the approval of the Master and Fellows. This occasioned sufficient controversy to bring it to the attention of the Chancellor, Bishop Stephen Gardiner (himself a member of the Privy Council), who immediately ordered the Vice-Chancellor, Matthew Parker (a subsequent Elizabethan Archbishop of Canterbury), to set up an enquiry and to provide the Privy Council with an explanation of how this performance had come to be authorised. Luckily for us, virtually all of the correspondence covering this dispute has survived in the University's own archives; and from this it becomes clear that from then onwards the universities of both Cambridge and Oxford, together with the legal training centres at the Inns of Court in London, had been placed on probation: any repetition of this incident would carry with it the near-certainty that the privileges and financial advantages that they still retained, notwithstanding the earlier dissolution of monastic foundations, would be annulled and confiscated to the Exchequer.[11] This message clearly struck home as there is no record of any repetition of so flagrantly provocative a challenge to government policy as set out in Henry VIII's Statute—An Act for the Advancement of True Religion and for the Abolition of the Contrary—in 1543.[12]

A warning, similar to that delivered to the University of Cambridge in 1545, was issued by the City Fathers in London to groups of actors who posted playbills advertising performances on Sundays in any ward of the city without the prior consent of the Court of Aldermen.[13] This attempt to prohibit (or at least to restrict) dramatic entertainments on the one day in the week that thitherto had been universally regarded as a day of rest and recreation, heralds the battle still to be fought out between the most zealous of Protestant Reformers and their most reactionary Anglo-Catholic opponents concerning the weight of God's claims over respect for his Sabbath on the one hand and those of civic liberties as previously allowed on public holidays. A fourth complication was added in 1545 when London's City Fathers, alarmed by the Court's encroachments upon its own claims to regulate dramatic performances both within the city itself and in its immediate suburbs, issued an Edict from Guildhall so worded as to reassert its own jurisdiction over such matters.[14] Such then was the situation both in and outside London when Henry VIII died in 1547.

Worse, however, was to follow for both amateur and quasi-professional players and their play-makers when he was succeeded by his nine-year-old son, Edward VI, acting under the guidance of Lord Protector Somerset as his Regent; for Somerset was a convinced Lutheran Reformer with leanings towards those views advocated by John Calvin in Geneva. Within a year of his accession, Edward had decided to advance upon his father's dissolution of the monasteries by introducing a Statute—the Chantries Act—dissolving religious Guilds and with it the abolition of public holidays dedicated to the commemoration of those many Saints and Martyrs to whose services these Guilds had been dedicated. By far the most important of these holidays, at least where dramatic performances were concerned, was the Feast of Corpus Christi which, up till then, had provided the *raison d'être* for the most ambitious and elaborate expressions of medieval theatrical achievement—the dramatisation of the history of the world from its Creation to Judgement Day in time to come, and the representation of it on stages in all major cities. In York the performances occupied a single day from dawn to dusk; in Chester and in Cornwall three whole days; and in London seven. These were 'community events' in the fullest sense of those words, occupying the minds, time and energies for months beforehand of all the writers, actors, craftsmen and fund-raisers needed to stage them, and attracting crowds of spectators from smaller and more isolated communities within the region to support them as both devotional and festive occasions.

In the city of Hereford, where responsibility for organising its

Cycle of Mystery Plays lay with Corpus Christi Guild, the Council decided in December 1548 that, with the Guild dissolved, no performance could take place in the following year; and so it proceeded to make arrangements for all the funds provided by all the craft guilds associated with its production to be diverted in future to the upkeep and maintenance of the city itself.[15] Elsewhere, a large question mark hung over the future prospects of all such theatrical celebrations; for, with the disestablishment of the religious guilds, it became difficult to foresee who would replace them as the organisational authorities responsible for the mounting of these almost wholly amateur dramatic celebrations marking other Calendar holidays throughout the year.

In 1548, however, no one could have guessed that the volatile pendulum of religious orthodoxy would swing back within five years to admit wholesale reversion to allegiance to the Vatican in Rome under Edward VI's Roman Catholic successor, his step-sister Mary I and her consort Philip II of Spain in 1553, and with it to the restoration of legitimacy to theatrical performances presented as accompaniments to Calendar Festivals. Nor could they have guessed that this reversion would be as short-lived as its immediate predecessor lasting a mere five years. When Mary I was succeeded by her step-sister, Elizabeth I, in 1558, allegiance to Rome was again severed and, with that, the debate on the legitimacy of theatrical performances resumed.

This time, however, it would proceed within a noticeably changed context: for, within the intervening decade, the Crown had been taking every opportunity that lay open to it to take as much control as it could over all forms of dramatic entertainment out of the hands of ecclesiastical leaders into its own. And there the Church was to discover that, having already surrendered supremacy over the ordering of religious affairs in England to the sovereign, many other related areas of its formerly undisputed hegemony would have to be vigorously defended if control of them was not to pass irretrievably into the hands of the Crown and its secular officials; for the time had passed when the Crown had to seek servants well enough educated to staff its own Judiciary and its Civil Service solely from monastically trained recruits.[16] Following the accession of Queen Elizabeth I, one of those disputed areas was to become control over *all* aspects of theatrical life from the 1570s onwards.

In arriving at this point, English thinking about the legitimacy of acting and playwriting had the advantage of having progressed erratically by jerks and starts allowing sufficient time to pass to

9

absorb the many far more radical changes that had been taking place simultaneously on the continent of Europe.

There, in Latin countries bordering upon the Mediterranean, the continuous threat of Islamic invasion from the Middle East and North Africa was considered to outweigh any threats of disruption from Lutheran and Calvinist sectarianism to the north. In consequence, a far more relaxed attitude was adopted in Italy, Spain and Portugal to the legitimacy of theatrical performances and their relationship to Calendar Festivals than was the case in France, Britain, Switzerland and all German-speaking states throughout the first half of the sixteenth century. Even so, it was there considered prudent to prune all religious festivals of such features as self-evidently lay open to accusations of superstition and, above all, of idolatry.

With that done, the Vatican could join forces with a clear conscience with the many self-governing Dukedoms and Republics bordering upon the southern flank of the Alps and stretching as far south as Rome and Naples, to subsidise and support an alternative form of dramatic entertainment that was currently emerging from academic research into those forms of theatrical life, licensed and enjoyed in the Graeco-Roman world five centuries before the birth of Christ, that appeared to offer an escape route from an exclusive diet of Roman Catholic religious drama. As these researches advanced, and as the fruits of them were transformed into experimental productions within roofed auditoria in Milan, Venice, Mantua and Florence, Ferrara and Rome, so it became possible to formulate theories of a strictly rational kind governing plays warranting description as tragedies, comedies and satyr-plays (*alias* lyrical fantasies), together with no less rational speculation about the forms of theatrical representation considered to be appropriate to each of these dramatic genres.[17]

Such was the *réclame* in diplomatic circles attaching to these very public experiments that by the middle of the century they could no longer be ignored elsewhere in Europe. In France they helped to precipitate the most radical of all possible responses: the total abolition by the Parliament of Paris in 1548 of all further performances of overtly religious plays formerly presented to celebrate major Calendar Festivals, notwithstanding the fact that those scripted, acted and financed in France had eclipsed all others organised and performed elsewhere in Europe (see *EES* II.i. Figs 1 and 2, pp. 5 and 7). A vacuum was thus formed for enthusiastic, neo-classical amateurs in leading schools, universities and Court circles to fill as they saw fit.

In the Iberian Peninsula where threats—real or imagined—to

Roman Catholicism from Jewish and Moorish residents still took precedence, these innovations were less enthusiastically received and, paradoxically, resulted in a compromise between actors (and even actresses in some places) and the Catholic hierarchy. This allowed the former to persist in their trade on a professional basis on strictly enforced provisos. First, all plays, having been duly submitted to the local ecclesiastical authorities for censorship, should then be performed within performance-spaces owned by monastic communities and used as hospitals or for other charitable purposes. The spaces in question were the enclosed courtyards (corrals) of these same charitable institutions that were then rented out to the actors with further provision made for receipt of a percentage of all profits taken from daily performances being donated to the monastic owners of these properties.[18] As this solution offered by the Church met with the approval of the Imperial Governments in Spain (and in its Portuguese neighbour), it was one that proved capable of sustaining the continuance of overtly religious plays in conjunction with the development of those with a more broadly secular content on a commercial, and thus professional, basis.

In Switzerland, however, John Calvin and his disciples, while continuing to uphold the legitimacy of play-acting, insisted that, if allowed, it should be to promote the advancement of 'true religion' (*alias* the Reformation) thus bringing its doctrines to the notice of still largely illiterate audiences. In other words licence must go hand in hand with evangelism.

In German-speaking states and the Netherlands, however, no such clear-cut solutions could be reached, despite growing awareness of the escape route from these problems that was on offer from the Italian city states. Among the former, divisions of religious belief were so extreme and intense as to boil over into civil wars. In the latter, Spanish attempts at colonisation reduced them to appealing to Queen Elizabeth I for assistance in preserving their independence.

What path then remained open to the English in the second half of the sixteenth century to determine the future of players, play-acting and performance-spaces—whether for amateurs or would-be professionals—through the latter half of the century? Faced with this question, successive Elizabethan governments recognised that the making of martyrs out of Roman Catholic play-makers and players during the 1540s, and out of Protestant ones during the 1550s, made the continuance of all dramatisations of religious belief for what had become primarily propagandist purposes a serious liability. On the other hand, they could also recognise that ever since Kings Henry VII and VIII had encouraged the importation of Italian neo-classical dramatic theory and practice into English schools, universities and Court circles, the escape route provided by these innovations was still on offer for them to exploit through the preferment of those already quasi-professional companies of players maintained and licensed with royal approval as 'Household Servants' for nearly a hundred years by most leading members of the aristocracy. On her accession in 1558, Elizabeth I could hardly have done better than to decide to try to preserve the *status quo*. Yet, as every aspiring player and play-maker must have recognised at that time, the days of the amateurs were already numbered and those of the aspiring professionals were still to come. Radical change and innovation was thus already well advanced as the 1560s gave way to the next decade and any lingering respect for the attachment of theatrical performances to Christian Calendar Festivals was rapidly fading out of view.

II

ECCLESIASTICAL FESTIVALS AND THE SUPERIMPOSITION OF CHRISTIAN FESTIVALS UPON THEIR PAGAN ANTECEDENTS

'Thou shalt not make unto thee any graven image.'

BY the start of the fourth century AD, the founding fathers of the Christian Church had arrived at the conclusion that all play-acting, as practised within the Graeco-Roman Empire, was a subversive, corrupting and Satanic abomination that must be banished from the Utopian new world they were aspiring to create.

They can hardly be blamed for reaching this conclusion given what, by then, they had already experienced in Hellenistic theatres and amphitheatres in Asia Minor, Greece, Italy and North Africa. Three centuries of steady decline from performances of plays so scripted as to supply society with a literary, visual and educative portrait of itself, together with visions of outstanding athletic prowess, had reduced both to little more than decadent, lewd and brutal public spectacles. For not only were converts new to the Christian faith there held up to ridicule by mimes in satires, songs and dances on public holidays in honour of pagan deities, but offered as human fodder to satisfy the blood-lust of vast crowds of spectators at the *Ludis Gladiatores* and *Ludis Venalis* (games involving the baiting of wild animals) in the Colosseum in Rome and similar amphitheatres throughout the Empire (see Plate I, No. 1).

Thus, while posterity continues to hold those buildings erected to contain these debased spectacular entertainments which have survived the ravages of time in high regard, the leaders of Christian communities in lands bordering upon the Mediterranean who suffered in them must also be forgiven for yielding to a growing clamour for revenge upon such Emperors as Nero and Diocletian who actively promoted the creation of Christian martyrs by throwing converts loyal to their faith into these amphitheatres to defend themselves as best they could against attack from hungry lions, tigers, bulls and bears imported from Africa and Asia for this purpose (see Plate I, No. 2). No wonder, therefore, that the emergent Christian hierarchies in both Eastern and Western Churches, centred on Byzantium and Rome respectively, began to seek assistance in discouraging attendance at such spectacles. This they found to be forthcoming from members of the liberal-minded intelligentsia in both academic and senior government circles, well-read in the writings of Plato, Aristotle, Cicero, Virgil and Horace.

By the end of the second century AD they had secured the support of the North African lawyer and critic, Tertullian who, in his *De Spectaculis* (*c.* 195 AD), launched a frontal attack both upon mimes, singers, dancers, pugilists and other representatives of contemporary, populist culture and on those patricians upon whose patronage these theatrical performers depended for protection. Thus, by condemning both the entertainers and their backers as corrupt and morally indefensible, he placed the first large question mark over the future of such decadent *spectacula* which, sooner or later, would have to be confronted and answered; and as the wealth needed to protect the over-extended frontiers of the Empire itself came to be squandered in ever-more luxurious and materialist urban lifestyles, so ever larger numbers of concerned government officials chose to express their disenchantment and hopes for reform by joining the ranks of converts to Christian standards of moral conduct and social responsibility in both the Eastern and Western halves of the Empire.

Further assistance was forthcoming to this effect when the Emperor Constantine himself became a convert in 313 AD and decided to transfer the capital from Rome to the small trading outpost of Byzantium seventeen years later. Thenceforward it would become known as Constantinople, and with these changes came others affecting the balance of power within Christendom between the Greek Orthodox Patriarch and the Roman Catholic

Pope, and the use of Greek and Latin as the official languages of imperial rule, both of which would resurface as questions to trouble the consciences of all ecclesiastical reformers during the sixteenth century.

By the end of the fourth century, however, with the Empire already split and fraying at its edges as the funds and military resources needed to prevent rebellions in its western and northern extremities (and to keep the barbarians beyond these frontiers at a safe distance) had dwindled from bare sufficiency to exhaustion, so retrenchment and retreat became inevitable. As the fifth century dawned, Rome withdrew its legions from Britain leaving that country to determine its own future and to protect itself. Simultaneously, in the Empire's heartlands surrounding Rome and Constantinople, churchmen, politicians and army officers alike were finding themselves confronted by the prospect of imminent invasion from the north and east by barbarian tribesmen—Franks, Visigoths, Goths, Huns, Vandals, Slavs, Bulgars and Ostrogoths— awaiting opportunities to cross the rivers Rhone and Danube and then sweep south-westwards over the Alps into Italy and Dalmatia. By 410 AD Alaric I, King of the Visigoths, had penetrated all defences and succeeded in occupying Rome itself, forcing the Pope to flee to Ravenna while finally answering centuries of Christian prayer by ordering the closure of the Colosseum (see Plates I, II and III).

Yet despite these tumultuous upheavals which continued to rock the former Graeco-Roman imperial world throughout the fifth century, Christian bishops managed to find time and means to reach an accommodation between what had survived from the old order as the century drew to its close and the new one they were determined should replace it in the centuries to follow: an Empire dedicated to the service of the risen Christ, describable as Christendom and claiming the allegiance of Christian converts living within it, no matter what their earlier nationalities or ethnic origins.

Fundamental to the way ahead, if this vision was to be fulfilled, was the adoption—despite the differences of approach and emphasis likely to arise between one diocese and another—of a liberal-minded and pragmatic spirit of reconciliation and compromise with the past. Destroy and bury the most objectionable features of it; but rescue, preserve and adapt the best to assist in meeting present needs. Translate; allegorise; improve. These precepts were then applied to classical literature, whether historical, philosophical, legal or poetic: to architecture, scripture and all attendant

15

arts and crafts, and even to the scripted plays of Greek and Roman authors.

Thus, as the growing cult of monasticism offered a means of nurturing and protecting all aspects of spiritual life as expressed in Christian doctrine, so new monasteries must be built and equipped with libraries to serve as repositories not only for the writings of the founding fathers of the Christian faith but for those of the most outstanding and respected of their pagan predecessors. Within all Roman Catholic monasteries in Western and Northern Europe such libraries could thus easily come to contain plays by Terence, Plautus and Seneca alongside the works of Virgil, Cicero, Horace, Ovid, Quintilian and Juvenal;[1] and likewise, within the domains of the Orthodox churches to the east, monastic libraries could easily contain the works of Homer, Plato, Aristotle and Greek dramatists alongside the original Greek and Hebrew texts of the Bible, together with works of Christian exegesis.[2]

It was in this spirit of firm spiritual resolve, tempered by tolerance, that the bishops and patriarchs then embarked upon the most urgent of the tasks that lay ahead of them—that of persuading their new temporal rulers (together with their civil and military retainers) to substitute Christian beliefs for those that they had formerly espoused.

The manner in which this was attempted is admirably illustrated by the instructions of Pope Gregory the Great offered to Abbot Miletus, shortly after his arrival in Britain in 601 AD, where he was to start his evangelistic crusade to persuade his British flock to transfer their allegiance from the pantheons of Roman and Celtic gods and goddesses to Christ's service:

'Allow existing temples to stand,' read these instructions, 'destroy the idols; purify the buildings with holy water; set relics there; and let them become temples of the true God [see Plates IV and V]. So, the people will have no need to change their places of concourse; and where of old they were wont to sacrifice cattle to demons, thither let them continue to resort on the day of the Saint to whom the church is dedicated and slay their beasts no longer as sacrifice, but for a social meal in honour of him whom they now worship.'[3]

It was within this compassionate spirit of tolerance and compromise that Christian Calendar Holydays had come to be aligned in both Rome and Constantinople with the most significant recurrent moments in the agricultural year—the winter and summer solstices and the vernal and autumnal equinoxes—as universally celebrated in previous pagan cultures: and from these instructions it is clear that this principle is to be extended throughout the widening frontiers of Christendom.

It was fortunate that the Christian Church had advanced that far in both its theological philosophy and in its doctrinal practice by the start of the seventh century; for both were shortly to be struck again by further seismic shock-waves centred this time on the Middle East and the Arabian Peninsula to the south.

It thus remains to remind ourselves of the nature of these attacks that were aimed against both Christianity itself and what had survived of the former Roman Empire, if only because of the enduring effects they were to have on future debates about the legitimacy of dramatic art and theatrical representation following the Protestant Reformation both in Britain and continental Europe through the sixteenth century and beyond.

The first of these catastrophes—at least as viewed by everyone living within the reduced frontiers of the old Empire—was the advent of a new and militant religious movement, Islam. This was brought to birth in Mecca and Medina by an Arabian prophet of extraordinary personal charisma, coupled with exceptional gifts of leadership, during the first half of the seventh century: Mahommed. The tenets of this new faith were received by him through divine revelations which were then recorded in the Arabic verses that were collected and set out in the *Qur'an* (Koran). These revelations from Allah embraced many features of both Jewish and Christian cultural values but rejected all ideas about a Divine Trinity of Father, Son and Holy Spirit in favour of a monotheism that was to prove to be as militant as it was unwaveringly autocratic.[4]

Within the next ninety years not only had the Roman and Hellenistic colonies comprising Egypt and what we call 'the Middle East' fallen under Islamic control, but so had the rest of North Africa to its Atlantic coast. Moorish armies then swept north through Spain and Portugal and over the Pyrenees to conquer most of southern France. Their advance was finally checked at the battle of Poitiers in 736, and thereafter they were steadily driven back south again to seek shelter behind the Pyrenees.

Memories of these alarms, however, lingered long enough for the first 'villain' who figures in Christian religious drama of the thiteenth and fourteenth centuries—Herod, King of Judea—to be depicted (anachronistically) as a disciple of Islam, swearing by Mahommed to put the infant Christ (together with all first-born

17

children under the age of two) to the sword. Indeed, the threat presented by Islam to Christian Europe was still potent enough to inspire English dramatists of the calibre of Marlowe, Shakespeare and Davenent in the sixteenth and seventeenth centuries to devise scenarios for plays constructed around scheming Turks, Jews, Moors and other infidels with which to chill and thrill their audiences.

The second seismic shock-wave to shake the fabric of both Eastern and Western churches within what remained of the old Empire during the seventh century took the form of a ferocious argument about the legitimacy of 'graven images' (*alias* pictorial representation) in all kinds of religious art. Known as 'Iconoclasm', this movement was grounded in the use that had come to be made of portraits of both the most revered figures in biblical history and subsequent saints and martyrs in churches and domestic dwellings alike. Copied initially from the Graeco-Roman examples preserved in wall paintings, mosaics and statues on display throughout the Empire, such portraits, or icons, came to be commissioned and paid for by Christian converts from local artists and tradesmen as emblems of their faith and devotion to these singular models of Christian virtues and self-sacrifice (see Plate VI, No. 7).

Trouble began when these strictly symbolic icons, or emblems, became equated in the minds and hearts of their beholders with real presences; and from there it was but a short step for illiterate and superstitiously minded converts to advance beyond simple veneration to personal involvement with their own emotional needs. Once that had happened, as it inevitably did, these portraits began to acquire lives of their own—almost as if they had been transformed into actors and actresses—able to smile, frown, deliver messages or bleed from wounds that had been inflicted upon them while still alive.

The attack on these images and the uses that were being made of them originated in Middle Eastern countries where Arabic, Islamic and Byzantine cultural values overlapped. The case raised against them was that as these supposedly innocuous *icons* were being everywhere metamorphosed into *idols* they must be destroyed and banned; and once the leaders of this small but vociferous movement had gained the support of such forceful Emperors as Constantine V and Leo III, the Iconoclasts quickly won their case, at least within the boundaries of the Eastern, Orthodox Church as the argument raged onwards from the seventh into the eighth century.[5]

In the West, however, where the Iconoclasts had attracted less

18

support, efforts to suppress pictorial representation of the terrestrial world were at best half-hearted, and had virtually lapsed as the seventh century reached its close.

Nevertheless, the example that had been set by the force of the argument itself, and by the use made of it in the Greek- (as opposed to Latin-) speaking Byzantine Church, was one that would be resurrected following the Reformation in North-western Christendom and directed with equal ferocity to both inanimate images as portrayed in stained glass and ecclesiastical statuary and those animated ones depicted on public stages by actors. To our eyes and ears the vandalism displayed by the most extreme of Protestant reformers in the attitude they chose to adopt towards all pictorial graven images, together with the denunciations they levelled against plays and players in their tracts and sermons, may seem to have been as un-Christian in spirit as intolerant in intention; but, before we dismiss them outright as sectarian bigots, we could do worse than reflect upon the growing cult of idols (singled out from among film stars, sporting personalities and television celebrities) within our own society.

Perhaps the best answer that can be given to that question as we enter a new millennium is to be found in the abiding Dionysiac spirit of mimesis as defined, personified and worshipped in ancient Greece that can never be killed off while it continues to form an integral part of the human psyche. It can be temporarily suppressed by recourse to edicts, arrest, imprisonment and even execution, but only to re-emerge as soon as local conditions permit it to do so. By 'local conditions', I mean market places, fairgrounds and other such places of public assembly, small groups of singers, dancers or other nomadic entertainers ready to offer their wares to curious bystanders, and the possession of a hat or dish to pass around in the hope of some small reward for pleasure given.

As this is a subject that will be more fully discussed in the next chapter—Secular Festivals—it suffices here to say that it was by these means that many of the pantomime actors, acrobats (tumblers) and trainers of performing bears, dogs and monkeys survived the closure of all Roman theatres during the fifth century AD to scrape a living of sorts as *vagantes*—nomadic students, singers, dancers and vagabonds, gypsies and beggars—excommunicated by the Christian Church but received and even welcomed both by illiterate peasants in holiday mood, and by members of the nobility and landed gentry to enliven guests at wedding feasts and other domestic celebrations.

19

In their success, despite every imaginable form of social upheaval through the next three centuries, lay a lesson that the Roman Catholic Church would itself have to learn in the hardest of all possible ways eight centuries later: for, as some semblance of political and economic stability began to return to life in Europe following the Coronation of the Frankish King, Charlemagne, as Holy Roman Emperor in Aachen (Aix-la-Chapelle) on Christmas Day in the year 800 AD, it was shortly to discover that it was harbouring this same Dionysiac mimetic virus within one of its own most cherished institutions.

As a matter of known fact, and as fully recorded already in *EES* III, pp. 26–34, this message was delivered to the Vatican in Rome by one of the many Monastic Orders which it had encouraged to develop both as wealthy landlords and as institutions dedicated to devotional study and charitable good works—the followers of St. Benedict, familiarly known as the Benedictines.

Animation of liturgical icons at Calendar Festivals, 975–1375

As the ninth century passed into the tenth, most monastic communities found themselves with time enough on their hands to contemplate elaboration of the liturgies prescribed for their many devotional exercises which were conducted at regular intervals through every day and night.

At first this decorative process was primarily musical, building on what we describe as 'plain-chant'—a form of recitation that lifted sequences of spoken words onto a single melodic line of chant, or song. This was a practice that had come to be adopted in all monastic houses established within both the Eastern and Western Churches—as much to overcome both poor singing voices and the acoustic problems encountered in large, vaulted buildings as for any other reason—since it continued to accord supremacy to the words by projecting them more forcefully while largely eliminating the reverberances occasioned by echoes.

Among the many Monastic Orders of that time, it was the Benedictines who appear to have taken the lead in ornamenting plain-chant with a view to highlighting the significance of the principal historical events celebrated within the ritual year of the Christian calendar, starting with Advent and concluding with All Saints and All Souls. These festive holy days were noted and distinguished within the Mass from normal working ones by appropriate introductions (Introits) and additions known collectively as 'The Proper' (items particular to the Calendar Feast in question) in contrast to 'The Ordinary', or liturgy prescribed for daily use. Following the Anglican Reformation, this distinction would be reinforced descriptively in England for clergy and laymen alike by reference to Calendar Festivals as Red Letter Days and to all others as Black Letter Days.

During the tenth and eleventh centuries such ornamentation of plain-chant took two forms, the first of which was simply to split the choir of singing voices into two halves with one group leading the chanting and the other responding to it on an alternating pattern. Both halves continued to sing the words allocated to them in unison, but with a semblance of variety supplied by the responsorial, or 'antiphonal' method of singing adopted. This was at its most noticeable wherever these antiphons or 'tropes' took the form of a question followed by an answer.

The second and more decorative addition to simple plain-chant was provision of a second melodic line to rise above or below the original, known as Descanthus; this provided harmonic variety (in an exclusively musical sense) and offered a way forward to more complex polyphony through the addition of further melodic lines and rhythmic variations. Such decorative devices as these, however, could only be regarded as questionable since recourse to them served simultaneously to downgrade the supremacy that had thitherto been accorded to the texts by the use of plain-chant alone.

Records documenting the introduction of these practices survive from four Benedictine communities: one at St. Gall in Switzerland; two in France at Fleury and Limoges; and one in England at Winchester. Of these, the *Concordia Regularis* (c. 975) of St. Ethelwold, Bishop of Winchester, is the fullest. There, detailed instructions are set out for the ceremonies to be observed in all Benedictine houses in England when celebrating Mass on Easter Sunday morning, to which primacy of place had already been given within the Christian calendar since it signalled Christ's Resurrection from the Dead.[6]

Clearly the miraculous quality of this event in eclipsing and outshining all others, supplied its own incentive to press all existing forms of musical and iconic art beyond their own frontiers into creating a liturgy of praise and joyous thanksgiving so heightened as to outshine all others in proclaiming its significance to all mankind.

The method chosen to achieve this was a simple one. First, lift the words from St. Matthew's Gospel recording the meeting of the three women equipped to embalm Christ's corpse laid out in the sepulchre with the angel guarding its entrance on Easter Sunday morning (Chapter 28, vv. 1–6); then add these words to the Mass as an appropriate text, or Introit, with which to introduce it. As the words chosen take the form of question and answer, sing them antiphonally. Finally, since it is life not death that is to be celebrated—Resurrection *not* Crucifixion—animate the singers of this antiphon and let them re-enact this miraculous event for everyone participating at this Mass to witness with their own eyes and ears.

All that was needed to effect this was for one priest (the cantor), followed by three others carrying thuribles (incense-burners), to lead all the other brothers attending this Mass from the vestry into the body of the church; and then, as the brothers broke away from this procession to occupy their customary seats, for the four chosen to re-enact the event to move forward into the choir and towards the altar. The Cantor, on arriving at the altar, there assumes the role—in a strictly emblematic or iconic sense— of the guardian angel at the sepulchre, by simply standing beside the darkened altar table, its candles still unlit. After a brief pause, the other three priests swinging their incense-burners then approach the altar and halt at the steps leading up to it. For there they see the Cantor (this sepulchre's guardian angel) who then moves in front of it to bar their further advance. The Introit can then begin:

Cantor (guardian angel):	Whom seek ye in the sepulchre?
Responders (the three Marys):	Jesus of Nazareth.
Cantor:	He is not here: he is risen as predicted when it was prophesied that he would rise from the dead.
Responders:	Alleluia! The Lord is risen!
Unison:	Come and see the place.

The candles can then be lit and the Mass can proceed along its accustomed lines, but it has already been effectively singled out verbally, musically and pictorially as one of especial significance for all believers. St. Ethelwold, in his *Concordia Regularis*, reinforces this for the brethren in all Benedictine houses within his diocese by instructing them to conclude this Mass by singing the *Te Deum*, a hymn of praise and thanksgiving, and to follow that up by ringing their Abbeys' bells to inform the outside world of the miraculous event that has just been celebrated within their walls.

The importance of this choice of decorative elaboration of the liturgy in marking the rebirth of dramatic art in Christian Europe can scarcely be exaggerated; but at the same time the many ambiguities contained within the manner of its birth make it seem highly unlikely that any of those men responsible for it had any preconceived idea or intention of effecting this deliberately. Nevertheless, despite the severe stylisation of this consistently symbolic form of re-enactment of event, recourse has here unquestionably been taken to the principles underpinning the arts of drama and theatrical representation to effect it. Yet the result remained unrecognised and unidentified as such by the leaders of the Benedictine communities in which this practice had originated and in which it was to be repeated annually in future.

In the absence of any direct evidence to the contrary, this can best be accounted for by the ambiguities contained within so highly stylised a depiction of the original event. Chief among these is the Latin words *quasi* (as if) and *quomodo* (in the manner of) in the rubrics governing both the ordering of this ceremony, as recorded by St. Ethelwold, and the actions of all participants. Should the latter be described as priests? Or dare we describe them as actors? Were they not both, at one and the same time, since they were certainly heard and seen as such by everyone assembled to partake of this Mass, and thus as witnesses to the re-enactment of this historical event. Should we regard these witnesses as 'brothers' or as an audience? Here again they were present at first as witnesses but then as participants when called upon to join in the singing of *Te Deum Laudamus* (we praise thee, O God ...) to conclude what has been at once a sacred act of worship and a dramatic performance.

A performance it undoubtedly was; but it was one firmly contained within a devotional exercise that was one of Christian worship reinforced by recourse to dramatic art designed to heighten both the quality of praise and thanksgiving offered to God, and the degree of joy and comfort received from him in return by all witnesses to this performance. In short, the liturgy prescribed for the celebration of Mass on Easter morning has thus been transformed from a perfunctory ritual repeated annually into a unique cathartic experience.

> *Non est hic*! ... *Resurrexit*! ... Alleluia!
> (He is not here! ... He has risen! ... Alleluia!)
> Light all the candles and ring all the bells.

Once established, this innovative format for liturgical celebration could easily be built upon as a precedent for use at other major Calendar Festivals such as Ascension Day, Whitsunday (or Pentecost), Christmas or Epiphany. Since all of these extensions have already been fully covered in earlier volumes of this book (see I and III) they need not be repeated here, but there still remain three aspects of them which do require attention since all three of them were to influence the directions that dramatic art and theatrical representation, as licensed within a Christian context of devotional exercises for festive occasions, would take during the course of the next three centuries.

Of these the first was the discord to be caused by the arrival of the first villain to figure in the cast list of a liturgical music drama: Herod, King of Judea and mass-murderer of innocent children. His presence was central to any re-enactment of the Visit of the Magi to Bethlehem and the subsequent flight of the holy family into Egypt, both of which were recalled and commemorated in the liturgical offices for the Feast of the Epiphany.[7] Clearly he could not simply be excised from this story, yet the nature of his behaviour within it was such as to raise questions about the propriety of retaining this script (or others like it) in any strictly liturgical context or environment in future (see Volume III, pp. 34–5).

In other words, while dramatic re-enactment of biblically documented events might still be encouraged as means to shorten the ever-lengthening gap between the recording of these events and time present, it should no longer be permitted to take place as an integral component of the Mass itself nor within the most sacred precincts of the Abbey itself or in any other church. As these decisions came to be put into effect, however, during the twelfth century, so it was recognised that skilled clerical writers and actors could usefully (and thus legitimately) extend the restricted horizons of monastic communities to take notice of the secular world that continued to exist beyond monastic gates and graveyards, thus permitting them to turn their attention to aspects of scriptural history outside of those celebrated on the Red Letter Days of the Christian calendar.

One of the first of these to be dramatised for evangelical purposes was the story of Adam and Eve and, with it, the Christian doctrine of Original Sin.[8] Another was that of Mary Magdalene, the common prostitute whose faith and deeds of atonement secured both her redemption and ultimate elevation to sainthood;[9] and as such subjects as these came to be expanded both in content and length of treatment, so they began to attract the attention of laymen, not only as spectators and listeners but as craftsmen who could provide costumes and the scenic emblems of location needed to present these plays, and even as performers.

It was through such ways as these, therefore, that dramatic art and theatrical representation as reborn within the confines of plainchant and liturgical ceremonial as first practised in Benedictine monasteries, came slowly to be transformed into an educational and evangelistic medium that the clergy could continue to support and that their leaders could continue or authorise. Such performances, however, whether in England or in other European countries, remained sporadic, occasional and amateur without any particular pattern emerging to unify them or to govern the whereabouts or frequency of their occurrence, and it was in that condition that they remained until the end of the thirteenth century.[10]

What was needed, if dramatic art was to advance from being an almost exclusively ecclesiastical preserve into one that could become broadly acceptable throughout all forms of social and civic life in Christian countries, was an initiative stemming from the Vatican in Rome itself. Yet this, when it came, began as ambiguously as had that of its original rebirth at the hands of Benedictine monks within the confines of their own communities three centuries earlier.

In 1264 Pope Urban IV was persuaded to authorise the addition of a new festival to the Christian calendar. It was to be named as the Feast of Corpus Christi and to be observed on the Thursday following Trinity Sunday (i.e. in early June and thus close to the annual summer solstice). When finally promulgated from the Vatican in 1311 by Pope Clement V, all bishops were accorded freedom to determine for themselves how best to celebrate it within their own dioceses.[11]

To this end Guilds of priesthood clerks were created to devise appropriately festive ceremonies and to take responsibility for their execution. The only requirement specifically prescribed from Rome was that they should be framed within a procession that was everywhere to start out from a church and be led by its clergy carrying the Host (symbolising the Holy Trinity). This was then to proceed through the streets with the Host prominently displayed for all to venerate as it passed by and so to return again to the church where the Host was to be used for a festive Mass 'proper' to this new Calendar Feast. Beyond these simple provisions, it was left to bishops and city councils to determine what other celebrations might be added to explain and emphasise the significance of this Feast to a largely illiterate laity.

It is greatly to be doubted whether this innovation could, of itself, have provoked the swift and massive expansion of dramatic art that was to occur within the next two centuries had other steps not been taken at this same time to prepare ways forward to its realisation.

Of these, the first was the arrival on the stage of world history of St. Francis and St. Dominic, both of whom were to establish a new kind of spiritual community—itinerant and mendicant—during the thirteenth century by obtaining Papal permission to add Orders of preaching friars, dependent upon charity to maintain their lifestyle as travellers and beggars, to the long-established and wealthy monastic communities that devoted their time to scholarship, meditation and good works.

These Franciscan and Dominican brothers, recognisable by their brown and black habits respectively, sought to abandon monastic seclusion in order to spearhead an evangelistic crusade aimed at restoring an understanding of, and respect for, a Christian style of life among the thousands of illiterate and hedonistic peasants and urban workers throughout Europe. To this end they persuaded the Vatican to authorise them to convey their message outside of the walls of churches into market places and to wayside pulpits and shrines in the countryside, by preaching in vernacular languages instead of addressing their audiences in incomprehensible Latin, and to follow Christ's own example by teaching through parables and by drawing their metaphors and similes from the local occupations, pastimes and domestic concerns of those laymen they could persuade to listen to them. A third break to be made by them with past ecclesiastical precedents lay in their equally radical decision to replace earlier liturgical concerns with Christ's divinity (as revealed in his miraculous Nativity, Resurrection and Ascension) by making the mortality of his human existence central to their teaching as expressed in his dealings with overlords and officials and, above all, through his Passion and Crucifixion.[12]

Taken collectively, these several forward-looking changes in Christian philosophical thought and practical exegesis (as authorised by the papal *curia* in Rome and as implemented throughout Western Christendom by the new Orders of Franciscan and Dominican friar-preachers at the start of the fourteenth century) offered bishops, parish priests and laymen within all strata of society new forms of dramatic re-enactment of Christian history with which to adorn the freshly created Feast of Corpus Christi; and by the end of that century these were all meeting with enthusiastic responses in both theological and secular quarters.

Originating in Italian Passion Plays scripted in Latin, these responses developed in all continental countries from Spain and France to Switzerland and many German-speaking states into greatly extended plays in vernacular languages oriented around that theme.[13] In England, this theme was widened still further—both backwards and forwards in historical time—to span God the Father's creation of the world with the final day of judgement in plays that we now describe as Mysteries, or Miracle Cycles. All of them are anachronistic, both in their scripting and their theatrical representation, since their devisers were of one mind in electing to prefer relevance to daily life, as then lived in the secular world of the fourteenth and fifteenth centuries, to either strict historical accuracy or any lingering attachment to earlier liturgical treatments.

In this, they were rewarded by the enthusiasm that greeted these changes, not only among illiterate laymen but in powerful ecclesiastical and civic circles alike, which made it relatively easy to finance, police and stage biblical plays at midsummer in market places and other open spaces for at least an entire day or even longer. Likewise, because these plays called for the active involvement of greatly enlarged companies of actors and craftsmen needed to stage them, they secured the collaboration of laymen on an unprecedented scale in the evangelistic objectives of both the Vatican itself and the priesthood at large.

From this there could be no looking back. The art of drama, as first reborn within the liturgies of the Christian Church, had escaped—albeit while still under strictly authoritarian ecclesiastical control—not only into market places and onto village greens, but into baronial and civic banquet halls, all of which lay under secular control. Thenceforward, its future legitimacy would inevitably have to be determined by arguments advanced from these quarters rather than from sources emanating from the Church alone.

Firm foundations had thus come to be laid for the creation of a theatrical world to which further and more varied additions could be made but which, while still faithful to its liturgical origins in Red Letter Calendar Festivals, would remain familiar to play-makers, actors and their audiences alike during the opening decades of the sixteenth century, when a growing clamour for the reformation of sleaze, corruption and superstition in all aspects of ecclesiastical life and practice would open all of these long-inherited theatrical

27

assumptions to vigorous questioning, and to violently expressed divisions of public opinion in Germany, Switzerland and France.

One further innovation of thirteenth-century origin, however, remains to be taken into account here, since it was to have still wider implications for the subsequent development of dramatic art and the several forms of theatrical presentation that both could take by then. This was the founding of what we now call 'Universities'. These came into existence when the Vatican was persuaded to allow the creation of collective groups of monastic houses, or colleges, in certain European cities devoted principally to the teaching and training of students between the ages of fourteen and eighteen to ensure a regular supply of young men well enough prepared intellectually to embark upon careers in the priesthood, the law and the civil service as clerks.

While all of these colleges followed the rule of one or other of the many established Monastic Orders—whether Benedictine or Cistercian, Carthusian, Dominican or Franciscan, Carmelite or Augustine—the creation of such large inter-disciplinary communities living in close proximity with one another was a new departure in itself. As such, universities were certain from their inception—whether in Bologna or Krakow, Paris, Oxford or Cambridge—to encourage exchanges of theological and philosophical beliefs and opinions that, up till then, had been unimaginable: and when to that is added the wide social mix of adolescent novices recruited into these colleges (financed either by wealthy parents or from charitable endowments) the scale of this cultural and social revolution at once becomes apparent. For not only were these students immature and self-opinionated, but young enough to be still possessed of the *joie de vivre* which propels every new generation into questioning all authoritarian values imposed upon its members by their forebears with a view to enlarging their own freedom of action.

Obliged as they were to attend to their studies and acquire proficiency in Latin, Rhetoric, Grammar and Theology, they were still left with leisure time enough to explore new possibilities of enjoying themselves and entertaining others. Music, drama and the illumination of manuscripts offered obvious ways forward for those talented enough to pursue them. For others, the resources of the libraries they were encouraged to use offered further possibilities, and for some there remained the pleasures inherent in pressing radical viewpoints as far as—and if possible beyond—all previously permitted limits. Outside of term-time they were free to travel, to attract attention from potential patrons and to enlarge their acquaintanceships in the wider, secular world which, in their several ways, they were aspiring to transform into the New Jerusalem.

Many of them were doubtless to be disappointed in these youthful expectations, but some succeeded in defining the idealism, heroism and romance inspired by the Crusades as poets and singers (*trouvères*), while others succeeded in renewing contact with the all-but-forgotten theatrical world of ancient Rome as revealed in the tragedies of Seneca, the comedies and farces of Terence and Plautus, and the dramatic theory articulated by Horace in his *Ars Poetica*. Whether this resulted from their own curiosity when browsing in university libraries or from conversations with their teachers is beside the point: what mattered at the time was the consequent broadening of their horizons respecting both alternative forms and subject matter as represented in plays and the occasions and style of their performance. Above all, the fruits of these researches included the possibility of reopening a door that had previously been tightly locked but which, if opened, could lead on towards the writing and acting of plays devised for performance on a regular, professional and commercial basis alongside those already licensed for presentation on Red Letter Calendar days as strictly occasional and amateur festive celebrations.

It was from these sources that there emerged during the late fourteenth and early fifteenth centuries several new forms of dramatic entertainment that we now refer to as Morality Plays, Saint Plays, Moral Interludes, Farces, Mummings and Disguisings presented, as often as not, at night in the banquet halls of baronial castles and major mercantile livery companies, as well as in monastic and collegiate refectories. By the middle of the fifteenth century, moreover, some of these were being scripted by domestic chaplains and performed by small groups of histrionically talented household servants who were handsomely rewarded for their services not only with supplements in their weekly wages but with passports enabling them to accept invitations to present their plays in places outside of their own domains.

It is, however, both more appropriate and more convenient to address these developments in the next chapter devoted to secular festivals than within those of the previous and present contexts of Calendar and Ecclesiastical Festivals, from the limitations of which they had already escaped.

III

SECULAR FESTIVALS AND THEIR ACCOMPANYING ENTERTAINMENTS

I N all country districts of England, as elsewhere in Northern and Western Europe, such discipline as the King and his Privy Council at Westminster and the two Archbishops resident at Canterbury and York could assert over the ordering of their subjects' lives and souls was exercised at a distance by their representatives whose own interests were more often local than centralist in both their political and theological orientation, and whose approaches to their appointed tasks were inescapably pragmatic.

Following the Norman Conquest in 1066 AD, rural life had thus come to be centred on the four largest buildings that were to be found in or near all village communities—the parish church; the castle or manor house; the Moothall, Guildhall or Town Hall; and the alehouse or 'pub'.

Of these, the parish church had already established its dominance where all matters concerning the moral and spiritual welfare of local parishioners were concerned including provision for a weekly day of rest from manual labour on Sundays and for festive celebration of all Red Letter Days in the Christian calendar.

From the castle or manor house—the prime source of the livelihoods of most villagers and their families—life extended beyond its fields and farms to the woodlands, rivers, moors and swamps that characterised the local area. Everyone thus remained in daily contact with all the phenomena of nature pertaining to climate, the seasons, weather, farm and wild animals, birds, crops, herbs and other wild flowers. And it was this intimacy between men, women and children in all walks of life and their ecological environment that directed them to respect it and to encapsulate it into proverbs and to transmit it from one family to another in the form of folklore, from one generation to the next, time out of mind. Indeed, in many areas folk custom continued to provide in mimetic games and dances vestigial evidence of religious rituals inherited from a time before Christian missionaries stepped ashore in these islands (see Plate VII, No. 9).[1]

Beyond these strictly rural concerns, however, the castle or manor house represented the secular arm of the law since its occupant—whether lord, duke, earl or lesser member of the baronial peerage—owed his or her allegiance to the Crown on appointment as Lord Lieutenant, Sheriff or Justice of the Peace as the case might be from one area to another. What was particular to this class of men was that by owning most of the lands surrounding their domestic domains they could regard all farmers and labourers resident within their boundaries as their tenants and thus as subject to the levying of taxes (other than those levied by the Church) and, in time of war, to military service under their command. Shakespeare's 'History Plays' bear eloquent testimony to this state of affairs which indicates clearly that it remained one that was still familiar to his audiences late in the sixteenth century.

In most market towns and all larger urban areas, the Moot, Town or Guildhall existed to provide a roofed and spacious meeting place where the Mayor and local councillors could discuss such legislative and administrative duties as directly concerned them. These duties varied between the policing and cleansing of the streets; the arrest, interrogation and either committal for trial or acquittal of vagrants, indigent beggars and other miscreants thought likely to occasion breaches of the King's peace; together with making arrangements for annual fairs and other local and occasional events such as episcopal, judicial or royal visitations.

The fourth building around which life in both rural and urban areas revolved was the alehouse, tavern, inn or simple 'pub'. This was immediately distinguishable by the large banner or wooden signboard suspended above its door carrying its name and an appropriately illuminated emblem. These could vary from the Green Man, the Turk's or Saracen's Head and the Red Dragon on the one hand, to the heraldic coat of arms of the owner of the local castle, or even of a former king, queen or prince with whom that town or village chose to regard itself as closely associated—a tradition that remains alive today throughout the land.

The alehouse acquired this degree of distinction within medieval society (as it had doubtless done in earlier centuries) as a

31

recreational sanctuary from both the physical fatigue induced by the working day and by the mental stress occasioned by mounting debts, domestic strife or simply a desire for convivial companionship. There, under the stimulation proffered by the supply of food and alcohol, human propensities to indulge in gossip, rumour, salacious banter (and even bribery, conspiracy and lechery) could flourish alongside many more respectable, if hedonistic, leisuretime activities like singing, dancing and competitive indoor and outdoor games, or political discussions and the organisation of local sporting events. Alongside that, however, it had to be acknowledged that the facilities which they offered to their customers encouraged drunkenness, gambling, brawling and lascivious behaviour.

It is thus not without reason that the ecclesiastical hierarchy came to regard the alehouse as Satan's Temple—the home of anti-Christ and all seven deadly sins—a view that was later to be forcefully expressed in many late medieval and subsequent Tudor Moral Interludes but one which, once again, remained familiar to Elizabethan and Jacobean audiences as exemplified in the behaviour of Sir John Falstaff, Prince Hal, Mistress Quickly and their companions in both parts of Shakespeare's *King Henry IV* at the Boar's Head in Cheapside, and repeated (at least where Falstaff is concerned) in *The Merry Wives of Windsor* at the Garter Inn.

Given the near-universal presence of all four of these buildings throughout England as far north as the Scottish borders and as far west as the Welsh Marches, and given the example already set by the Church where the rebirth of dramatic art in Christian society was concerned, it was predictable that the owners and patrons of the other three would seek to copy it in ways that suited their own needs and lifestyles from the tenth century onwards. As the *raison d'être* for the existence of the castle, Moothall and alehouse all differed from that of the parish church, so it is to be expected that each would come to adapt or extend those patterns of dramatic celebration of festive occasions already set by the Church. I shall thus take each of them in turn when considering the nature and extent of these adaptations, starting with castles.

Castles, tiltyards and banquet halls

From the Norman Conquest until the accession of the House of Tudor to the English throne in 1485, it was the castle that dominated English landscapes, justifying both its existence and its architectural style as a citadel designed and built to defend local communities against piratical attack or marauding invaders from Scotland, Wales or the continent of Europe: and, as such, castles thus came quickly to be regarded as battle-schools for the training of officers and other men in the skills required of them in time of war.

In the course of these four centuries, castles were modified in their design to provide greater comfort in those areas appointed for domestic use and to include a private chapel. They were also extended both in the scale and sophistication of their outer defences to incorporate stables, an armoury, dormitories and sufficient kitchen and storage accommodation to withstand a siege. An imperative within the walls was a well or spring to ensure a regular supply of water at all times.

From among these many extensions, two were destined to enlarge the frontiers of dramatic art (as reborn within the liturgical ceremonies of the Christian Church) in directions that could never have been licensed under ecclesiastical auspices.

The first of these was the war-games, training exercises or 'tournaments' that succeeded in reviving the Roman concept of athletic and pugilistic contests (the *ludi circenses*) conducted in arenas and amphitheatres which included the chariot-racing, gladiatorial combats and the baiting of wild animals that had so incensed Christian converts during the first three centuries AD.[2] The second was the use of a roofed and heated hall for banquets interspersed with story-telling, singing and dancing on festive occasions.

At first, the Church denounced both of these initiatives, regarding tournaments as morally unacceptable and the festivities in banquet halls as a reversion to idolatrous rites and customs venerating pagan deities. The need, however, to mount and finance Crusades to wrest control over Jerusalem from its Islamic conquerors swiftly softened ecclesiastical attitudes to these heroic and romantic wargames. Likewise, the claims of orderly social intercourse as a means to ensure the survival of the human race through Christian sacramental rites came quickly to override earlier ecclesiastical objections to singing and dancing when celebrating family weddings, and christenings and other notable national or local events. In this sense then, these two strictly secular innovations of the tenth and eleventh centuries that emanated from castles rather than churches became inextricably intertwined with the tiltyards constructed to stage tournaments in daylight hours providing the poetic, heraldic (or iconic) scenic and musical motifs needed to celebrate the award of prizes in the banquet hall at night.[3]

With the advent of the Crusades, ordered and organised by the Vatican, the incentive offered to promoters of tournaments in custom-built castle tiltyards to decorate and elaborate them through recourse to heroic and romantic poetic sources became irresistible, and in that context the incorporation of ladies in whose honour these festive contests—both national and international— were held, and who were called upon to present the prizes at night, became a driving force in determining the varying forms that these spectacular entertainments would take.[4]

Since these developments have already been covered both in descriptive records and pictorial illustrations in Volumes I and II (Part 1) there is no need to repeat them here. Readers, however, may like to be reminded that tournaments took three principal forms, all of which, as challenges to excel in military skills, were designed to train cavalry officers in the arts of tilting (i.e. charging at each other on horseback when fully armed with spears or lances); jousting (i.e. fighting on foot, when unhorsed, with swords and daggers); and in laying siege to a specially constructed gateway or fortress (known as a *Pas d'Armes*).

From the first of these developed the heraldic, iconographic and emblematic devices needed to identify each combatant, concealed as he was by his elaborate protective armour consisting of helmet, breastplate and metal gloves, armshields and leggings, and by the draperies protecting his horse. These heraldic identification devices applied equally to jousting but with the difference that this kind of spectacular pugilistic and competitive entertainment could easily be imported into banquet halls as an appropriate accompaniment to festive celebrations illuminated by torchlight at night.[5]

The most elaborate form of tournament was the *Pas d'Armes* which obliged the construction of a substantial scenic device to represent the fortress under siege. By the start of the fifteenth century it had been recognised that this kind of combat could be varied allegorically and emblematically to allow both the object under siege and its attackers and defenders respectively to depict a much wider range of dramatic and theatrical themes and characters than had formerly been allowed.

It is to this source that we owe the finest of all English Morality Plays, *The Castle of Perseverance* (c. 1405–25), with its long cast list of Vices and Virtues. And it was still to this source that Sir Philip Sidney, the Earl of Arundel and others turned when devising *The Fortress of Perfect Beauty* for the entertainment of Queen Elizabeth I and her Maids of Honour in the tiltyard at Whitehall Palace (to which they laid siege—unsuccessfully—on 15th and 16th May 1581) on the occasion of the Duc d'Alençon's visit to London as her suitor.[6]

The banquet hall likewise offered opportunities for the widening of theatrical horizons by paving a way forward from the mere recital or chanting of heroic saga by Anglo-Saxon golliards and subsequent Norman and Provençal trouvères and troubadours towards the animation of chivalric romances derived from the Crusades and from the legendary lives and exploits of Saints and Martyrs in the form of Moral Interludes, Mummings or Disguisings. Many of these owed both their form and content to sermons preached by household chaplains and mendicant friars; others to a dawning interest in classical mythology or to more familiar characters and situations drawn from domestic and social life.

Since these have been discussed at length in Volume I, it is only necessary here to remind readers of the entertainments scripted by John Lydgate between 1425 and 1432 (which he describes variously as 'ballads', 'mummings' and 'disguisings') and such anonymous plays as *Wisdom* or *Anima Christi, Mankind* and *Everyman* from the latter half of the fifteenth century, most of which seem to have been written to provide theatrical entertainment to punctuate intervals or interludes between courses at banquets on the Red Letter Days of annual Calendar Festivals.[7]

These plays, together with many since lost, offered firm foundation stones for further development by such early Tudor playmakers as Henry Medwall, John Skelton, John Heywood, John Bale and John Redford to pass on to their successors (see Volume III, pp. 195–205 and 228–9; see also Chapter 6, pp. 109–11 below).

The introduction of jousting on foot into banquet halls at night likewise pointed forward to those 'soft and silken wars' of the Jacobean Court that were to be ornamented with music, dances and texts by Ben Jonson and other poets by the start of the seventeenth century and to become known as Masques at Barriers.[8]

Before moving on from palaces and castles to other secular environments that assisted in widening popular conceptions of dramatic entertainment and its theatrical realisation, it is useful to consider the scale of the staffing employed to maintain them and the high degree of organisation needed to ensure that everyone involved was aware of his or her status and duties in the orderly regulation and execution of daily life as conducted within these large establishments. Not surprisingly, life in all palaces and castles, given the origins of their construction, was regulated on regimental lines. Household Order Books, modelled on that provided to govern life at Court, were drawn up that set out in writing how this was to be achieved.

Responsibility for the ordering of daily life within such exceptionally large and self-contained communities was accordingly delegated by the owner or master to four principal officials.

Placed in overall control of the entire household were the Chamberlain and Comptroller. The former was charged with responsibility for the appointment and conduct of all members of the household and the latter with accountability for balancing income against expenditure.

Working directly under their orders were the Chaplain, responsible for conduct of spiritual affairs and the musicians employed in the chapel, and as a tutor to the owner's children in the arts of reading, writing, numeracy and music; the Steward, in charge of the hall and its adjacent kitchens, pantry, buttery and cellars together with the delivery and storage of all food supplies; and the Marshall who supervised the stabling of the horses and their grooms, the armoury, tiltyard and such domestic accommodation as was made for the castle's garrison. The physical preparations and arrangements for the staging of tournaments in the tiltyard in daylight hours were normally delegated by the Chamberlain to the Marshall, and those for entertainments provided in the hall at night to the Steward.

Virtually all of these arrangements survived the Reformation to be passed on, with only minor modification, into the great Tudor manor houses (like Longleat, Hatfield House and Hardwick Hall) which came to replace castles during the sixteenth and seventeenth centuries, as remains apparent in such Shakespearean depictions of these officials as Polonius and Philostrate (in *Hamlet* and *A Midsummer Night's Dream* respectively); Malvolio in *Twelfth Night* and the Lord Marshall in *King Richard II*.

Moot, town, guild and livery halls and civic pageantry

Outside of castle precincts, a roofed and heated hall became a necessity in Anglo-Saxon England as a place of assembly for use throughout each year to supply a meeting place for the discussion and regulation of all strictly secular aspects of daily life at local level. Known as Moothalls, they thus served as the administrative headquarters of local government in all communities large enough to warrant description as market towns.

Town halls came into existence some centuries later, as did the Guildhalls erected by some religious guilds and by the largest livery companies, to serve a similar purpose; but where the religious (i.e. clerical) guilds were created by the Church to organise Calendar Festivities dedicated to particular saints and martyrs (most notably those pertaining to the Feast of Corpus Christi after 1313), the commercial ones were formed only by the largest and wealthiest companies of merchants, sea-farers, manufacturers and retailers to promote their own vested interests within secular society and to safeguard them when once secured (see *EES* I, pp. 293–9, and Volume II; Plate VII).

Town halls were simply the Norman and later successors to Moothalls, but they were also a product of greater social stability and economic prosperity as towns and cities developed throughout the single kingdom that replaced the earlier regional ones. They were thus frequently required to meet local judicial as well as administrative needs, and from the thirteenth century onwards all of them played a part in the development of dramatic art and theatrical entertainment following the removal of liturgical music-drama from ecclesiastical precincts owned by the Church into those under the legislative control of secular organisations (see *EES* II; Plate VI).

Most of the burghers or councillors chosen to speak for the residents of towns and cities as law-makers and regulators of local life from within these halls were drawn from those groups of artisans whose professions (or 'mysteries') supplied the residents with the necessities of daily life: water-drawers, butchers, fishmongers, weavers, drapers, grocers, carpenters, metal-workers and so on. By banding themselves into trade-guilds, each of these groups became responsible for its own organisation and for the regulation of its affairs from the training imposed upon its apprentices to the advancement of its material interests under the protection of an appropriate patron-saint, while guided by a chaplain and fellow-clerks who were both literate and numerate enough to record the decisions taken at their meetings and to handle their order-books and accounts.

As time passed, so many of these trade-guilds grew to become wealthy enough, both in London and in such major provincial cities as Bristol, Chester, Coventry, Newcastle and York to build halls and chapels of their own and to vie with one another in the support they could afford to offer to hospitals, schools and other charitable causes. It is thus natural to expect that the Church would turn to these guilds for help in providing costumes, scenic requirements, actors and money when staging religious plays as elaborate as those scripted to celebrate the Feast of Corpus Christi in city streets and market places. Many of the chapels came to be described as Chantries.

An active partnership thus came to be established between the Church and town halls to engage the laity in all aspects of the organisation and production at secular level of the annual theatrical re-enactment of biblical history at a spiritual level: and so successful did this prove to be as to persuade many guilds in many towns and cities to adopt near-wholesale responsibility for a particular play in these Corpus Christi (or Mystery) Cycles which seemed to be especially relevant and appropriate to its own craft, skills and professional interests. In this way the shipwrights in Newcastle came to adopt the play of Noah's Flood as its own; Chester's goldsmiths that of the Magi as theirs; or York's vintners the play of the Marriage Feast at Cana in Galilee (see Plate VI, No. 8). Where the Church was concerned, it was from this partnership that the anonymous clerical writers or 'makers' of these plays learned how to broaden their appeal to laymen and their families. Through recourse to use of local dialect and anachronistic allusions to contemporary life in dialogue, characterisation and dress, they succeeded in transforming long stretches of biblical narrative into an educational and morally instructive experience that was theatrically both moving and entertaining for their audiences. In doing so they also acquired the skills needed to alternate sequences of comic and tragic incidents and to integrate both within a strong story-line that commanded close attention from standing spectators in holiday mood.[9]

This partnership between Church and town hall, moreover, was to prove fruitful in other ways that would expand theatrical horizons in primarily secular directions during the fifteenth and sixteenth centuries.

First, it convinced Mayors and their Councils that they could adapt this method of celebrating festive occasions to their own use when called upon to welcome reigning kings and queens into their towns by devising civic pageantry requiring the employment of singers, musicians, actors and the craftsmen needed to provide scenic devices to greet them at the city's gates and to provide relevant entertainment at fountains, market crosses and other local monuments as they processed through the streets to the town hall and, finally, to the residence chosen by the Lord Lieutenant and

Sheriffs to accommodate them and their many retainers during their visit.[10]

Secondly, it offered a precedent for those livery companies rich enough to be possessed of their own halls to imitate or adapt when celebrating such major Calendar Festivals as Christmas and Carnival, the feasts of their respective patron-saints, or the installation of a new Master or Warden. Entertainment at banquets on these festive occasions was at first offered by visitors disguised as strangers—popes and cardinals, knights and esquires, or foreign ambassadors—bearing gifts and known as mummers because they arrived and departed in silence, relying upon the surprise and appropriateness of their disguises, gifts and dances to enliven proceedings during the evening. Later, small groups of amateur actors capable of providing guests with short comic Interludes were engaged for a fee to provide entertainment.[11]

This was an innovation first introduced at Court during the fifteenth century, which was to be extended later in long-established schools and university colleges into the revival of Roman comedies and farces (at first in Latin and then in translation as an aid to the study of Rhetoric, or the Art of Oratory) during the first three decades of the sixteenth century. It was in the halls of these schools and choir schools that groups of boys were to make their first appearance as companies of child actors.[12]

Alehouses, taverns and inns

Among the buildings listed for discussion in this section, alehouses must be considered as the odd-men-out since, despite their near-universal presence in all English villages, towns and cities, they played no part in the administrative regulation of the spiritual, political or economic life of the country. On the other hand, alehouses and their larger and more ambitious extensions into taverns (which provided meals and other amenities as well as drink) and inns (which were the equivalent of today's hotels, catering principally for the needs of travellers) were unquestionably the focal point of daily social life, for they alone could provide a meeting place for everyone, regardless of rank or occupation, to exchange domestic gossip, to play games with cards and dice, to receive news both from neighbouring villages and more distant towns, and to learn something of the wider world outside the county boundaries from passing strangers (see *EES* II.i, Plate X).

Alehouses can thus claim to have exercised as strong an influence over the formation of collective opinion and identity within the local communities that they served as the parish church or the nearest castle or town hall. So, before we dismiss them as unlikely to have added much to our knowledge of the return of drama and theatre to Christian Europe and its subsequent development in other secular environments, we should recall that it was within these same alehouses that the many and varied folk customs, songs and dances celebrating the principal festive events of the agricultural year in Celtic, Roman and Anglo-Saxon times were preserved for posterity to retain beyond the Norman Conquest. There they survived, lovingly passed on from one generation to the next, both in their own right and for subsequent incorporation into the Mummings, Disguisings, Masques and plays of later centuries in other more spacious, wealthier and more sophisticated environments. By offering a secular place of public assembly (not unlike a sports clubhouse today), alehouses, or 'public houses', supplied a base from which it was possible to organise and carry into effect all the time-honoured festivities associated with the annual celebration of Wassail, Yule, May-Day, sheep-shearings, Harvest Home, fundraising fêtes or fairs and the passing of both the winter and summer solstices.[13] It was such celebrations as these (together with several more of equal antiquity that survived in remoter parts of the country) that were then bequeathed from Chaucer's, Lydgate's and Gower's worlds to that of the Elizabethan and Jacobean poets and playmakers. In these ways alehouses laid the foundation stones of those visions of an Arcadian and 'merry' England—a world replete with shepherds and shepherdesses, Dryads and Naiads, witches and demons, love and sorrow, joys and pain—which a galaxy of poets, madrigalists and musicians led by Edmund Spenser, Sir Philip Sidney, William Byrd, Thomas Dowland and Orlando Gibbons could then ornament and embroider with such additional characters and subject matter as they had themselves borrowed from classical mythology derived from Italian and French Renaissance sources. And it is this world that we will find encapsulated for posterity in many plays by John Lyly, George Peele, Thomas Nashe, William Shakespeare, Ben Jonson and John Fletcher written between 1580 and 1620.

Of the larger English taverns and inns, the first to make its mark in a literary context was the Tabard Inn in Southwark, just south of London Bridge, where Geoffrey Chaucer's jovial band of pilgrims— a rich assortment of monks, nuns, knights, lawyers, merchants, millers, shipmen, not forgetting a certain Wife of Bath—assembled to embark upon their journey to St. Thomas à Becket's tomb at Canterbury, late in the fourteenth century. Until recently, a public house of that name still existed near the High Street in Southwark, but it has now been demolished. Nevertheless, what remains of the George Inn in adjoining Southwark High Street after the bomb damage inflicted upon it during the Second World War, still offers us a fine pictorial record of a typical late medieval inn, with its railed galleries rising one above another and surrounding a spacious gated courtyard. Another, and better preserved, example may still be seen at the New Inn in Gloucester.

Chaucer himself, as a clerk to King Richard II's Exchequer, became responsible for constructing one of the earliest multi-storeyed arenas to contain a type of tournament known as 'trial by combat' of the kind depicted between Henry Bolingbroke and Thomas Mowbray in Shakespeare's *King Richard II* (see Volume I, pp. 31–4). These, in their turn, set a precedent for the construction of the later bull- and bear-baiting arenas that were also to be erected in Southwark during the fifteenth and sixteenth centuries (see Volume II.2, Plates III to VII). Smaller polygonal buildings, but of similar design and known as cockpits, were constructed to contain the equally popular sport of cockfighting both in London and in the provinces, some of which were later converted into playhouses, as were several inns (see *EES* II.2, Plates XVI to XXI).

Virtually all taverns and inns in medieval and Tudor times were large enough to be possessed of spacious gardens as well as reception rooms that their landlords could lease out to individuals in need of open spaces (both in summer and winter) in which to entertain their guests with food and drink when in festive mood following baptisms, weddings and wakes. It is thus natural to expect that when leaders of small travelling groups of quasi-professional players began touring plays that had been well received in their masters' banquet halls during the fifteenth century, they should turn to these landlords for help in providing them with a performance space large enough to contain an audience, for not only were landlords already accustomed to such lettings for occasional public use, but the buildings themselves with their heavy gates and courtyards offered a ready means for controlling admissions in return for a fixed fee. Since the only alternative available to these nomadic companies was an open space in busy market places where any speculative reward would have to be gathered from the spectators assembled there by passing a hat or dish around amongst them either during or after the performance, controlled admission with a fee payable in advance

41

of the kind possessed by taverns and inns offered self-evident advantages.

Surviving records offer little help in determining when this practice first started, but they do prove that well before the death of King Henry VIII in 1547 it had become one that was both well established in several large provincial cities and troublesome enough to be causing grave concern to city councillors and Magistrates in London. By then, however, the continuance of all aspects of play-making, play-acting and public performances had come to be threatened by both Church and State as an unanticipated result of the Anglican Reformation that began in 1531.

When Henry VIII ascended the throne in 1509, plays and play-acting had come to be universally accepted through all levels of social life (and sanctioned by ecclesiastical and secular authorities alike) as a way in which to celebrate all special occasions. By dramatising the occasion itself, it had thus become possible to highlight and define the significance of that occasion in an entertaining and enjoyable manner. All dramatic activity had thus come to be regarded as a special form of 'game' or 'play' which, by providing pleasurable recreational entertainment, served simultaneously to reveal 'earnest', or the significance of the occasion celebrated by this 'game' or 'play' as it affected the stern realities of life in this world, and the inevitability of final judgement with everlasting salvation or damnation as the reward for the conduct of it.

This concept was derived directly from St. Augustine's grand vision which, with good reason, he had described as 'the Great Theatre of the World'; by that he sought to depict mortal life as a play enacted on a large circular stage surrounded by an auditorium seating God the Father, Son and Holy Ghost and the angelic host watching Everyman, together with his family, friends and enemies, act out in 'game' and 'play' the story of his life. In doing this, he would reveal in 'earnest' the use he chose to make of God's most precious gift of Free Will to all Mankind and thus invite a final judgement offering alternative verdicts of eternal salvation or damnation in Heaven or Hell respectively.

This was a vision that still remained familiar to Shakespeare, the Burbage family and their London audiences when naming their first playhouse in the northern suburb or Shoreditch as 'The Theater' in 1576, and its successor on the south bank of the Thames in Southwark as 'The Globe' in 1598/9. Likewise, it remained relevant enough to the Spanish poet and play-maker, Pedro Calderón de la Barca, and to his actors and audiences, when choosing to use it as a title for his play, *El Gran Teatro del Mondo*, some thirty years later.

If, then, we are to assess with any claim to accuracy the legacy bequeathed to their children and grandchildren by men and women of the Middle Ages—those priests, city councillors, noblemen, merchants and citizens from many humbler walks of life who collectively encouraged and supported the constant growth and expansion of dramatic art and theatrical entertainment throughout those five centuries—we become obliged to summarise their achievements. This is no easy task, but it is one to which we must now turn our attention in the next two chapters in attempting to arrive at an answer.

IV

THE MAKING OF RELIGIOUS DRAMA

Play-makers and actors: their status, repertoires and performance spaces

Since neither the words 'dramatist' nor 'playwright', nor the word 'actor' existed in either Anglo-Saxon or Anglo-Norman as written and spoken in the tenth and eleventh centuries AD, let us start with their vocabulary.

Two words that were in common use at this time were 'pleg' (play) and 'gomen' (game). Derived from them were the words 'player' and 'gamester' describing the active participants in these activities, whether employed in an athletic or a mimetic context.

Likewise, in literate monastic and clerical establishments, three Latin words that had survived from Roman times—*mimes, lusores* and *histriones*—continued to be used to describe these same participants in plays and games, whether athletic or mimetic.[1] These words, however, could commonly be extended in their use to embrace musicians, both instrumentalists and singers; so when we encounter either of these words used to cover payments to performers in monastic or civic account books and other documents, we need to be on our guard when attempting to decide which kind of performer was intended by the scribe.

Such ambiguity also attaches to the occasional use of the Norman French words *jeu, jouer, trouvère* and *jongleur*. Between them, however, this little posy of Anglo-Saxon, Latin, Norman and Provençal words suffices to supply us with a rough-and-ready equivalent to the word 'actor' as we use it today. Yet if we seek for a similar equivalent during the tenth and eleventh centuries to what we would describe today as a playwright or dramatist, none will be found. Why?

The answer, as I see it, lies in the circumstances that accounted for the rebirth of dramatic art in Christian Europe during the closing decades of the tenth century AD as already described in Chapter 2 (pp. 20–2).

In short, re-enactment of an historical event within the liturgical celebration of Mass on Easter Sunday morning was not recognised by anyone *at that time* as a play. No writer or author was involved other than St. Matthew, whose record of this event in his Gospel supplied the text for the Introit used to begin the Mass in question. Nor was it thought that any 'plegmen', '*lusores*', '*histriones*', '*jouers*' or 'actors' were involved, since this simple re-enactment of the visit of the Three Marys to Christ's tomb and their brief encounter with its angelic guardian at the High Altar was executed by Benedictine priests in their own abbeys, and for no purpose other than to celebrate the singular significance of Christ's resurrection from the dead. Indeed, it was on the grounds that the text for this 'play' was authenticated by the Bible that it came to be licensed by the Vatican for repeated use (or performance) in subsequent years in all Benedictine houses in England.[2] Hence the need for the promulgation by St. Ethelwold, Bishop of Winchester, of his *Concordia Regularis* of 975 AD obliging its continued use in all Benedictine monasteries in future (see Chapter 2, pp. 22–3); hence also its further extensions to the liturgies celebrating the significance of two other great Calendar Feasts—Christmas and Epiphany—with strictly liturgical re-enactments of the respective visits of the shepherds and the Magi to Bethlehem as recorded in texts supplied from the Bible presented in an identical manner.

It is thus only with the appearance of these additional extensions during the twelfth and thirteenth centuries of less strictly biblical authorship that it becomes recognisable both to the Pope and his advisers that dramatic art (as recognised in Greek and Roman times) had emerged within Christian society, and that its further development must thus be either suppressed, or such licence as was to be accorded to it must be more tightly controlled.

This change of stance is marked in part by decisions taken to distance these simple liturgical music-dramas both from the Mass itself and from the Sanctuary surrounding the High Altar. It was achieved by removing them to Matins and confining re-enactment to the nave and to the vestry or porch behind it. More controversial was the question of whether or not to license further expansion of strictly liturgical re-enactments of well authenticated scriptural events to include dramatisations of other aspects of biblical history and accompanying moral instruction.

As no documentation of precisely how and when these decisions were reached has survived, we have to rely on such factual evidence as we do possess of the greatly extended length and subject matter of those plays which began to appear all over Western Europe during the twelfth century, and which survive in manuscript for us to study, to supply us with our answers. Collectively they tell us unequivocally that as those occasions within the Christian calendar significant enough to warrant re-enactment as short music-dramas within the liturgy began to dry up, so pressure built up to extend the licence already accorded to them to topics of a more broadly educational kind like Original Sin, the coming of Anti-Christ (in a context provoked by the threat from Islam), or veneration of the faith, deeds and self-sacrifice of particular saints and martyrs.

It would be misguided to suppose that these pressures were of so uniform and centralised a kind as to warrant any form of legislation by Papal Decree or through ecclesiastical Councils or Courts. Rather did these pressures accumulate piecemeal from one source in one diocese here, and from another there, with the licence needed to proceed being granted or refused on a localised basis and dependent on the strength of the case advanced to support the request.

Only on such grounds can we explain the advent of the Latin *Ludus de Anti-Christus* presented in the Imperial Court of the Holy Roman Emperor, Frederick Barbarossa in 1160, as Richard Axton has so clearly demonstrated in *European Drama of the Early Middle Ages* (pp. 88–94). This is a long play, making extravagant demands in its cast list, costumes and scenic representation, with no precedent and no immediate sequels. Likewise, the unique Anglo-Norman plays of *La Sainte Resureccion* and *La Mystère d'Adam* possess strong affinities with liturgical ceremonial but stray at times from Latin into the vernacular and lack parallels in other parts of Europe. Both plays are long and have large casts. Such is also the case with the *Ludus Danielis* which proclaims itself to be the work of a group of clerical students from the Cathedral town of Beauvais in Northern France in celebration of the twelve-day Feast of Christmas. A second, but shorter, version of this play exists scripted by an English scholar-poet, Hilarius, who studied under Abelard in the University of Paris, *c.* 1130.[3]

The sudden appearance of plays venerating the lives and deeds of the Virgin Mary, St. Mary Magdalene and St. Nicholas during the twelfth century can be attributed to the formation of clerical brotherhoods known as *confrèries* or Guilds, specifically established to honour them.

It is thus obvious that during the course of the twelfth century at the latest it had become necessary to call upon priests, clerks and students both literate enough and skilled enough to reshape scriptural, apocalyptic and legendary narrative into recognisably dramatic forms. Just as writers employed today by the film and television industry are required to transform novels and biographies into scripts which replace narrative with dialogue amplified by appropriate stage-directions to assist with the visual realisation of the narrative in pictorial terms, so literate men and women in medieval monastic communities were called upon to supply similar services. They were thus rarely, if ever, called upon as renowned poets or authors to perform this task but invariably as artificers or play 'makers'; hence the survival of only three individual names (two of whom were noteworthy German nuns: Hrostwitha of Gandelsheim and Hildegard of Bingen) amongst these 'makers' during the twelfth and early thirteenth centuries, together with one collective group of students from the French Cathedral of Beauvais.

The fourteenth century supplies a few other names, most of whom were French—Adam de la Halle, Rutebeuf and Jehan Bodel for example—but both in England and elsewhere, despite rapid extension and expansion of religious plays in the wake of the establishment of the Feast of Corpus Christi in 1313, no named 'makers' of these plays survives. This becomes understandable to us if we remember that the calls made upon their services remained strictly occasional because they were still tied to Calendar Festivals. Once these plays existed in manuscript, moreover, they were carefully preserved as 'prompt-books' for repeated use in future years, together with copies of the lines and cues for each individual character. These copies were then distributed among the performers to enable them to commit these lines to memory, and then collected in after the performance to be safely stored until needed again when the play was next performed.

Since the copyright in each of these play-scripts was retained by the Abbey Church, religious Guild or Confraternity responsible for staging performances (whether in London, Coventry, Chester, York or elsewhere), it is scarcely surprising that the original makers of them should have remained both anonymous and regarded as artificers rather than as poets, historians or philosophers of sufficient individual distinction and renown to warrant recognition by name. Indeed, in the case of the three- or seven-day Cycles of Mystery Plays in England, and the even longer ones in France, Switzerland

and many German-speaking states scripted during the fifteenth century, authorship of these plays may even have been collective rather than individual.[4]

Long before the start of the fifteenth century, however, we must expect to find changes in this situation being brought about by the impact of secular interest in dramatic entertainments of the kind listed in the preceding chapter—that is to say in castles, town halls, livery halls and universities—upon the erstwhile near-monopoly of the Catholic Church itself.

Remarking on this in Volume I of *Early English Stages* (pp. 181–2), I said that it was in Provence during the eleventh and twelfth centuries that:

'... the Northern tradition of serious [secular] entertainment represented by the recited sagas of the gleeman and scôp fused with the Southern tradition of lighter amusements represented by the antics of the mime and pantomime; and it was there that a new language was fashioned which Southern and Western Europe were ready to accept as a vehicle for story-telling.* ... Those who experimented in the writing of this new poetry were called trouvères and the success of their pioneer efforts, as far as European literature is concerned, was to be as revolutionary as the invention of printing four hundred years later: for the trouvères managed to convince educated society in South-Western Europe that a modern language was as suitable for composition as the ancient ones.* Their verses conveyed stories in a familiar tongue, intelligible to the ladies as well as to the men. Recital of these verses thus rapidly became a popular form of courtly entertainment.'

What was significant about this achievement at that time was its correspondence with the Vatican's call for Crusades to be mounted by Christian kings and emperors to rescue Jerusalem from its Islamic occupants, since this assured the new literature of a far wider hearing than it might otherwise have obtained by providing it with romantic themes of chivalric adventure in far-off and exotic lands. Told in terms of contemporary ideals and contemporary manners, these heroic romances were described as *chansons de geste* and either recited or chanted to the accompaniment of musical instruments. The incentive already provided by the Church in its

* These notes refer to notes 2 and 3 respectively for Chapter V in Volume I, p. 378.

re-enactment of specific events in biblical history within its liturgical music-drama for its principal Calendar Festivals offered the trouvères an example to apply to their own, secular gestes; but, before this could be effected, the trouvères would have to recruit and employ small groups of *mimes, histriones* and *lusores* (i.e. musicians and actors), known collectively as *jongleurs.*

Both in Provence and further afield in France and in Italy, this was achieved during the thirteenth century. The resulting troupe of entertainers, under the leadership of the trouvère, comprised minstrels, tumblers (acrobats), dancers, puppeteers, mimes and actors (see *EES* I, Plate XXII, No. 3). This motley group of nomadic entertainers suffered a severe disadvantage when directly compared with the play-makers and performers of religious drama, for they lacked an ecclesiastical licence to perform and with it both performance-spaces and audiences that they could legitimately call upon to finance their activities.

Some of them, moreover, by taking recourse to mimetic actions and gestures, and verbal *double-entendres* and innuendos calculated to provoke laughter through appeals to commonly experienced human instincts and vulgar, if familiar, styles of behaviour, attracted attention from leading churchmen that invited condemnation of their activities. Among the sternest of such English critics were Robert Grosseteste, Bishop of Lincoln, Thomas de Cobham, Bishop of Salisbury and John Grandisson, Bishop of Exeter, all of whom were learned enough in the writings and pronouncements of the founding fathers of early Christendom to recognise links between the conduct of these nomadic entertainers and that of those mimes and pantomimes who had populated Roman theatres before they were finally closed in the fifth century AD (see *EES* III.1, pp. 183, 191 and 264–6; also *Med Stage* 1, pp. 57–60 and 262–3). In the event, and because their repertoire consisted of secular amusements, these obstacles were overcome by the social status of the leader of these troupes, the trouvère himself who, as a well-educated gentleman with the rank of an esquire, could hope to claim an entré to the baronial households of castles, priories and abbeys equipped with banquet halls and a desire to be entertained on festive occasions. This was far from automatic: rather was it grounded in reputation earned by achievement and then passed on by word of mouth or social correspondence.[5]

The importance of this development lies in the fact that these groups of secular entertainers, in offering an alternative to strictly amateur and occasional religious drama, had opened a way forward to the possibility of placing dramatic entertainment on a quasi-professional and commercial basis. This possibility advanced steadily towards probability as this pioneering, Provençal example spread northwards and eastwards into England and German-speaking states during the course of the fourteenth century.

In England, written testimony to the acceptance of this change in the nature of festive celebrations sponsored and maintained, not only at Court and in the castles of the nobility, but in wealthy ecclesiastical and academic communities as well, survives from the royal Wardrobe Accounts during the reign of King Edward III; and on either side of that from Durham Priory and the two St. Mary Colleges founded by William of Wykeham at Winchester and New College, Oxford.[6] More graphic descriptions of these entertainments are also offered in the poems of William of Nassyngton and *Piers Plowman* from which we learn that not only had it become common practice in the fourteenth century for the nobility to employ a gleeman or trouvère able to provide heroic romances about such notable English Crusaders as Bevis of Southampton and Sir Guy of Warwick but a melée of talented instrumentalists, clowns, dancers and jugglers.[7] Several other account rolls of this period amplify this picture still further by making it clear that these troupes, each known by the name and title of its employer, travelled widely (when their services were not required in their own households) and were rewarded by their hosts.

A question arising from this brief account that begs to be asked is, where did trouvères spring from with their remarkable gifts of leadership and their talent to please? Given the paucity of documentary evidence, the most obvious answer in point both of chronological fact and intelligent surmise must be from amongst the ranks of those relatively affluent young men who enrolled in the newly established universities founded in Bologna, Paris, Krakow, Oxford and Cambridge during the middle years of the twelfth century. From there they would have emerged as graduates well schooled in the *lingua franca* of Christendom, Latin; in Theology, Philosophy, Poetry and Rhetoric (or oratory) and equipped with a broad perspective embracing the opportunities on offer from which to choose a personal vocation. Many of these privileged young men, moreover, must have become closely acquainted while still *in statu pupilari* not only with liturgical music drama and its subsequent extensions into more explicitly dramatic biblical material respecting King Herod, St. Mary Magdalene and the Prophet Daniel, but the quasi-liturgical celebrations of the major feasts of social

50

inversion centred upon the twelve-day Feast of Christmas and the three-day festival of Shrovetide or Carnival.

The latter group, while theoretically redesignated by the Church itself either to venerate the humility of Christ's birth in a stable (Holy Innocents and the Boy Bishop) or as days in which to prepare for the onset of the ensuing forty days of Lenten penance and fasting, once placed in student hands, could scarcely avoid becoming intertwined with experimental reversions to those forms of social inversion and conduct governing celebration of the Roman Kalends and Saturnalia of pagan times (see *EES* II.i, Plate XXX, No. 4). Many descriptive records, contemporary with those events, had survived for them to read in both monastic libraries and those of their own colleges, as did illuminated copies of the comedies and farces of Terence, Plautus and other Roman play-makers; and from these it became clear that the licence accompanying these festivals of social inversion (restricted as they were in number each year) stretched even under the most dictatorial of emperors to sanction the lampooning of all forms of authority—both civic and domestic—in satire, parody and caricature. The Christian liturgies licensed for the Feasts of the Holy Innocents and the Boy Bishops thus invited such treatment from the young clerks and students principally concerned with their fulfilment and quickly found expression in such extensions of them as the Feast of Fools and of the Ass, and above all in the institution of an official Lord of Misrule elected to preside over and to regulate the whole twelve-day Feast of Christmas in all collegiate establishments. Shrovetide followed suit in the celebration of wine, women and song that accompanied Carnival as is amply testified in the *Carmina Burana* from Tegerensee in Bavaria and in the corresponding reprimands and prohibitions that began streaming from the pens of many bishops during the latter half of the thirteenth century and thereafter. Nowhere, however, was this expressed more clearly than in the sudden emergence of *faiblieux* and farces (such as the anonymous English *Interludium de Clerico et Puella* (*c.* 1300) and the earlier French ones of Jehan Bodel and Adam de la Halle scripted in the vernacular).[8]

None of this could have happened, however, without the spectacular accompanying growth of villages into towns and of existing towns into cities that was so central and distinctive a feature of what we now describe as the twelfth-century Renaissance throughout Western Europe; for, with the rapid growth in their populations, there developed a corresponding sense of rivalry and a no less vigorous spirit of competition between them. This applied not only to architects and builders but to the artists and craftsmen of all descriptions needed to furnish and decorate their new buildings, together with the purveyors of building materials, food and clothing.

Thus the rise of largely autonomous cities (authorised in England by the grant of a Royal Charter) served also to create a new class of citizen who owed the wealth and status that they came to acquire within their own communities neither to noble birth nor to ecclesiastical preferment but rather to their own labour and their own creative and commercial acumen—in short, a bourgeois society of radically-minded entrepreneurs.[9]

In discussing the many changes of substance and direction that overtook both dramatic art and theatrical representation during the thirteenth, fourteenth and fifteenth centuries, therefore, especial care must be taken not to forget or ignore the emergence of this new 'middle class' in Christian society, nor to overlook its impact upon the provision of incentives for change emanating from both the clergy and the literate nobility.

If we bear this constantly in mind, we can, I think, begin to comprehend how it became possible during the late twelfth century for Provençal trouvères and their student associates and imitators in the newly established universities to succeed in usurping the initiative, formerly exercised exclusively by the Church in dramatising selected aspects of liturgical ceremonial, and adapting it to suit the secular needs for leisure recreation that were developing in castles and in town and city halls as the twelfth century gave place to its successors.

In this context it is worth recalling that the word *Universitas*, when translated literally, means group, 'guild', fraternity or corporation, all of which words convey an image of an association of like-minded people engaged in forwarding a particular pursuit in a professional sense. This also applies to the French word *mystère* (lit., 'mystery') which was frequently used to define groups or guilds of manual workers skilled enough in particular crafts to describe themselves as builders, weavers or bakers equipped through apprenticeship to practise a trade from which to earn a living.[10]

All such confraternities or guilds were strictly regulated on an hierarchical basis with promotion governed by degrees of skill and experience. The crucial difference separating those guilds created from within a university or ecclesiastical environment and those created in city market places of the fourteenth century was literacy.

This was essential for anyone hoping to engage in a career in the church, the law, medicine and even the making of both plays and music; for those engaged in construction, crafts and commerce it was not. What the trouvères of the twelfth and thirteenth centuries discovered—Chaucer would describe them a century later as 'tregetoures'—was that this rapidly developing gulf within European society could be bridged by story-telling, singing and dance for, as any mother or father quickly learns, nothing is more comforting, reassuring and endearing to children too young to read or write than a bedtime story and a lullaby. It was this discovery that in due course of time would prepare a path towards the creation of a fully professional theatre before the end of the sixteenth century.

This was an eventuality which, during the eleventh and twelfth centuries, the Catholic Church could not be expected to contemplate. We have only to recall the traumas it had endured at pagan hands in its centuries of struggle to establish its right to exist within the Roman Empire, and the fate of its many martyrs, to understand why this was so. This situation, moreover, was still further compounded by the many fulminations of its founding fathers directed against plays, theatres and actors of all descriptions faithfully preserved in monastic libraries as warnings to future generations. Indeed, it was itself becoming sufficiently alarmed during the twelfth century as I have already remarked (p. 49 above) by the reversion to pagan cultures apparent by then throughout secular society to yield to internal pressures to launch an evangelical crusade to counter it. Monastic communities were such closed societies as to be accused by many laymen of giving up so much of their time to their devotional duties as virtually to have ignored the spiritual instruction and edification of laymen.

In this instance, change began late in the thirteenth century with the authorisation accorded to Saints Dominic and Francis to found new Orders of mendicant friars whose principal duties would be to suppress the cult of heresy among the Cathars in Southern France and Navarre and to bring the message prescribed in the Bible to a seemingly heathen and uncaring world through preaching in vernacular languages intelligible to everyone who chose to listen to them. Bonded together by their missionary zeal, and willing to forgo the luxury of a cloistered existence, they chose rather to travel as beggars dependent for their board and lodge on the charity of those responsive to their message. In this, their achievement during the fourteenth century rivalled that of the trouvères a century earlier in coining a new language of moralistic story-telling upon the daily lives and experiences of their hearers whether assembled around civic market crosses or remote and isolated rural shrines. Using biblical texts as their starting point, they then embroidered them in the local dialect and idiom of the districts through which they travelled, to make their messages explicit to their listeners whether they were literate or not. The only requirement obliged upon them in the exercise of this new freedom was that they would abide strictly by the vernacular translations of the Latin Bible authorised for their use by the Papal Curia in Rome to avoid all danger of heretical opinion colouring the texts that they used to begin their sermons.[11]

Simultaneously with the start of this evangelical crusade, the Vatican decided to launch a new Calendar Festival in honour of the Eucharist: the Feast of Corpus Christi. As already remarked earlier, this was first promulgated by Pope Urban IV in 1264 and finally instituted by Pope Clement V in 1311. The nature of this new festival, together with the regulations prescribed for its observance having already been covered in Chapter 2 above (see pp. 25–6), we need only consider here the rapid growth in both the numbers and types of religious plays that swiftly resulted from it during the fourteenth and fifteenth centuries throughout the whole of Western Europe.

In justifying the promulgation of the Feast, Pope Urban IV had referred all Christians to the Eucharist itself, saying:

'For the day of the Supper of our Lord [i.e. Maundy Thursday, or the eve of Good Friday]—the day on which Christ himself instituted this sacrament—the entire church, fully occupied as it is with the reconciliation of penitents, the ritual administration of the holy oil, the fulfilling of the commandment concerning the washing of feet, and other matters, does not have adequate time for the celebration of this greatest sacrament [i.e. the Eucharist itself].'

Thus, since Maundy Thursday is inappropriate, Pope Urban recommended another Thursday—the first after Trinity Sunday, when priests and parishioners alike are less preoccupied—for uninterrupted celebration of the redemptive power of the Eucharist for all believers.

In this sense, then, the new festival was not created to celebrate the significance of a particular calendar event like Christmas Day or Easter Sunday, but to establish a feast of commemoration and thanksgiving for man's salvation through God's decision to become man (in the person of his Son) and to pay the price, through Christ's crucifixion, of man's redemption from Original Sin. This takes us *out of ritual into universal time,* for the Eucharist lacks significance in the context of man's salvation without acknowledging either the Fall of Lucifer and Adam before Christ's birth or Christ's subsequent Harrowing of Hell and Doomsday when all of mankind will be called before his Maker to answer for his life as lived in St. Augustine's 'Great Theatre of the World'.

Therein lies the key to an understanding of the need to 'make' new plays to accompany or supplement the simple procession displaying the Eucharist to public view in city, town and village streets. Here the steady growth in the popularity of both liturgical and more secularly-orientated plays that had manifested itself during the thirteenth century made it well-nigh certain that this would be the method chosen as clerical guilds were established to organise and regulate Corpus Christi processions during the early years of the fourteenth century—more particularly since this new festival would be celebrated in summer weather. No less important was the need, implicit in Pope Urban's instructions regarding the nature of the obligatory procession, to explain its significance to a predominantly illiterate laity. This in itself involved the civic authorities as well as the clergy, and in such circumstances it seems probable that, at the very least, all of these freshly constituted Corpus Christi guilds would have included one experienced play-maker among its members. It was just as likely that some degree of competition would quickly develop both between guilds and between cities.

If this were to have been the case (although no documentary evidence survives to prove it), it would readily explain both why and how so many stories abstracted from both the Old and New Testaments came to be dramatised for the first time within a mere thirty to forty years. What we know for certain is that long sequences of such plays, all scripted in vernacular languages, were being regularly staged for the edification and enjoyment of large public audiences in France, Germany, Spain and England during the last quarter of the fourteenth century at the latest. For this to happen, the organisational arrangements respecting the civic ordering and advertising of such events must have been discussed, tried out and set in place, together with all provisions for the preparation of actors' parts, rehearsals, costuming, scenic devices and funding of these productions in earlier years. It must, moreover, have been far easier to undertake this in large and influential cities than in any single rural parish or group of parishes. It is not until the fifteenth century, however, that we become possessed of sufficient factual evidence from surviving records to acquire an adequate picture of *how* this was achieved.

Essential to almost every aspect of it was the close partnership that swiftly developed between the ecclesiastical and civic authorities within those early years. With the Church providing the *raison d'être* for this public holiday, the licences, the playscripts, the copies of each actor's lines and the music—and in some cases with further assistance from the neighbouring nobility—it was then left to the town halls and civic trade guilds to handle the policing, rehearsing and most aspects of the staging of these productions. Funding and the necessary provision of actors was shared between them on a localised basis, as were such items contributed by, or requested from the nobility resident in that area for supplementary musicians, actors and costumes. This is a subject that will be treated at greater length in the next chapter. When considered collectively, however, it is already apparent that this bonding of social and spiritual aspirations resulted in the creation of the great continental European Passion Plays and the English Mystery Cycles of the fourteenth and fifteenth centuries which rival, in their literary and theatrical dimensions, the monumental architectural and engineering achievements represented by medieval cathedrals. As such, these plays would continue to underpin all aspects of English drama, both religious and secular, for another hundred and fifty years, yet the social standing of both the playmakers and actors failed to change. They thus continued to remain anonymous and regarded as amateurs in a world where professionalism and its attendant modes of self-promotion and self-protection were becoming ever more pronounced in almost all other walks of life.

The reasons for this are twofold. The first was that their services (at least until the early years of the fifteenth century) were so rarely called upon—in most cases no more often than once or twice a year. The second, no less self-evidently, was that the attachment and performance of lengthy sequences of religious plays to the procession celebrating the newly created Calendar Festival of Corpus Christi was universally regarded as an annual event involving entire communities of clergy and laymen alike, all of whom viewed themselves as participants in an act of thanksgiving to God for His redemption of mankind from bondage to sin. That in itself sufficed at least to retard (and possibly to preclude) the singling out of particular individuals for their services in what everyone regarded as an act of worship and celebration undertaken by the whole community in a corporate sense.

The number of cities in Western Europe in which cosmic sequences of biblical plays, all scripted in vernacular languages, had become firmly established before the end of the fourteenth century is impressive. Among the English ones, Chester laid claim to having been the first to do so, c. 1350.[12] If so, its example was quickly followed in York, Beverley, London and Coventry, possibly in Cornwall, and probably in both Ipswich and Shrewsbury.

The earliest surviving ecclesiastical and municipal records attribute some twenty-five plays to Chester by 1377 (together with a Civic Proclamation advertising their performance two months in advance of the event); but York is said to have been already possessed of forty-eight plays by 1375. In York these plays were presented between dawn and dusk on Corpus Christi Day itself, but in Chester they were spread over the three-day holiday of Pentecost (Whitsuntide).

Some idea of the size, wealth and power that enabled city councils in England to contemplate the production of such long and complex sequences of plays before the end of the fourteenth century can be gleaned from an event in London in 1392. During the early summer, King Richard II demanded a loan to help finance his wars in France which the City Council refused to grant. In retaliation for this rebuff, the King deprived the Mayor and Aldermen of their offices and removed his Court from Westminster to York. He stayed there from,

'... the Feast of St. John Baptist unto the Feast of Christmas next coming after [i.e. for six months]. And then the King and his constables saw it not so profitable there as he was in London.'

A condition exacted by Londoners for his return was the restoration (to the City Council) of its civil liberties granted to the city under charter by King Edward I. For that, he was thanked with a variety of gifts and a lavish theatrical civic welcome back to the city. For a full account of this remarkable affair, including the texts of the pageants prepared for the civic welcome, see *EES* I, pp. 64–70.

Common sense dictates that neither in London, Chester nor York could responsibility for the scripting of so many plays have been entrusted to a single play-maker; rather must that have been committed to several literate and experienced priests working as a well-co-ordinated team in close co-operation with the many trade-guilds to whom responsibility for the acting and production of these plays had been allocated. Small wonder therefore that authorship remained anonymous and that no provision appears to have been made to record the names of any of the actors for the simple reason that the leading roles of God the Father, Jesus Christ, St. Peter, St. Mary Magdalene and the Virgin Mary must likewise have been shared out amongst several actors, play by play and guild by guild. Adam and Eve, for example, appear both in the Old Testament play covering their banishment from the Garden of Eden near the start of the Cycles, and in the New Testament play of the Harrowing of Hell towards the end, with each of these plays handled by different guilds.

Responsibility for change, when that began during the early decades of the fifteenth century, passed from the Church and from town and city councils to the domestic chaplains and household servants of the nobility. Encouraged by the evangelical success story of the Corpus Christi Cycles of biblical historical cosmology, governed in both structure and content by story-telling, many members of the new mendicant orders of friar-preachers chose to become dependent for their board and lodgement on the hospitality of the Court and the provincial nobility in return for their services as private chaplains and domestic tutors within their households, and it was they who began to turn their attention to exploiting the dramatic and theatrical possibilities of moral exegesis in plays deliberately scripted for largely literate audiences assembled in the banquet halls of kings, dukes, earls, abbots and priors and in the livery halls of wealthy merchants and bankers. Their resulting plays have since come to be described as Moralities or, in the case of those of relatively short duration, as Moral Enterludes (later, as Interludes).

Precedent for this can of course be said to have been set both in respect of residential employment and in the scripting of shorter, more secularly-orientated plays, from the thirteenth century onwards by the Provençal trouvères and by their student successors in the newly established universities during the fourteenth century; for it was they who began experimenting with the writing of shorter and more tightly self-contained plays described as *Entremets* (when using the French word for them) or 'Enterludes' in English. Scripted to fill intervals of about an hour's duration between the several courses of a festive banquet which could last from 3.00 p.m. until well after midnight, these short plays could be tailored to encompass chivalric and pastoral romances or even farcical fables of domestic strife designed to convey a moral message in their cast lists to include personifications of Virtues and Vices who could then engage in battles to seize control of human souls reflecting the fashionable tournaments of the nobility as conducted in open-air tiltyards in daylight hours[13] (see *EES* I, Plate IV, No. V and Plate VI, No. 8).

A pioneer among this new breed of play-maker in England was John Lydgate, a Dominican priest and a poet of distinction and the natural successor to Geoffrey Chaucer. Between 1427 and 1430 he acquired commissions not only from the boy king, Henry VI, when celebrating Christmas at Hertford Castle, but also from 'the great Estates of this land', the Mayor of London, and the Goldsmiths' and Mercers' Livery Companies in that city. Drawing his scenarios from town life, classical mythology and biblical parables that pointed a moral, he described these entertainments indeterminately as 'Ballads', 'Mummings' and 'Disguisings', yet all of these texts are clearly intended to be spoken by a 'Presenter' accompanied by simultaneous mimetic action by appropriately costumed actors (see *EES* II, Plate XXX, No. 43). The advent of this form of intimate domestic entertainment laid the foundations for its eventual elaboration into the highly spectacular and theatrical Disguisings and Court Masques of the late Elizabethan and early Stuart era.

Shortly after Lydgate introduced his sophisticated Mummings and Disguisings to courtly households, yet another type of short play was added to the range of subject matter on offer to English play-makers for dramatisation through the rest of the fifteenth century. This took the form of a reversion to the use of simple storytelling by recourse to dramatising the lives of legendary saints and martyrs. Three such plays are recorded in Lincoln between 1440 and 1455/6: St. Lawrence, St. Susanna and St. Clara. York records another (St. Dionysys) and Coventry another (St. Catherine) in 1455 and 1490/1 respectively.[14] Authorship of all these plays remains anonymous and the texts have all been lost or destroyed, but it can hardly be coincidental that eleven of these religious plays should have been scripted and performed in cities possessed of cathedrals.

Some idea, however, of their likely shape and content can still be gleaned from two such plays that survive in a manuscript that has since become known as 'The Digby Plays', now in the Bodleian Library at Oxford. These are *The Conversion of St. Paul* and *St. Mary Magdalene*, both written towards the end of the fifteenth century and by authors who still remain anonymous. Both plays are strikingly spectacular in their content and demanding in the requirements made of the actors and craftsmen responsible for their production; both will accordingly be discussed at greater length in the next chapter covering the visual iconography of medieval theatrical representation.

Such further additions to the repertoire of plays offered to public and privately invited audiences in the latter half of the fifteenth century continued to be derived in part from popular sermons, preached in English, urging repentance and atonement for sins of commission and omission while time allowed, and in part from the formal structure of debates as conducted in schools and universities as a component of a student's training in rhetoric (i.e. as orators). In most cases the two went hand in hand since it was obvious that if argument was to take precedence over narrative as the driving force behind the stage action, the storyline must be chosen from topical sources that would help to point the moral through characters, situations and images that were already familiar as depicted in countless frescoes, stained-glass windows and tapestries in churches, castles and town halls alike throughout the country.

Where actors were concerned, however, the addition of comic and romantic *Entremets* (Enterludes), Disguisings and short moral Interludes to the repertoire of licensed festive entertainments during the fourteenth and early fifteenth centuries brought with it a discernible change in their social status.

This change is attributable to the fact that, since none of these entertainments was tied directly to Calendar Festivals (as were those devised to celebrate the Feast of Corpus Christi and particular saints' days), performances of them could be repeated—at least theoretically—both on holidays other than those which had first brought them into being and in places other than that in which the first performance had been given. Before this could start to happen, however, recognition had to be accorded to the performers both *as actors* and as household servants of a named patron who could license them to travel beyond the boundaries of their respective local domains, and since this was unlikely to be offered by the Church, permission for so radical a departure from past precedent could only come from one source—the highest secular authority in the Kingdom, the Court.

The extant records are too scanty to allow us to state precisely when this step forward was first taken, but the probability is that the young Henry VI was the first king to maintain his own small company of actors since both household and civic account books from the 1450s onwards reveal that payments were being made not only to the *lusores regis* (King's players) but to those of some of the wealthiest and most powerful members of the baronial nobility to whom this privilege had been extended by the King. Precedent for this already existed in the case of privately maintained companies of musicians whose services were regularly called upon both in the chapel and in military quarters of most castles: but, where the Church had never raised objections to them, its latent hostility to actors (except when called upon in an amateur capacity on a strictly occasional basis to further its own evangelical ends) remained an abiding concern to many senior members of the Catholic hierarchy. Since no evidence exists to suggest that the Church challenged the Court in this instance, we must assume that the King's use of his own prerogative to bestow licences to maintain small troupes of actors in addition to musicians upon request from powerful members of the aristocracy was accepted as unlikely to change the existing *status quo* in any heretically objectionable way. So here a random selection of entries in surviving account books recording rewards paid out to privately maintained companies of players during the latter half of the fifteenth century must suffice to illustrate this point.

The earliest is a payment, entered in the Account Rolls of Selby Abbey in Yorkshire, 'to players of our Lord the King this year (*c.* 1450) of six shillings and eightpence', followed up later that year by a further payment to 'the players of the Duke of York' of exactly half of that amount. In 1479/80, no less than six such companies visited the Abbey—the King's, the Duke of Gloucester's, the Earl of Northumberland's and groups of actors maintained by Lord Scrope, Sir John Conyers and Sir James Tyrell. Where the King's players continued to receive six shillings and eightpence, the Earl of Northumberland's were given five shillings for their performances; those of Lord Scrope and Sir John Conyers, however, were awarded payments of only a shilling each, and those of Sir James Tyrell even less—a mere eightpence. Yet in 1483 the Abbey Rolls surprisingly record a payment of three shillings and fourpence 'to the players of the Duchess of Norfolk'. From that entry we must assume that widows inherited their dead husbands' responsibilities, respecting their household servants as an integral part of his estate.[15]

Other records from other places confirm that 'payments in reward' of these kinds had already come to be recognised as standard fees geared to accord with both the social status of the player's patron and local expectations of the quality of the entertainment likely to be on offer. Thus in 1467 the Warden and Fellows of

Winchester College rewarded the Duke of Arundel's players with two shillings, while in 1482 the Duke of Norfolk rewarded 'four players of my Lord of Gloucester' with three shillings and fourpence.[16]

The most revealing of all such figures supplied in surviving account books is perhaps the one recorded by the Treasurer of the Corporation of Shrewsbury respecting a visit from the King's (Richard III) players in 1483. While this fails to provide the fee actually awarded, it does specify that the number of players in this company was six and that the payment was given *pro honestate villae* (as a gift in expression of thanks from the town).[17] This entry strongly suggests that all such payments to visiting companies of players were still regarded as gratuities paid out partly as a token of thanks due to their patron and partly to cover their travelling expenses rather than as fees demanded by professional actors in our sense of those words.

Records of these privately maintained groups of players travelling abroad during the fifteenth century are matched, moreover, by those relating to small troupes claiming to represent particular towns who appear to have obtained permission from the Mayor or Council to visit other towns in the vicinity on festive occasions. Such were the players from Coventry and Daventry who were rewarded for visits to Maxstoke Priory in Warwickshire (*c.* 1450) with payments of a shilling and eightpence respectively.[18] Likewise in Kent and Sussex, players from Lydd, Heme, Folkestone and Rye all brought plays to neighbouring New Romney in 1422, 1429, 1474 and 1489 respectively. Yet while some of these plays were particular to religious Calendar Festivals, there were others— described in account books as 'games' rather than 'plays'—which more nearly resembled folk-dramas variously associated with May Day, Yule, Wassail, St. George, Robin Hood, Morris dances, Hocking and Mumming.[19] Such were 'Lopham Game', 'Garblesham Game' and 'Kenningale Game', all of which visited the neighbouring village of Harling in Norfolk in 1457, 1463 and 1467 respectively.[20]

While these 'rewards', whether paid to actors primarily employed as servants in noble households or to players travelling to neighbouring towns as representatives of particular townships in more localised areas, must be regarded as gifts to amateurs rather than as wages supporting them in a regular profession throughout the year, it becomes increasingly difficult to believe that some of the more enterprising and ambitious members of these troupes had not begun to entertain hopes, before the end of the fifteenth century, of using their mimetic talents to forge an escape route from serfdom by establishing themselves on an economically stable basis as professional actors just as many musicians had succeeded in doing a century earlier.

Such thoughts, if readers were to consider them, are not far removed from those grasped at by many teenagers today who, on leaving school with no recognised qualifications, turn to football, the boxing ring or the world of 'pop' music to rescue them from the prospects of drudgery that otherwise look likely to pursue them for the rest of their lives. If this were to have been in the minds of these small troupes of medieval players they would not have had long to wait to see their dream fulfilled for, within a decade or two of the accession of the House of Tudor to the English throne in 1485, many of the assumptions and regulations that had governed medieval life and thought for centuries would be forced to give way to a new era of radical change and innovation imported from Italian-, Dutch- and German-speaking states.

A question relating both to these actors and to those who devoted their time and talent to rehearsal and performance of biblical Corpus Christi Cycles and their long Morality and Saint Plays has yet to be addressed: the expectances entertained of them all by their audiences. In other words, what was understood by the words 'acting' or 'playing' during the Middle Ages? Here we find ourselves obliged by lack of contemporary descriptive evidence to take recourse to what is at best 'informed speculation', and since that can be interpreted with better chances of success in a broader context of all those visual aspects of medieval theatrical representation which is to form the subject of the next chapter, I propose to postpone any attempt to answer this question until then, and to return here to take note of a change that was about to overtake play-makers between the 1450s and the 1480s which would prove to be even more radical in its consequences for them than those that were already confronting actors—the invention of printing.

This revolutionary discovery was first made in Europe at Mainz in Germany in 1454/5 and arrived in London twenty years later when William Caxton established his printing press at Westminster in 1476. From then onwards all play-makers could begin to entertain ambitions to free themselves from their previous thraldom to anonymity for, instead of having to hand over the single, hand-written texts of their plays for a token fee to the group of players who were to bring it to life in performance, these play-makers could foresee an era in which their plays could appear in printed editions available to such interested readers as could afford to buy a copy, as well as to other groups of actors. And if well-educated noblemen and gentlemen could already afford to maintain a personal company of players to entertain themselves and other guests at Calendar Festivals in their banquet halls, why should they not also elect to support play-makers of their own choosing with their patronage? What was still needed if this scenario was to be realised was a return to more stable social and economic conditions, both of which had been severely disrupted, at first by the Hundred Years War with France and then by the accompanying civil wars occasioned by the rivalries of Lancastrian and Yorkist claimants to rightful possession of the English throne through most of the fifteenth century.

Within a decade of William Caxton establishing his printing press in London, the accession of Henry Tudor in 1485 and his marriage to Elizabeth of York in 1486, brought both of these wars to an end. And with that accomplished, play-makers and actors alike could look forward to exploiting the new opportunities that had so suddenly and unexpectedly been offered to them.

V

VISUAL AND ECONOMIC ASPECTS OF PLAY-PRODUCTION DURING THE MIDDLE AGES

Just as the original re-enactment of the Visit of the Three Marys to Christ's tomb on Easter Sunday morning in Benedictine Abbeys of the tenth century AD was protected within the Christian liturgy by the Latin words *quasi* (as if) and *quomodo* (in the manner of), so all aspects of its visual realisation—from actors and acting to costume and scenic representation—were protected iconographically by the Church. In other words, what was *done* in the naves and chancels of these abbeys and by these priests was not to be regarded by its witnesses as either pictorially or representationally realistic in any historical sense, but only emblematically (or symbolically) and within a context of ritual time appropriate to the most notable of all Calendar Festivals—Easter Sunday (see Chapter 2, pp. 22–3 above).

This was a concept that came to be shared and accepted by all subsequent priests, play-makers, players and audiences alike throughout the Middle Ages. Slowly, as century followed century, it was relaxed and modified as the repertoire of plays on offer came to be extended from the earliest liturgical music-dramas of the tenth and eleventh centuries to embrace other subject matter abstracted from biblical, legendary and chivalric literature. Still further concessions came to be made to both verbal and visual realism as the narrative content of plays came to be scripted in vernacular languages and to be extended to include moralistic debate and even occasional secular subject matter during the thirteenth and fourteenth centuries. Nevertheless, the legacy bequeathed by these clerical, largely anonymous and almost exclusively amateur

English play-makers and players of the early Middle Ages to their Tudor successors towards the close of the fifteenth century remained true to its origins in liturgical music drama of the tenth and eleventh centuries A.D.

Grounded in the iconography of the Byzantine rather than that of the Roman Church, but reinforced by Roman Catholic faith and doctrine, it then expanded as an aid to an evangelistic Crusade to educate an illiterate laity by recourse to the use both of vernacular languages instead of classical Latin, and to historical anachronism and local dialect to assist comprehension during the fourteenth century. This iconography was stretched to its limits by the inclusion of familiar, topical and comic incidents snatched briefly from contemporary country, municipal and domestic life; but with all of them so interlocked and presented to viewers of Church altarpieces, wall-paintings and dramatic performances as to seem to have remained faithful to its emblematic starting point through five hundred years.

What then did the play-makers and players, and the craftsmen whom they called upon to supply them with the costumes and scenic devices required to identify characters and locations in their scenarios, offer to their audiences?

The answer, at its simplest, lies in a choice made by a play-maker (the story-teller) to appeal directly to one or more bright-eyed and eager listeners to embark upon a journey with him or her, starting out from a given place at a given time, but with its destination only revealed to them at its end.

This invitation, if accepted, will then be transmuted through words, deeds and costume into a mimetic game to be played out by its animators, actors or gamesters for as long as the play-maker and his company of players can retain the interest and attention of those watching and listening to them.

The rules by which this game were to proceed were simple. On the one hand, listener-spectators for their part must temporarily suspend all disbelief in order to create a level playing field, or performance space, for this game to begin. With that half of the bargain fulfilled, play-makers and gamesters must then fulfil theirs by peopling the designated world of make-believe chosen as the acting area with readily identifiable characters. With the entry of the first of these characters this game or play has begun.

There is no need for this character to say a single word on first stepping into public view before he or she will start revealing important facts about him- or herself, for the play-maker's choice of the clothes in which this character is dressed will do that. Thus, just as rags and grime instantly declare themselves as indicative of penury, deprivation or oppression, so furred gowns, flashing jewels, crowns and mitres suggest positions of power, wealth and privilege. With that done, the play-maker need only endow his character with some such simple phrase as 'I King Herod am!' to enable his audience to begin to regard him as a real person who has come among them already equipped with an identity of his own.

From that point forwards the play-maker may choose to allow this character to harangue his hearers as if they were his subjects to impress his personality upon them in greater detail, or he may choose to advance his storyline by introducing another character or characters with news, to communicate to King Herod requiring action.

While, however, it may be relatively easy for us to recognise how an experienced play-maker can develop his craft to supply him- or herself with many unexpected twists and turns in the storyline and many unsuspected facets in a character's behaviour, we must oblige ourselves to recall that no English play-maker working during the tenth and eleventh centuries was as yet either expected or allowed to exercise such a degree of independence of mind or creative initiative when called upon to dramatise a biblical event to celebrate a principal Calendar Festival. These festivals—Advent, Christmas, Epiphany, Easter, Whitsun and the Ascension—were already familiar events in New Testament history and only called for modest adjustments to transpose the original *oratio obliqua* (indirect address) of the Latin Gospel text into the *oratio recta* (direct address) of dramatic dialogue and re-enactment. Yet because recourse has been taken to pretence and make-believe ('game' and 'play'), it has become possible to transpose historical time into ritual time, thereby transforming the single, actual historical event into one that can repeat itself annually for all eternity. Therein, moreover, lay the justification for licensing both play-maker and actors to assist the Church to establish faith in the first instance and, having done so, to reinforce it annually thereafter; for that was something they, and they alone, could effect between them.

What St. Ethelwold, in promulgating his *Concordia Regularis* (*c.* 975) for observance in all Benedictine abbeys in England, had thus ensured was that the mimetic play or game (which he himself described as *Ordo Quem Quaeritis in Sepulchro*) would not only be repeated annually on every Easter Sunday morning thereafter, but would result in a cathartic experience for all who participated in it (see p. 21 above). In short, the recreational element of play or game authorised within this rite would be transmuted through re-enactment into 'earnest'—the serious, educative and doctrinal significance of this event as lifted out of the distant, historical past into the immediate present.

Apart from some five other liturgical music dramas licensed for enactment on major Calendar Festivals—notably Advent, Christmas, Epiphany, Whitsun and Ascension—there was little pressure for change for the next two hundred years. All plays continued to be sung rather than spoken; to be dressed in costumes derived from vestments normally worn by the clergy; and for authors and actors alike to remain veiled in anonymity. However, with the passing of time, performances of these plays came slowly to be distanced both from the Mass itself and the Sanctuary as pressures to expand the text, introduce new characters and even to dramatise biblical narrative drawn from Old Testament sources rather than exclusively from the New, began to develop during the closing years of the twelfth century. The *Ludus de Anti-Christo* (1160), *Ludus Danielis* (*c.* 1150) and *Jeu d'Adam* or *Ordo representacionis Ade* (*c.* 1160) offer the most striking examples. No less significant in this context is that the original Latin descriptive rubric *Ordo* can by then be seen to be yielding place to the more self-evidently theatrical *Ludus* or *Representacionis*, or even *Jeu*.[1]

If change was slow until late in the twelfth century, it accelerated more rapidly thereafter following the reforms introduced by Pope Innocent III: the creation of two new Orders of Mendicant Friars—the Dominicans and the Franciscans (see Chapters II and IV, pp. 26 and 53–4 above) authorised by the Vatican to preach in vernacular languages; and the Institution of the New Calendar Feast of Corpus Christi in 1311; for between them, these events served to attach the instructional possibilities of dramatic art and theatrical representation far more closely to the evangelistic service of the Church than had ever been the case before. Thus, where liturgical music-drama had confined itself largely to conserving devotional and introspective aspects of Christian worship for nearly two centuries, the Vatican, in embarking upon an unprecedented sequence of reforms within the next hundred years, itself opened the way forward to radical and rapid change.

These changes, when they came during the first half of the fourteenth century, brought with them new demands upon the play-makers, actors and the many men and women whose services would soon be required to provide a greatly expanded repertoire of plays.

These included not only many more actors to perform them, but a much wider range of craftsmen to supply them with the costumes and locational scenic and pyrotechnical devices needed to stage them; and beyond all these questions lay that of how all these additional production costs were to be met.

Since the pressures that had precipitated these changes were primarily doctrinal and evangelistic, it was natural for the Church to seek help in mounting this Crusade from both its own members and its converts—a fact that it was honest and open enough to declare when creating the new Calendar Feast of Corpus Christi in 1311. In electing to establish this Festival and by placing it on a level with Easter and other major feasts of the ritual year, it effectively proclaimed its intention of switching public attention away from the concerns of monastic life outwards to those of a largely illiterate laity and its alarmingly obsessive preoccupation with those of the secular world outside.

This message it chose to deliver in three specific ways. First, it instructed its own Archbishops, Cardinals and Bishops to take immediate steps within their own diocese to ensure that the Host would be carried out of the Sanctuary of every parish church in a solemn procession through the streets, prominently displayed for all to see and venerate, and back again on the first Thursday after Trinity Sunday, in all future years.[2]

Beyond that, it was left open to them to consult with their local parish priests and civic officials about what further measures should be taken to reinforce the significance and importance of the new festival. This measure, as it was hoped, would then lead on to still greater involvement of laymen at all levels of the celebrations finally adopted. The advent of *The Play Called Corpus Christi* spells out for us the answer that in English cities won the greatest measure of approval.

The consequences that followed from this decision for the future of the theatre, both in England and elsewhere in Europe, can scarcely be exaggerated. First, it must be remarked that it was those towns already large enough to contain abbeys or cathedrals of their own that seized the initiative in formulating the directions change would take, for they could be relied upon to supply enough clergy in residence already equipped with the skills needed to devise long sequences of new plays embracing the history of the Christian world from Creation to Doomsday, and to provide the many copies of individual actors' lines that would be needed for them to learn and recite. Such cities, moreover, as Chester, York,

London and Coventry, also already possessed a wide range of well-organised Trade Guilds to meet most of the demands likely to be made upon them in helping to service the production requirements of these long sequences of new plays. It must also be remembered that these cities already possessed the powers required to levy local taxes to assist in meeting the production costs of the many new plays that were to become the central corporate feature of the new Calendar Holyday.

With that said, however, virtually no documentation of the many meetings and discussions that must have taken place in Cathedral Chapter Houses and City Halls during the forty years between 1311 and the 1350s to arrive at decisions on the form that local celebrations should take, appears to have survived. This unfortunately leaves only speculation open to us if we are to bridge the time-gap of some forty years that separates the two sets of facts that we do possess at either end of this period: those surrounding the Institution of the new Festival in 1311, and those describing the celebrations in Beverley, York and Chester during the 1370s which offer us proof of the inclusion of performances of new biblical plays in English involving both clergy and laymen.

We are, however, assisted in such speculative quests as we may elect to undertake in any attempt to explain this transformation by other relevant items of information which have reached us from both clerical and civic sources during this period. Among the most important of these are:

1. The sudden emergence from within the ranks of the junior clergy of Corpus Christi Guilds charged with devising appropriate celebrations to mark the new Festival.[3]
2. The direct involvement of long-established trade guilds in responsibility for performances when these begin.
3. The prior adoption by all such trade guilds of a patron saint, together with funds needed to support a Guild Chapel and chaplain.
4. The existing relationships between the elected leaders of these trade guilds and City Councils as represented by the Mayor, Chamberlain and other civic officials.[4]

Collectively, this information at least testifies to the existence between 1311 and the 1370s of a nexus of close connections already in place between clergy and laymen in regular communication with one another and thus able to collaborate in the pursuit of common

70

objectives; and during those years a priority among these was to reach agreement on the most appropriate and practical ways in which to celebrate the new Feast.

The answer that had been arrived at in most English cities by the start of the fifteenth century or shortly after, was a predominantly theatrical one encouraging dramatisation of the history of the world as recorded in the Old and New Testaments, but allowing wide variations both in allocating responsibility for presenting it and in the manner of executing and financing it.

As these variations have already been examined and illustrated in Volumes I and II (Part 1),[5] I shall not repeat them here, so let us proceed at once to the single exception—the supply of texts for the new plays, for here we can be certain that the Church retained to itself not only the right to license the performance of biblical plays as an appropriate method of celebrating the Feast of Corpus Christi, but also exclusive control over the provision of all new texts—more especially if these were to be scripted in English.

What is equally certain here is that, in requiring a public procession through town and city streets as an obligatory component of these celebrations, the Church was exceeding the limits of its own jurisdiction in this respect. It required both the permission of the resident civic officials in the City Hall if this procession was to proceed and, hopefully, their active co-operation in implementing such other public celebrations as might accompany or supplement it; but if this permission was to be granted, and active assistance to be forthcoming, there would be a price to pay for it. In the event, permission was granted, and the price tag attached was the surrender to town and city halls of control over the ordering of the procession, together with a dominant voice in determining the arrangements to be made for the production of such new plays as the Church itself might see fit to authorise and supply; and herein may lie an explanation of how York chose to confine its plays to a single day and combine them with the procession, while Chester elected to shift its plays to Whitsun and to spread them over three full days.

An inevitable consequence of this bargain was that most of the arrangements for the production of these plays would have to be subcontracted to the officers of the many wealthy trade guilds on whom most of the City Councillors from the Mayor downwards were themselves electorally dependent for their seats, since control of the labour market lay effectively in their hands. This, however, was a condition that corresponded closely with the Church's own

71

needs—both material and evangelistic—since it not only ensured a much wider involvement of laymen than would otherwise have been the case, but also a substantial reduction in the financial burden accruing from the production of so many new plays. It thus proved to be a bargain that was acceptable enough to both parties to have been put into effect during the closing decades of the fourteenth century not only in Beverley, York and Chester (and possibly in Coventry) but also in London.

In this context, London has to be regarded as exceptional, not only because it was larger and richer than any other city in the Kingdom, but also because its residents included a far greater number of parish priests and clerks than any provincial city. Record, moreover, of a rapid growth in the number, frequency and type of theatrical performance offered to its citizens antedates those to be found in any provincial city by nearly a hundred years. Our datum point is provided by William Fitzstephen who, in a prefatory description of London in his *Life of Thomas à Becket* (*c.* 1175), tells us that Londoners could already expect to be edified *pro ludis theatricalibus, pro ludis scenicis sanctiones,* re-enacting miracles, performed by saints, or *representationes* (plays) about the constancy and self-sacrifice of martyrs.[6] Given this early date, it must be presumed that these plays were still being scripted and performed in Latin since, as yet, no sanction had been accorded by the Vatican to write or present them in English.

Nothing more is heard of plays in London until 1378 when the priests in charge of the scholars of St. Paul's Cathedral Choir School had cause to petition King Richard II 'to prohibit some inexpert persons from representing the History of the Old Testament, to the great prejudice of the said clergy, who have been at great expense in order to represent it at Christmas'. Choice of that Calendar Festival for this performance suggests that it had originally been devised to celebrate Advent—the start of the Christian year—and as an extension of the earlier liturgical music-drama, *Ordo Prophetarum.* As there is no record of any action being taken to stop these 'inexpert' intruders, and since, by 1384, London's parish clerks are recorded as presenting long sequences of plays scripted from biblical texts drawn equally from both the Old and New Testaments at Skinners' Well in August, it seems probable that they were the 'inexpert persons' complained of by the student players at St. Paul's.[7]

In 1391, and again in 1409, these same plays at Skinners' Well are claimed to have lasted for four whole days and, in 1411, for 'seven days continually'. As this corresponds with what by then was occurring regularly in several provincial cities—most notably Beverley, York, Chester, Wakefield and Coventry—in celebration of the Feast of Corpus Christi, it is to be presumed these long sequences of new plays in London had been created under the same initial auspices, but that performances had been shifted to August for local reasons. Just as Chester had chosen to present its plays during the three-day holiday at Whitsun, London may have opted to attach performances of its plays to one or other of its two great summer trade fairs—Lammastide (1st August) and St. Bartholomew (24th August)—both of which had been regarded as Harvest Festivals since Roman times. A further local reason for doing this, given the fact that in London it was the parish clerks and not the trade guilds who were responsible for both staging these plays and meeting the production costs, may well have been commercial, for fairs and markets have always attracted not only exceptional numbers of customers from within the towns where they were held, but also from surrounding districts, together with entertainers eager to exploit the audience potential offered by the large crowds in holiday mood already so conveniently assembled.[8]

Thus from the start of the fifteenth century we may safely regard ourselves as possessed of enough factual evidence to assume that from that time onwards other towns and cities throughout the country would seek to emulate them as and when their own financial resources allowed them to do so. As this is an assumption confirmed by surviving records from Hereford, Ipswich, Norwich, Lincoln and other places, we may safely move on to consider the theatrical consequences of these midsummer festivals, harnessed as they were by the Church to the Christian calendar for its own evangelistic purposes but involving both clergy and laymen in the organising, scripting, acting, costuming and other aspects of the staging of this greatly enlarged repertoire of religious plays, not the least of which was the financial provisions needed to cover the costs of production.

The driving force behind all the changes in staging conventions that accompanied this rapid expansion of the dramatic repertoire can only have been the play-makers since they, and they alone, possessed the authority from the Church to translate the new play-scripts from the Latin Bible (the Vulgate) into local vernacular dialects, add new characters and thus control both the shape and context of the performances actually presented to greatly enlarged audiences of largely illiterate laymen. These same play-makers, moreover, were also already possessed of the iconic vocabulary required to control every aspect of the theatrical representation of their plays. This they had acquired through their familiarity, as priests working in the *scriptorium* (or writing-room) of their respective monastic libraries, with the emblematic approach consistently adopted by the Church towards pictorial depiction of all biblical characters and such scenic landscapes in which they figured. This emblematic visual *lingua franca*, or pictorial dictionary, as it had evolved through a thousand years of practical experiment and achievement in mosaic, illuminated manuscripts, statuary, oil-painting, fresco and finally stained glass, covered every aspect of cosmology as interpreted within Christian theology.

The universe had thus come to be viewed as made up of three distinct and separate worlds, all of which had been created by God as Pantocrater to reflect the moral order of its entirety as seen through Christian eyes, but each of which operated independently of the others according to the rules appointed for it by its creator.

Central to this vision was the terrestrial world which St. Augustine had described as 'The Great Theatre of the World' (thus likening it to those that he himself had attended in Rome and in its North African colonies before his conversion), containing a circular auditorium from which God and the whole hierarchy of Heaven could watch the uses made by mortal men and women of their gift of Free Will as acted out on its stage.[9]

Directly above it was the celestial world (described either as Heaven, Paradise or the New Jerusalem) populated by hierarchies of Archangels, Angels, Seraphs and Cherubim, together with the souls of saints and martyrs and all those mortal men and women who had repented of their sins and earned their redemption (and with it their passage to salvation and everlasting life) by their subsequent penance and atonement through good works.

Below both lay the infernal world, or Hell. This was presided over by Lucifer (the disobedient Archangel who, in his presumption, had challenged God Himself for supremacy) and occupied by his fellow conspirators, or devils, together with those souls who, in the course of their mortal lives, had sinned and who, in failing to repent, had thus invited the everlasting Damnation to which they would be assigned on Judgement Day.[10]

Pictorially, all three of these worlds were represented as walled cities, or citadels, fortified and defended by their occupants but with strikingly different interiors. Heaven was seen as a walled garden replete with birds and flowers and peopled by choirs of angelic children either singing or playing assorted instruments. Earth was likewise depicted as a city retaining features of the Paradise Garden before the Fall, but inhabited by people engaged in constant toil, wars and commerce, addicted to pleasure, luxury and idleness but as often wracked by pain and grief, and presided over by the skeletal figures of Time and Death—the former identified by a long, white beard and hand-held hourglass, and the latter by his hooded cloak and scythe. Hell was represented as a grim castle with a gaping mouth of dragon's teeth for a gatehouse and portcullis (see Plate VIII, No. 10). Its interior consisted of dungeons, torture chambers and greasy, smoke-filled kitchens. Ruled by Lucifer (or Satan), assisted by Belial and Beelzebub, it was peopled by grotesques— half beast and half man—and the many damned souls everlastingly assigned to their sadistic care.

The starkness of this emblematic view of the universe, as formulated during the first millennium AD, invited all succeeding generations of artists to use their own creative imaginations to embellish the distinctions between each segment of the tripartite whole in order to illuminate and clarify the cautionary tale contained within the original icon.

When this came to be applied to theatrical representation of biblical narrative and incident as scripted by Corpus Christi vernacular plays of the fourteenth and fifteenth centuries, this icon could then easily be subdivided into more detailed pictorial emblems of those components needed for the staging of each play and thus assist audiences to recognise the location of the stage action. This task was only made easier by the play-makers' decision to restrict such biblical narrative as was chosen for dramatisation to specific incidents, each of which was possessed of a self-contained storyline of its own: Cain's murder of his brother Abel; Abraham's sacrifice of his son Isaac; the Annunciation; the visit of the Magi; the entry into Jerusalem; the trial before Pilate; and so on.

An advantage accompanying this decision was to offer play-makers the freedom to link their choice of incidents in order to dramatise their typological significance—that is, to correspondences between events recorded in the Old Testament and those chosen from the New. In these terms of reference, Abraham's sacrifice of his son Isaac can thus be seen to prefigure the Crucifixion just as Noah's Flood prefigures Doomsday.[11] So Christ replaces Adam, Mary replaces Eve, and the Cross on Calvary replaces the Tree of Knowledge in the Garden of Eden as the list of New Testament plays moves to its conclusion.

This goes far to explain why only some five or six incidents from the Old Testament were regularly chosen for inclusion in most of the surviving English Cycles, while at least two or three times as many as that were taken from the New Testament. The 1591 manuscript of the Chester Cycle, for example, comprises five plays selected from six stories recorded in the Old Testament—Fall of Lucifer, Creation (Adam, Eve, Cain and Abel), Noah's Flood, Abraham and Isaac together with those of Moses, Balaam and Balak—while including seventeen from the New Testament and three taken from the Book of Revelation. The Townley (or N-Town) manuscript likewise dramatises the same five incidents from the Old Testament and adds another, but varies the choices made from the New while adding another seven.[12]

By 1440, York had commissioned forty-nine, but of these only nine were taken from the New Testament and all of them are shorter than those presented in Chester and Wakefield. Of the many other provincial cities in which we know processional performances to have been staged during the fifteenth and early sixteenth centuries, too many playscripts, play-lists and other documents have been destroyed or lost to permit us to arrive at any reliable judgement of what was actually offered to those audiences.

In places, however, where stationary staging was preferred—notably Cornwall, London and East Anglia—enough documentary evidence has survived to assure us that the same pattern of choice was followed in selecting those incidents considered to be obligatory where dramatisation was concerned, while allowing greater elbow-room for the inclusion of additional incidents of especial relevance to the local population.[13]

When taken collectively, this information suffices to illustrate the extraordinarily ambitious scale of the productions envisaged by both the clerical play-makers of Corpus Christi religious drama scripted in English, and the many leaders of town and city councils whom they called upon for assistance in staging them. Nothing to match it, either in terms of length or breadth of subject matter, had previously existed on which to model it; nor has any theatrical creative endeavour to match it emerged since, unless it is argued that Richard Wagner's four-part *Der Ring des Nibelungen* got close to doing so when it received its first performance in the newly built Festspielhaus in Bayreuth in 1876. This achievement of scores of anonymous medieval play-makers thus needs to be recalled to mind if we are to appreciate today the many problems that had to be faced and overcome before any such creative concept could be transmuted from a land of literary and theological wishful thinking into one of practicable theatrical reality.

Let us make a start therefore by confronting the problems raised by scenic representation, since it is invariably in this respect that prospective audiences first make their presence felt as indispensable participants in any such enterprise. In this case, the first question to arise was that of representing the three separate but inter-related ideological worlds of Heaven, Earth and Hell as demanded by the play-makers. Here, the solution adopted took its starting point from the particular incidents chosen for dramatisation from both the Old and New Testaments. Since most of these took place in the terrestrial world, it was thought necessary to identify the particular scenic locations of the stage-action in greater detail there than in either Heaven or Hell. The technique adopted to effect this, therefore, was to simplify depiction of each terrestrial location by reducing it (in a manner copied from earlier liturgical music-drama) to an emblem that would *suggest* it to viewers while leaving them free to supply further details from their individual imaginations.

Thus the Garden of Eden, for instance, could be presented to audiences as an adjunct of Heaven (or Paradise) represented by a single fruit-bearing tree, placed in the centre of a circular or rectangular performance space ringed by a fence with a gate in it and a ladder opposite leading up to a dais on which to seat *Deus Pater* with St. Michael in attendance. Other trees, bushes and flowers could be added as fancied, if funds permitted.

Two or more trees could similarly be stretched in the viewer's imagination, when assisted by dialogue and mimetic action, to represent a wood or a forest, while a simple bench, surmounted by an arch with a vine or climbing rose entwined around it, sufficed to supply an arbour to represent a summer garden which, in its turn, could be supplemented by a fountain to provide greater pictorial realism where financial and technical resources allowed.

A useful variant on the arbour was the pavilion, or tent, since it could identify an interior scene whether used as a bed-chamber, a law-court or military encampment. Other, more elaborate, variants were the tomb or monument; the mountain, with or without a curtained cave; and the prison or dungeon. All of these devices, however, were normally conceived and constructed as two-storey structures possessed either of exterior steps or an interior ladder to link its upper to its lower level.[14]

In this make-believe theatrical world of emblematic rather than pictorially realistic representation, the challenge presented by a need to provide a desert landscape, or wilderness, as a scenic location could be met by deploying the mountain with its curtained cave, thereby enabling Moses to receive the tablet containing the Ten Commandments from God on Mount Sinai, the Devil to tempt Christ to defy gravity and the Crucifixion to be re-enacted on Golgotha.

Noah's Ark could likewise be built on stage by his sons and neighbours from prefabricated panels that only needed to be hammered together to provide a three-dimensional ship into which two-dimensional painted cut-outs of birds and beasts (including the indispensable dove and raven) could be carried to escape the ensuing storm. Even the still more daunting task of parting the Red Sea to allow Moses and the Israelites to escape from Egypt and closing it up again to drown Pharoah's army while still in hot pursuit, could be achieved with the use of cloths painted to suggest the waves of the sea, and so manipulated by stage-hands as to create the desired effect. Recourse, moreover, to this same conjuring trick could persuade audiences that Noah's Ark was floating on the stormwaters of the flood until they began to subside on the return of the dove, for then a painted rainbow could be raised above the Ark to signify God's forgiveness and with it a new start to life on earth.

A singular advantage of this emblematic technique of representing both the location of the stage action and the ensuing demands made upon the actors and craftsmen responsible for presenting it to their audiences, was its adaptability; for, whether the plays were to be produced processionally (as at York or Chester), in the round (as in Cornwall) or in an approximation to a Roman theatre equipped with a raised stage encircled by its auditorium (as in London and probably in Lincoln), this method of handling all visual aspects of theatrical representation was equally efficient and effective. And, once that is understood, it becomes clear that the choice between these three styles of production could safely be left to the administrative authorities whether municipal or ecclesiastical, in every individual town or city possessed of a cycle of Corpus Christi plays as best suited its own, local facilities and convenience.

Thus in those places where responsibility for the production of the plays had been handed over by the Church to City Councils, and then delegated to their own trade guilds, it was virtually inevitable that each biblical incident chosen for dramatisation would be parcelled out to a single guild. It was just as likely that the assignment of plays to guilds would be governed, in part, by the appropriateness of each play's subject-matter to the trade, craft or 'mystery' professed by each guild;[15] in part by the ability of each guild to cast this play from its own members and to provide a 'pageant master' capable of allotting roles to them, organising a rehearsal schedule and overseeing all other aspects of the play's production, and in part by the guild's ability to finance the production costs of the play assigned to it from its own resources.[16]

The principal advantage of adopting this form of play production was that it enabled the municipal authorities to hand over all casting and production responsibilities to those guilds nominated by the Council for inclusion in the procession, thereby restricting its own contribution to such civic supervisory tasks as fell within its normal range of statutory and executive duties.[17] These included:

1 Choice of those sites within the city limits where the procession would halt to allow performances to be given.
2 Policing of streets along the chosen route to ensure that the procession could proceed without risk of gridlock, or interruptions caused by drunken or unruly members of the crowd jostling to secure a better view of the performances whenever the procession came to a halt to allow this to happen.
3 Determining the date (or dates) of performance year by year.
4 Advertising them at least a full month in advance with a formal Proclamation, drawn up by the Town Clerk on the Mayor's behalf, and delivered by the Town Crier escorted by a procession of representatives of the participating guilds known as 'The Riding of the Banns'.
5 Imposing penalties (normally fines published in a fixed code familiar to everyone concerned) both upon those guilds whose performances of their plays were judged to have fallen below the standards expected of them, and on members of the audiences arrested and charged with disrupting them.

A final responsibility that rested with city councils was the occasional need to reallocate a play from one guild to another (sometimes to two or more) when serious fluctuations in trading conditions made this essential to ensure that adequate financial resources remained available to meet the production costs of that play.[18]

In those places, however, where the Church chose (or found itself obliged) to retain exclusive control of play production—notably in London, Lincoln and Cornwall—radically different criteria had to be applied if this ambition was to be transformed into a practicable proposition.

79

Since 'control', in this context, had to be placed in the hands of the religious guilds already established in the area, or of those specifically created to forward the celebrations attendant upon the new Feast of Corpus Christi, the first question demanding an answer was whether the collective membership of these guilds sufficed to cast the plays offered by the play-makers for performance. The second was whether adequate funding was available to meet the costs of production; and the third was the method of theatrical representation to be chosen if the answers to the first and second of these questions were both positive.

In a city as large as London had become by the end of the fourteenth century, this was certainly the case, given both the number of parish clerks resident within it and the wealth of its livery companies, all of whom could by then afford to maintain a Guild Chapel or Chantry together with a Chaplain of its own. Supplementary income, moreover, should that be needed, could also be confidently anticipated from charitable donations and bequests.

Since we are reliably informed by the author of the *Grey Friars Chronicle* that, by 1411, the audience for 'a great play from the beginning of the world . . . that lasted vij days continually' included, 'the most part of the Lords and Gentils of England', the guest list must have been a long one; and with special scaffolds erected to accommodate them, the price tag attaching to the best seats was likely to have been as costly as those for all gala theatrical and sporting events today.[19] There was thus no need in London to contemplate processional performances since enough large open spaces normally used as markets existed to permit the erection (albeit on a temporary basis) of a theatre approximating to such literary and architectural features as still remained to copy from Roman theatres at St. Albans, Cirencester and Caerleon, and from illuminated manuscripts of Terence's plays in many monastic libraries.[20]

It would therefore seem that it was this kind of fragmentary antiquarian evidence that provided the parish clerks, who were already staging plays at Skinners' Well by 1384,[21] with their model for a fixed performance-space containing a raised stage surrounded by a semi-circular or rectangular auditorium built in wood, that could be erected and as quickly demolished for storage against future use.

Conditions in Cornwall, however, were altogether different from those in London and other English provincial towns and cities. In the first place there were no cathedral cities comparable in size and resources with those elsewhere in England; in the second, Cornwall itself remained a predominantly rural and Celtic county, still possessed of its own language and cultural inheritance.

Thus, if the establishment of the Feast of Corpus Christi was to be celebrated there by any ceremony additional to the obligatory procession, this could only be initiated by a large and wealthy monastic community capable of taking responsibility upon itself both for determining what form it was to take and how it was to be paid for. Such slender documentary evidence as survives suggests that it was the collegiate monks of Glasney Abbey in Penryn who shouldered these burdens and that they tackled them on an extraordinarily ambitious scale.

At some time during the fifteenth century a decision was reached to dramatise sufficient incidents from both Old and New Testament sources to create a celebratory event spanning three whole days. The prompt-script of the resulting thirty-three plays (described in its Latin rubrics as the *Ordinale*, or Ordinalia) survives in the Bodleian Library at Oxford (Ms. 791) and is divided into three, self-contained sections: *Origo Mundi* (The Creation); *Passio* (The Passion of Our Lord Jesus Christ); and *Resurrectio* (Resurrection, Harrowing of Hell and Ascension). All three of these day-long plays were scripted in the Cornish language. Thirteen biblical stories are contained within *Origo Mundi* totalling nearly 2,300 lines; twenty in *Passio* with two incidents sandwiched together in one case and three in another, totalling some 3,200 lines; and ten in *Resurrectio*, with two distinct incidents again compressed into one in the penultimate play, totalling 2,630 lines. Each group of plays is accompanied by a diagram depicting an arena surrounded by a circular auditorium, on the top of which eight scaffolds are shown, together with the names of the principal characters who are to occupy them throughout the whole of each day's stage-actions.

All three ground-plans assume both continuous action throughout each day and use of an iconic method of theatrical representation that allows scenic location to be identified by the scaffolds from which characters descend into the arena to participate in the action and to which they then return when no longer needed in the action, or when the scene reaches its conclusion. Two of these scaffolds are reserved for the same occupants on each of the three days: that facing east for God in Heaven and that placed in the north for Lucifer in Hell.

The factual information provided within these three diagrams that accompany the manuscripts of these plays serves to define the

celum
heaven

tortores

Ortno

infernum

Abraham

Rex Pharoah

Rex Solomon

Rex David

FIG. 5.1 Diagram of the staging arrangements for *Origo Mundi*, occupying the first day of the three–day Cornish Cycle of Mystery Plays, as set out for performance in an earthwork arena in Penwyth.

Source: Reprinted from Edwin Norris, *The Ancient Cornish Drama* 2 vols., Oxford University Press, 1859 (from Bodleian Library, Ms. 791).

method chosen by the monks of Glasney Abbey for staging them. This was unquestionably 'in the round' or, more particularly in Cornwall, within one of several earthwork arenas surviving as 'game-places' from earlier times.[22] That chosen was almost certainly St. Piran's Round, situated near the small village of Perranzabuloe on the moors above Perranporth some ten miles south-west of Newquay and fifteen miles north of Penryn and Falmouth. The logic informing this choice lay in the fact that it relieved the brothers of all anxieties, both constructional and financial, attendant upon the provision of an auditorium.

The earthwork 'round' itself rises some twenty feet above the surrounding moor and measures about a hundred feet in diameter.

Its circumference is punctuated by two openings (one in the north and one in the south) that have the effect of cutting the circular arena into two semi-circles. The southern opening served the double purpose of providing an entrance to and exit from the auditorium for all spectators and of allowing characters who are expelled from the acting-area in the course of the stage-action (like Adam and Eve), or who are required to enter it when riding donkeys or mules (like Balaam on his Ass, or Christ riding into Jerusalem). The northern opening likewise allowed Lucifer and his cohort of devils to carry the corpses of all Old Testament characters who die on stage (like Abel when murdered by Cain, or Pharoah's army when drowned in the Red Sea as its waters close over them) out of the arena through the gate of Hell-Castle into the infernal world beyond. Meanwhile, God and his angels, mounted high on their scaffold in the east, could watch from above while awaiting the moment in *Resurrectio* on day three, when Christ would lay siege to Hell and lead all saved souls back into the arena to join him (now arrayed as Christus Rex) on the Heaven scaffold.

Blessed as we are today by the survival of the Cornish records of the ground-plans of both the staging and seating arrangements for all three days of this Cycle of 43 plays, we lack—as we do in London—all documentary evidence of the kind so frequently preserved by the trade guilds in York, Chester, Coventry and other English cities relating to the expenses incurred in staging these plays.[23]

Nevertheless, we still possess enough information to be sure that a third method of presenting long sequences of biblical plays in vernacular languages (frequently chosen in France and German-speaking countries) was also adopted in England. This involved the construction of a wide, raised stage with all the scenic devices needed to identify the location of stage-action laid out laterally across the back of it, of which the best and most familiar graphic example survives from Valenciennes in north-eastern France (see *EES* II, Pt. 2, Fig. 2, p. 7). There, Heaven (Paradise) is set up to face spectators on the extreme left of the platform (actors' right) with Hell Castle on the extreme right, and with all terrestrial locations so arranged as to fit in between them.[24]

In England this was the method chosen by the parish clerks at Skinners' Well in London, as also by the East Anglian authors of *Ludus Coventriae*—a manuscript that has no connection with Coventry but which most scholars today attribute to Lincoln.[25] If this mode of stationary play-production originated in continental Europe, the most probable source for it would then have been the architectural remains of Roman theatres spread out in the Rhône valley from Lyon, Orange and Vienne in the north to Arles and Nîmes in the south. Similar ruins existed in England at St. Albans and Cirencester but they were not as well preserved as those in France (see *EES* II, Pt. 1, Plate I, Nos 1 and 2).

Given the many social and economic upheavals and casualties that accompanied the virulent epidemic of plague (known today as the Black Death) during the closing decades of the fourteenth century, followed up through most of the fifteenth century by both the disastrous resumption of war with France and the equally disruptive 'Papal Schism' (with rival popes presiding simultaneously in Rome and Avignon) and the civil war (now referred to as the Wars of the Roses), the sudden surge of creative energy and innovation that characterised the growth and popularity of all theatrical activity throughout this period is astonishing.

Here the facts speak for themselves. The first to figure in this reckoning must be the long list of towns from Carlisle and Newcastle in the north to Ipswich, Chelmsford, Reading, Canterbury, Bath and Salisbury in the south that appear to have acquired self-confidence and resources enough during these troubled times to emulate Beverley, York, Chester and London in staging sequences of at least twelve biblical plays of their own during the summer months in June or August. In the Midlands, the cathedral cities of Hereford, Coventry and Lincoln each excelled them by succeeding in scripting and producing nearly twice as many plays.[26]

A second striking testimony to the vitality of dramatic activity pioneered during the fifteenth century is to be found in the innovative additions to the dramatic repertoire represented by the long Morality and Saint plays intended for out-of-door performances in summer months, and by the shorter Moral Interludes devised for performance in the more intimate and sophisticated surroundings of roofed banquet halls both in winter and in summer as occasion demanded. Both have already been noticed in the context of the status and economy of play-makers and actors in the previous chapter (see pp. 58–9 above).

Of the former, only a few complete texts, *The Castle of Perseverance* (*c.* 1405–25) and the Cornish play of *St. Meriasek* (1504) being the most striking in the complexity of both their dramatic structure and their staging requirements, have survived. All Moral Interludes, by marked contrast, are not only much shorter but were scripted to meet the needs of much smaller companies of actors, all of whom were privately maintained as household servants.

The first text to have survived (albeit in fragmentary form) is that of *The Pride of Life* (*c.* 1425).[27] A time gap of some forty years separates that from its nearest sequels, *Mankind* and *Mind Will and Understanding* (often abbreviated to *Wisdom*), both written at some time between 1465 and 1470. Perhaps the most remarkable feature of Moral Interludes, however, lay in the impact they were to have on the lifestyles of both play-makers and actors during the final decades of the fifteenth century and throughout the sixteenth century, for not only did they provide actors with a type of play that could easily be transported from their home base to new audiences in other venues, but were also the first plays to be made accessible to readers in printed editions (see Chapter 4, pp. 63–4 above).

Innovation, however, could not stop with the creation of new dramatic forms, for Saint plays, Moralities and Moral Interludes all provoked questions about how they were to be staged and funded before they could be presented to audiences.

The least troublesome of the three were long Saint (or Miracle) plays, since they could be viewed as extensions to Old and New Testament plays containing legendary rather than biblical subject matter: and, as both the narrative content and style of presentation were already familiar to actors of cyclic Corpus Christi plays and to their audiences, only minor changes needed to be applied to existing methods of production when extended to include those legendary Christian heroes and heroines who had followed Christ's example in laying down their lives for their faith. Prominent amongst these were St. Paul, St. Nicholas, Mary Magdalene and Saints Catherine, Lawrence and Thomas à Becket, together with many local patronal saints like St. Meriasek in Cornwall, St. Anne in Lincoln or, to cite a continental example, the Saints Séverin, Exupère and Félicien at Romans in Provence (see *EES* I, pp. 302–6).

The most popular method of staging such plays appears to have been on a fixed stage as in London, Lincoln, Valenciennes and Romans, or in the round as in Cornwall. The iconography governing costumes and the provision of scenic devices likewise presented only minor problems, since the emblematic vocabulary governing both was either already firmly established or could be borrowed from wall paintings, altar-pieces or stained-glass windows.

Moralities and Moral Interludes, however, presented more serious problems affecting play-makers, actors and craftsmen alike, but both offered new opportunities. These all stemmed from the fact that where all previous religious plays had been anchored in story-telling, both Moralities and Moral Interludes were constructed around an argument instead of an historical or legendary incident or sequence of incidents; and argument, if sustained over any length of time, assumes a predominantly literate audience. Since drama, however, must entertain if it is to educate, the element of 'earnest' contained within the 'game' or 'play' must be relieved by the provision of either a comic sub-plot (preferably presented as a recognisable parody of the play's central theme) or by the thrills and spectacle of armed combat between heroes and villains.

Both of these innovative new forms of play also required the invention of long lists of new characters plucked both from the imagined ranks of the Virtues attendant upon God in Heaven and from the diablerie surrounding Lucifer in Hell. This was essential, since the near-invariable subject of these moral debates was a medieval version of those 'virtual reality' games that are so popular today, backdated through time to depict the Day of Judgement when Mankind, *Humanum Genus* or Everyman will be called before their maker to account for the use that he or she has made of his or her transitory journey through life on earth. To this end life, as depicted on the stage, was simplified into a struggle between the Three Cardinal Virtues and the Four Daughters of God on the one hand, and the corresponding Seven Deadly Sins on the other, to acquire possession of Man's soul while time remained for him or her either to recognise their sins and beg for Grace, Mercy and Forgiveness, or to elect instead to tread what Shakespeare would later describe as 'the primrose way to the everlasting bonfire'.[28] The nature of this choice was such as to open a way forward for playmakers during the sixteenth century towards the composition of recognisably Christian forms of tragedy and comedy to compete with those that had been rescued from Graeco-Roman sources during the Italian Renaissance.

Identification of these new cast lists of abstract personifications, both angelic and diabolic, could remain emblematic since all of them had already been depicted in tapestries, frescoes and other forms of pictorial art long enough for contemporary audiences to recognise them: so an iconic style of visual representation could continue to be used.

All the Virtues seem thus to have been clothed in long gowns and regarded as females equipped with personal emblems of their own either hand-held or integrated into their costumes or headgear. 'Justice', for example, could thus be distinguished from 'Faith' by the sword and scales held by the former and the cross and chalice carried by the latter. These aids to identification were supplemented

86

by the colours of their gowns; so, if the actors cast in these roles wished to rid themselves of hand-held stage properties to recover the use of their hands when called upon to enter into the stage action and speak, they could quickly dispose of them and allow the dialogue to assist them instead, and with their hands and arms free to supplement the emotional content of their contributions to it.

All characters chosen to represent the diablerie on the other hand seem to have been portrayed as males—possibly to accord with the bodily strength required of them and the aggressive barbarity of their treatment of those damned souls committed to their care. A hierarchy was also created for them by the play-makers to resemble that in Heaven, ranging from Lucifer (or Satan) himself as its commander-in-chief, through such other fallen angels as Belial and Beelzebub down to those humbler members of the infernal host who were given lines to speak but only identified as first, second and third devil. As in pictorial art, all of them were normally visualised as bestial caricatures of human beings equipped with tails, horns and claws. Beyond these physical attributes, however, devils were required to be masters of cunning and disguise.

To effect this, both play-makers and actors drew heavily upon the contrasting emblems of 'mask' and 'face', by burying the demon under the outward show of the clothes (referred to as 'gear') in which they dressed themselves when leaving Hell Castle to walk abroad in the terrestrial world. For this, an early model had already been set in the Chester Corpus Christi play of *The Creation* where Lucifer decides to disguise himself in transvestite attire by wearing an adder's coat topped by a woman's face, a flaxen wig and falsetto voice.[29] Thus the preferred technique came to be the super-imposition of an outward semblance of charm, authority and reassurance upon a concealed determination to deceive, betray and destroy—not unlike that of serial killers today. That it proved to be highly successful when put into action is undeniable since it remained in constant use over the next one hundred and fifty years to enable Shakespeare to epitomise it in Lady Macbeth's advice to her husband on learning of King Duncan's approach to their castle:

> '. . . look like the innocent flower,
> But be the serpent under it.' (I.v.63–4)

Indeed, it still survives as a cliché in English pantomimes to inform the conduct of the Demon King.

Makers of Moral Interludes, however, were here confronted with a problem unique to themselves: the severe restriction imposed upon the number of actors who could be called upon to perform them. For, unlike those clerics employed in devising the texts for Corpus Christi Cycles and long Morality and Saint plays, who could rely upon the supply of at least fifty actors to fill the roles created for them, they found themselves limited to a maximum of six of their master's household servants, including one borrowed from the chapel choir. They were thus obliged to rethink their approach to the writing of such plays if they wished to include more than six characters in their cast lists.

The solution adopted was so to order each incident in the action as to allow at least one actor to leave the stage with time enough provided to change his costume and make-up before returning in another role. The same scripting device, if adopted for a second or third time, could then permit this actor to revert to his original character at a later point in the play. Depending on each actor's personal skills and talents, this technique made it possible for the play-maker to 'double' one male role with that of a second role that could be either that of another man or that of a woman as the plot dictated.

Successful as this solution was to the problem of matching characters chosen to represent the mortal world in Moral Interludes with the small number of actors available to portray them, it failed to meet the larger one arising from having to add yet more characters to represent the spiritual worlds of Heaven and Hell. Here, the restricted number of actors available to the play-makers enforced a more draconian answer. Since the nature of the debates and combats conducted and fought out verbally and physically in the mortal world in such plays precluded wholesale elimination of stage representation of either of these extra-terrestrial worlds, the only practicable solution was to reduce it to a single character from each of them who, preferably, was already active in the mortal world. Thus, in the case of Heaven, the figure chosen could either be *Deus Pater* himself depicted as spectator and adjudicator (as in *Everyman*), or as a priest-*cum*-father confessor (like Mercy in *Mankind*). In the case of Hell, however, a more subtle and inventive answer was found. This was to exploit Satan's notorious proclivities for disguise and deception in ways that served between them to create a new theatrical character that came to be widely known as 'The Vice'.

As the prototype of all subsequent stage-villains, The Vice owed much of its popularity with audiences to the many opportunities provided by this role to surprise, charm and amuse them. It would take another century, however, for this character to reveal its full theatrical potential in such vivid stage portraits as Marlowe's Mephistopheles in *Dr Faustus*, Jonson's Mosca in *Volpone* or Shakespeare's Iago in *Othello*. In *Hamlet*, Shakespeare went further by providing his young Prince with five lines that give us a definitive picture of the shock-waves of disillusionment and despair that flow from the discovery by its victim of the depth of the deception and treachery to which he has been exposed. When informed by his father's ghost that he has been murdered by his brother Claudius, Hamlet exclaims:

> 'O villain, villain, smiling, damned villain!
> My tables (i.e. *Notebook*). Meet it is I set it down,
> That one may smile, and smile, and be a villain:
> At least I'm sure it may be so in Denmark.
> So, uncle, there you are.' (*Hamlet*, I.v.106–10)

It remains to consider what expectancies were entertained by audiences of actors in medieval plays, and the ways in which actors prepared themselves (or were trained) to meet them; but here we enter an almost impenetrable land of shadows, partly on account of the dearth of reliable records covering rehearsals and performances, and partly because every live performance, whether athletic, musical or theatrical, vanishes from public view as soon as it is over. From that moment onwards posterity becomes dependent upon the viewpoints of those few literate spectators who, for one reason or another, either choose or are required to record their private responses in writing. As no considered responses of this kind have reached us respecting plays written and performed before the end of the fifteenth century, we have to content ourselves with such dry twigs of information as can be gleaned from civic and monastic Minute Books and Account Rolls.

These sources, however, suffice to assure us that, well before the end of the fourteenth century, chains of command had been established between senior representatives of the Church and the civic authorities, both in London and in several provincial cities, charged with responsibility for organising the production of Corpus Christi processions and plays (see pp. 78–9 above). Yet, while these can safely be regarded as having been broadly uniform in their structure and composition, allowance has to be made for variants between those adopted in one city here and another there to accord with local resources and convenience. These embrace not only the days and dates chosen for the performance of the plays, but also the disciplinary codes of conduct imposed upon those guilds elected by the Mayor in Council to organise the production of specific plays, the players chosen to perform them and the audiences who travelled from near and far to see them. As full a picture of all these municipal regulations as could be given in 1959, when Volume I of *Early English Stages* was first published, is set out there between pages 292 and 300. Since none of the records discovered and published between then and now has served to change that account in any serious way, only a brief résumé is offered here.

Starting then with audiences, we know that in Chester—at least until 1531—audiences were warned in the Proclamation issued annually by the Town Clerk on behalf of the Mayor (as the King's Deputy) that 'every person disturbing the same plays in any manner wise [is] to be accursed by the authority of Pope's Bull unto such time as he or they may be absolved thereof ... '. An even stronger warning is there given to anyone found wearing or using 'unlawful weapons' within the precincts of the city during the time of performances, 'upon pain of imprisonment of their bodies and making fine to the King at Master Mayor's pleasure' (see *EES* I, pp. 342–3).

With that spelt out to every individual attending performances of these biblical plays, city councils then moved on to formulate regulations to govern the conduct of all guilds accorded the privilege of being awarded responsibility for presenting one of the many plays authorised for performance annually within the city. These were inclusive enough to cover both the guilds (when regarded as corporate institutions) and all individual members of that guild charged by its officers with specific responsibilities for the production and performance of its own play.

Thus in Beverley, for example, a fixed penalty of forty shillings was laid down by the Corporation in 1390 for failure by any guild to present the play allotted to it. At the same time overall responsibility for each of the thirty-eight pageants was placed under the rule of a single Alderman. In cases where individual actors or pageant-masters were held to blame for failure to achieve the standards expected of them, smaller fines were levied for what was known as 'the common good', or benefit of the Guild itself as a corporate whole.

One such fine was imposed at Beverley in 1452. When Henry Couper, Weaver (or Webster), 'did not know his part on Corpus Christi day', he was fined 'six shillings and fourpence to the common good'; but in this instance, since this actor is said to have been 'a poor man', Robert Thomskrew, Alderman, was instructed '. . . to lay down six shillings and eightpence because the players of the Carpenters craft did not know their play.'[30]

Similar disciplinary measures were set in place in York in 1394 to ensure that each guild only performed its pageant in those places (stations) appointed by the City Council. It was then left to each guild to provide 'good players, well arrayed and openly speaking'. Failures attributable to neglect or other inadequacies in rehearsal or performance were penalised, as at Beverley, with fines.[31]

Further regulations were introduced at York in 1476 which throw some light on the methods adopted there to select and train actors for the tasks that lay ahead of them. These stipulated:

'That yearly in the time of Lent there shall be called before the Mayor for the time being iiij of the most cunning, discreet and able players within this City, to search, hear, and examine all the players and plays and pageants throughout all the artificers belonging to Corpus Christi Play. And all such as they shall find sufficient in person and cunning, to the honour of the City and worship of the said Crafts, for to admit and able [? *enable, assist*]; and all other insufficient persons, either in cunning, voice, or person to discharge, ammove [? *remove*] and avoid. And that no player that shall play in the said Corpus Christi Play be conduct and retained to play but twice on the day of the said play [i.e. *in not more than two different pageants*]: and that he or they so playing play not over twice the said day, upon pain of 40 shillings forfeit unto the Chamber [i.e. *the City Treasury*] as often times as he or they shall be found defaulty in the same.'[32]

Collectively, these and other records assure us that civic pride was the dominant factor motivating the actions taken by City Fathers to obtain the best actors locally available. This they aimed to achieve through competitive auditions and by setting a premium upon stage-presence, coupled with good diction ('open speaking') and an ability to project lines both forcefully and loudly enough to be heard by large audiences assembled in performance-spaces open to winds and weather.

By today's standards, the time allotted to rehearsals seems very short. In Coventry, for instance, the number of rehearsals varied for each pageant between a minimum of two and a maximum of five. In 1493 these were held during Easter and Whitsun weeks in the presence of members of their respective guilds at breakfast time between 6.00 and 7.00 in the morning,[33] but with five months elapsing between auditions in Lent (February/March), rehearsals in April and May and performance in June, actors clearly had time enough to master their lines before rehearsals began. Thereafter, given the stylised acting conventions expected of amateur actors of that time, an experienced 'pageant master' or 'dresser' needed only to equip them with their cues for entrances and exits; to tutor them in those movements and gestures required of them when on stage; to accustom them to wearing their stage costumes, wigs and head-dresses, and to adjust the speaking of their lines to meet the conditions of performance in the open air. When, moreover, these relatively simple requirements were backed up by the prospect of fines being imposed for failure to meet them, the rehearsal time provided for appears to have been at least adequate, if not generous. With audiences already known to be pleased enough with what was given to them to wish to return for repeat performances year after year, it becomes very difficult for us to believe that it was not.

The self-evident success of these productions as staged all over England by the end of the fifteenth century can, I think, be confidently attributed to the fact that they were universally received in the same spirit as they were conceived, organised and funded; that is, as major community events involving almost as many people as active participants (in many varying capacities) as took advantage of an extended summer holiday to support them for other, more mundane reasons.

By marked contrast, it is virtually impossible to provide readers with any comparably detailed picture of those many organisational procedures and arrangements that were put into place to facilitate production of the elaborate Morality and Saint plays written and performed during the fifteenth century, for lack of reliable documentary evidence on which to base it. Beyond the diagrammatic ground-plans for the staging of *The Castle of Perseverance* and the Cornish *Life of St. Meriazek* appended respectively to the manuscripts of these texts, and the exceptionally full stage directions offered by the anonymous authors of such relatively late Saint plays as the Digby texts of *St. Mary Magdalene* and *The Conversion of St. Paul*,[34] nothing has survived either in monastic or civic Account Rolls or in other documents that can help us to reconstruct a picture of the organisation and funding arrangements governing their production, or even the precise whereabouts of the monastic communities under whose auspices they were staged.

Reduced as we thus are to speculative surmises, the best answer that is likely to be forthcoming must lie in the examples already firmly established in many town halls and cathedral Chapter Houses for handling long sequences of Corpus Christi plays, since these could easily be copied or adapted to comply with the special requirements of these novel extensions to the dramatic repertoire and to the local facilities prevailing in or near the places in which they were written to be performed.

Sadly, a similar fog-blanket of ignorance surrounds all attempts to offer anything beyond the most cautious and heavily qualified descriptions of the theatrical conditions governing the production of the much shorter Moral Interludes devised for the entertainment of guests at banquets in castle halls and monastic refectories on festive occasions.

We know that the actors were recruited from household servants equipped with talents both to edify and amuse; that these were restricted to a maximum of six throughout the fifteenth century, thus obliging some of them to appear in more than one role wherever scripts included more than six characters; and that their masters often allowed these privileged servants to present these plays in other places when requested to do so, and to receive payments, partly to cover their travel expenses and partly as thanks for the service rendered, thus prompting them to seek escape from serfdom by aspiring to acquire professional status in the course of the sixteenth century.[35] It is also reasonable to suppose that, given the environments in which these plays were staged, the players' needs respecting costumes and the minimal scenic and musical requirements called for in the texts could readily be met from within their respective households, at a little or no cost to themselves.

The distance thus travelled between the first re-enactments of the *Quem Quaeritus* Introit during the Latin liturgy presented for Easter Sunday in the late tenth century and the wide range of vernacular Corpus Christi biblical plays, together with the Moralities, Saint plays and Moral Interludes that jostled each other for performance during the fifteenth century is strikingly impressive. Not only had the number of actors required risen from a mere four to a figure nearer a hundred in each Cycle of Corpus Christi plays alone, but audiences likewise had grown from relatively small monastic brotherhoods into crowds of both clerical and secular participants and spectators numbering thousands in many cathedral cities throughout the country.

Production costs had also risen proportionately to provide a sense of occasion together with a degree of pageantry and spectacle unimaginable in the tenth, eleventh or twelfth centuries. Combining with all of this were the many alternative dramatic entertainments provided with ever-increasing frequency by mummers, mimes, trouvères, jongleurs and musicians in secular environments that embraced not only palaces, castles, town and livery halls but the humbler courtyards, gardens and reception rooms of inns and taverns.

When, therefore, following the death of King Richard III at the battle of Bosworth Field in Leicestershire in 1485, Henry Tudor succeeded to the throne, all Englishmen had cause enough to believe that they were the heirs to a tradition of dramatic art that was as firmly grounded in their religious beliefs as it was in the community spirit that had promoted its development into the most popular of all forms of social recreation on offer on public holidays throughout the calendar year.

By then, however, signs that the winds of change were beginning to blow had already appeared above the horizon: among them were Wycliffe and his Lollards; the building of new schools and university colleges with revised statutes; the arrival of gunpowder in Europe; the fall of Byzantium to the Turks; and William Caxton and his printing press. What no one could have guessed at that time was that these winds would gather force enough to erode the foundations on which all forms of English dramatic art and theatrical representation had hitherto been grounded, and thus as to cause the whole of this noble edifice to collapse within the next one hundred and fifty years.

BOOK TWO

Change and Innovation in Tudor England, 1485–1580

VI

RENEWAL AND REFORM,
1485–1530

THE first, and most urgent, task confronting Henry Tudor, Duke of Richmond, after his triumphant entry into London for his coronation in 1485, was to restore some semblance of political stability to a kingdom ravaged by nearly half a century of civil strife occasioned by the remorseless rivalry between Lancastrian and Yorkist claimants to the English throne. A hundred years later this still remained an experience so debilitating in its consequences for many of his subjects as to enable Shakespeare to recall it when electing to dramatise it in his sequence of nine 'History Plays' (starting with Richard II and concluding with Richard III) from which most theatre-goers still derive such knowledge of the 'Wars of the Roses' as they possess today.[1]

In approaching this formidable task of exchanging past discord and deprivation for a vision of future peace, stability and prosperity, Henry VII appears to have set himself three principal objectives, the first of which was to secure his own position as England's rightful king.

The second was to purge his Court and, with it, the ranks of those clerical civil servants and lawyers upon whom both he and his Privy Council relied to govern his subjects both in London and throughout the provinces, by entrusting ecclesiastical and political positions of power to men who owed everything to him rather than to their claims to inherited titles and wealth.

The third was to try to change the nation's view of itself by focusing public attention upon the many innovative discoveries and entrepreneurial enterprises that were already well advanced in several countries in continental Europe instead of continuing to accept a blinkered lifestyle bounded by feudal grudge-fights largely motivated by unbridled self-interest, supported by flagrant breaches of the law in the name of revenge.

Fulfilment of all three of these objectives, if successful, was likely to bring changes with them in social attitudes subsequently adopted to both theoretical and representational aspects of dramatic art regarded as expressions of *avant-garde* thought and politically acceptable practice.

In securing his position as the rightful successor to the English throne, Henry VII was fortunate to be still a bachelor and thus free to strengthen it with a proposal of marriage to the heiress and eldest daughter of Edward IV, Elizabeth of York. This he did within six months of his accession; this marriage had received a papal blessing and, once Elizabeth herself was safely delivered of a son and heir—Prince Arthur—she was crowned as Queen of England at Westminster Abbey in November 1487 amidst great ceremony and splendour.

In the meantime, Henry had hastened to present himself to his subjects by embarking upon a provincial Progress during the summer of 1486 which took him to York, returning to London by way of Worcester and Bristol. In each of these cities, he was received in the time-honoured manner with eulogistic speeches of welcome and spectacular, allegorical street-pageants organised and financed by the respective civic authorities, as already described in Volume I (pp. 71–81).

With that achieved, his next priority was to equip himself with a strong, armed bodyguard—the Yeomen of the Guard, stationed at the Tower of London—and to set about distancing himself and his family from potential rivals and traitors among the surviving aristocratic clans of feudal dukes, earls and barons. This he sought to achieve by surrounding himself, both within his own household and within his Privy Council, by trusted friends of proven merit who owed their appointments and prospects directly to him. As a further precautionary measure, he chose to reduce the role of Parliament in government to a minimum while augmenting that of his own Privy Council by equipping it with a Law Court of its own (known subsequently as Star Chamber) to which all matters thought likely to raise legal questions or disputes could be referred for consultation and advice before decisions were reached.[2] A final self-protective measure was to call upon the second Parliament of his reign, in November 1487, to tighten up the powers previously delegated to Justices of the Peace and City Magistrates at local level throughout the country and to extend these powers to recover control over the recruitment of liveried servants and their subsequent maintenance in baronial households, which had been so often breached or ignored during the Wars of the Roses.[3]

Many of the above measures are to be seen theatrically reflected in *Fulgens and Lucres*, a long Moral Interlude written some ten years later by Henry Medwall, Chaplain to Cardinal John Morton. Morton had already been rewarded for his loyalty on his return from self-imposed exile in Flanders during the reign of Richard III, with promotion to the See of Canterbury as Archbishop, and then appointed by Henry himself as Lord President of his Privy Council[4]. This play, scripted in two self-contained parts for presentation between two sections, or courses, of a banquet, was probably directly commissioned by Morton for performance when entertaining the Flemish and Spanish ambassadors at Lambeth Palace during the Christmas season of 1497.

When introducing this Interlude in my edition of it in *English Moral Interludes* (J. M. Dent, 1976, pp. 37–101), I said that this play:

'... adapts a disputation in the manner of Cicero or Petrarch to contrast the rival claims of the old aristocracy and the new men of proven ability from the middle class for high office in Tudor England. Medwall's play is loosely structured on a variety of traditional Christmas games and pastimes—songs, wrestling, jousting, mumming and debates—which are then given coherence within a narrative that incorporates them either ... to supply variety or as parodies for dramatic and moral purposes.'

Medwall is explicit about his reasons for including them when describing them later (Pt. II, lines 22–4) as:

> 'Divers toys mingled in the same
> To stir folk to mirth and game
> And to do them solace.'

The core of the play's moral matter, the 'earnest' or significant aspect of it, is then expounded in Part 2 by Gaius Flaminius (Lucres' aristocratic suitor) in the course of the final debate with his rival—the plebian, Publius Cornelius:

'(Publius)   ... this I wot well
That both he and I came of Adam and Eve;
There is no difference that I can tell
Which maketh one man another to excell

So much as doth virtue and goodly manner
And therein I may well with him compare.' (II, lines 665–70)

This disposes of the claims of noble birth and inherited wealth at a stroke, substituting natural ability and personal achievement as the primary criteria for respect and promotion. Within this context Lucres, as the bride for whose hand the two men are contending, becomes figuratively translated into the personification of the State, or Commonwealth. The debate is then enlarged to reveal its full social and political significance.

Henry VII's third objective following his accession, as already noted, was the much broader one of trying to refocus his subjects' attention away from insular, domestic concerns and outwards to the wider horizons already opening up abroad—most noticeably in Spain, Italy, Flanders and German-speaking states. While he recognised that this could not be achieved overnight, measures were quickly taken to prepare the ground for significant changes in English outlooks and aspirations within the next two or three decades.

Among the most visible of these were the many invitations issued to Italian architects and to both Italian and Flemish painters, to reside at the English Court and accept commissions for work there. Those who accepted included Pietro Torrigiano, Antonio Toto del Nunziato and Hans Holbein. Among notable Italian scholars whom Henry invited to England was Polydore Vergil. Born in Urbino and brought up there at Court, he arrived in 1502 and was rewarded with a living in the parish of Langton in Leicestershire. In 1505 he was commissioned by Henry to write a history of England that could be relied upon to distinguish between established facts and legendary fiction of the kind that had been retained (or invented) by Geoffrey of Monmouth.

Efforts were also made to encourage talented young scholars to move in the opposite direction and to devote a year or two to acquiring some knowledge of Greek and to perfect themselves in their command of classical Latin and Roman literature in all its forms. At the same time wealthy merchants were urged to consider founding new grammar schools under the names of their own crafts and professions with a view to encouraging promising young apprentices to think about their prospects for preferment within the learned professions as churchmen, lawyers, teachers or civil servants. About this, more will be said later in this chapter.

Following Henry's visit to Bristol during his provincial Progress in 1486 (see p. 71 above), measures were also taken to revive the fortunes of English seafarers, both naval and merchant traders, which had fallen into decay from long neglect during the Wars of the Roses.

However tentative and exploratory these early initiatives may seem to have been, by 1500 they had begun to reveal positive results. The measures taken following Henry's visit to York in 1486, where he had been hailed in street pageants as a new Solomon and champion of justice, to control former abuses of laws restricting liveried servants in feudal households and their maintenance, and to create new ones to extend the powers of all Justices of the Peace and local Magistrates, had already served to emancipate Welshmen by starting to integrate the legal system in Wales with that applying in England.[5] They had also helped to make it much easier for the King to snuff out such Yorkist-inspired attempts to unseat him as had taken place since his coronation and marriage, with relative ease.[6] Unquestionably, however, the most eye-catching and news-worthy sequel to these measures was John Cabot's successful trans-Atlantic voyage, underwritten by the King himself, which started out from Bristol and ended with the discovery of Newfoundland in 1497. Almost simultaneous in its timing with Christopher Columbus's equally successful voyage from Cadiz to South America, and Vasco da Gama's return journey from Lisbon round the Cape of Good Hope to India and back between 1497 and 1499, Cabot's voyage opened English eyes to trading opportunities that had hitherto been unimaginable (see Plate IX, No. 12).

Perhaps most importantly of all, the combined effect of these successes was to convince both the Pope and the Kings of France, Spain and Scotland that Henry Tudor, Duke of Richmond, had secured his claim to be the rightful King of England and Wales safely enough for his overtures to begin negotiations for the arrangement of dynastic marriages between his own children (the Princes Arthur and Henry, and the Princesses Margaret and Mary) and theirs to be taken seriously. In days when the feelings of the children to be disposed of in this way were the last item to occasion concern to the brokers of such marriages, it should not be thought surprising, therefore, that negotiations for the betrothal of Henry and Elizabeth's eldest son and daughter should have begun in 1497/8 when they were respectively only twelve and ten years old.

Their parents' choice for Prince Arthur was the Princess Catherine, daughter of Ferdinand, King of Aragon, and his Queen, Isabella of Castile. After two years of stiff and protracted bargaining, a marriage contract was finally signed by proxies in April 1501, and the Princess duly arrived in Plymouth in October but without, as yet, her promised dowry of 100,000 crowns. There she was rapturously received and then escorted by heralds and other officers of the English Court in gentle stages on her journey to London. As she approached its outskirts, on 9th November, the King and Prince Arthur rode out to meet her and to conduct her to Lambeth Palace where she was to be allowed to rest for a few days.

Three days later, she left the Palace to make her official entry into the city by way of London Bridge where the Lord Mayor and the city's livery companies had prepared a spectacular display of street pageants of unprecedented cost and splendour.

Welcomed appropriately at the entrance to London Bridge by Saints Catherine and Ursula encircled by an angelic choir, she passed over it into Gracechurch Street to be addressed from a castle, built over the water-conduit by Policy, Noblesse and Virtue (for a route map see *EES* II, Pt. 1, p. 60). This castle, adorned with intertwined red and white climbing roses surmounted by niches built to contain its three speech-makers, was devised as an emblematic compliment to the royal couple whose daughter-in-law she was about to become.

From there, her cortège moved on into Cornhill where she was confronted with a spectacular Pageant of the Moon consisting of a wheel, or 'volvel', with the signs of the Zodiac circling around it, and the moon itself passing through its own orbit of light and darkness, surmounted by famous astronomers supporting King Alphonse X of Castile and such proverbial sages as Job and Boethius placed there to provide Catherine with her horoscope. As her procession entered Cheapside, she was greeted with another pageant that included stage machinery—this one representing her bridegroom-to-be as 'the sphere of the Sun', surrounded by moving stars. A full verbatim description of this has already been provided in *EES* I, pp. 96–7. Presided over by *Deus Pater*, its intention was to offer her a flattering horoscope for Prince Arthur as 'the once and future king' of European myth and legend. Alas, this horoscope was all too soon to prove to have been even more inaccurate than that which had just been given to her.

Two more of these street-pageant-theatres awaited her arrival at the Standard in Cheapside and at the little water-conduit adjacent to St. Paul's Cathedral. The first of these, described as 'the Temple of God', was dressed to contain a huge red rose encircling God Himself, flanked by Prophets who welcomed and blessed the Princess before she passed on. It was not by chance, therefore, that it should have been there that the King had chosen (or been advised) to ensconce himself and his family in the house of a wealthy member of the Haberdashers Company—William Geoffrey—to watch how the citizens of his capital city received his prospective daughter-in-law.[7]

Shortly before reaching the seventh and final pageant near St. Paul's, she was greeted by the Lord Mayor and leading citizens who then escorted her through the ranks of Aldermen mounted on horseback to view a Pageant of the Seven Virtues. On the upper level of this structure sat Honour flanked by two maidens holding the sceptres and coronets of the prospective Prince and Princess of Wales. Below them sat the other six virtues, ready to receive the gifts of gold and silver plate presented to them by the City Council as tokens of respect and good wishes.

And so these lavish 'triumphs' ended as the Princess left the City of London to return to lodgings at Lambeth Palace with the next day in hand to reflect upon her reception into England and to prepare herself for her wedding in St. Paul's Cathedral two days later. It had been a day, moreover, when the people of London had obliged their King with an unforgettable theatrical display, not only in terms of its wealth, its imaginative artistic skills and pietistic self-discipline, but one so ordered as to impress every crowned head in continental Europe that his island kingdom was one whose cosmopolitan interests and prospects must in future be taken as seriously as their own. In short, if ever there was a case of the medium—and in this case civic pageantry—being the message, this must surely have been it.

The Court itself then took on the task of impressing it even more firmly upon all continental and nearer neighbours by following up the wedding with equally theatrical celebrations throughout the next two weeks consisting of jousts and tournaments by day and banquets, prize-givings, music, dancing, plays and Disguisings at night. Details of these festivities are to be found in Volume I, pp. 217–18.

In the middle of these festivities, ambassadors from Scotland arrived to participate in the ceremonies marking the betrothal of Henry's eldest daughter, the Princess Margaret, to their master, King James IV; and by the end of November the Spanish Ambassador finally delivered Catherine's promised dowry of 100,000 crowns into the King's Exchequer.

Henry thus had good cause to celebrate the ensuing Christmas and New Year holidays in 1501/2 in the belief that the first two of the objectives that he had set himself after his coronation in 1485 (see pp. 97–8 above) had been fulfilled, while the first fruits of his third—the despatch of young scholars to update their acquaintance with Greek and their knowledge of Italian Renaissance thought and Latin literature—were about to deliver positive results.

Leading these English scholars were William Grocin, who came back to Oxford to teach Greek in 1491; Thomas Linacre, who likewise returned to Oxford to teach Greek a year later; and John Colet who, after two years spent studying law in Paris and Orléans, then moved on to Bologna (and probably to Florence) before coming home in 1497 to resume his teaching career in Oxford until he was appointed Dean of St. Paul's in 1505. By then all three of them had acquired the friendship of two other distinguished scholars, one of whom was the illegitimate son of a Dutchman—Desiderius Erasmus—who had first come to London in 1499 in search of preferment. The other, Thomas More, as the son of Sir Henry More (a distinguished lawyer), had learnt his Latin at St. Anthony's School in London and from there was received into Cardinal Morton's household to broaden his mind before proceeding to study law at Oxford.

It is hard to assess the influence of each of these five men of letters, once they had become bonded into an intimate circle of friendship and mutual respect, on the liberalisation of subsequent English thinking about all aspects of philosophical, educational, religious, medical and theatrical life. Here, it must suffice to say that it was profound.

By 1501, Linacre had joined the Royal Household as personal tutor to Prince Arthur to be promoted subsequently to the post of Physician to the King. By then all of them had become aware of the emancipating power of the new printing presses, together with the need to endow more schools both in London and the provinces. Colet was himself among the first to do this when, in 1509 (either shortly before or after Henry's death), he chose to build a new school at the eastern end of St. Paul's Churchyard to accommodate 153 boys and three tutors; and in 1512 he appointed another well-trained scholar, William Lily, as its first High Master under whose guidance the curriculum in Rhetoric (or public oratory) was opened up to include the regular study and performance of Latin plays, thereby setting an example soon to be copied in other schools and at several colleges at both Oxford and Cambridge Universities.[8]

Meanwhile, Erasmus had moved to Cambridge to promote the study of Greek, just as Grocin had for long been doing at Oxford;

but, when again disappointed in his hopes of preferment to finance his notoriously relaxed lifestyle, and anxious to publish his daringly satirical version of *The Ship of Fools* under the new title of *In Praise of Folly*, he chose to remove himself to Paris thinking it safer to do so there than in London. Given that his object in writing it was to launch an attack on the products of nepotism, lazy-mindedness and corruption in all walks of life, including those of the Church, he was probably wise to do so since, on its publication there in 1514, it was well enough received to be translated and reprinted in many languages thus establishing himself securely as the most eminent Renaissance scholar of his generation. However, his close and hospitable English friend, Thomas More, was soon to follow his example by publishing his *Utopia* in 1516, a literary masterpiece that was to win for him an international reputation of comparable distinction.

Against this background of scholarly enterprise and innovation, it may strike some readers as strange that English religious drama in all of its long-established forms should have continued to be presented annually along its traditional lines with few, if any, significant changes either in its content or method of performance throughout the twenty years between Henry Tudor's accession and the printing of Erasmus's *In Praise of Folly* and More's *Utopia*. This, however, conceals the eroding effects that the rationalist, Renaissance approaches to philosophical and religious patterns of thought (which Henry VII had initiated) were shortly to have on all ecclesiastically sponsored amateur, community drama; so it will become necessary to return to them later in this chapter.

Here, we must retrace our steps to 1502 when the King had to face two serious setbacks to the first of his primarily political objectives: the securing of his own claim to be the rightful King of England and, with it, that of his son and heir, Prince Arthur, to succeed him. The first of these was the sudden and unexpected death of his son in April of that year within six months of his wedding, and when still only sixteen years old. The acutely personal nature of this misfortune was then only made the more distressing by the serious diplomatic consequences that immediately arose respecting the future of his widow, Catherine of Aragon, Princess of Wales, and the handsome dowry that Henry had received from Spain in fulfilment of the marriage contract. The simplest answer to both of these problems lay in the swift betrothal of this unfortunate Princess to the King's younger son, Prince Henry; but before that could be effected, a Papal Dispensation was obligatory lest objections were to arise on grounds of consanguinity. This had then to be delayed because of the deaths of two Popes—that of Alexander VI who had sanctioned the first marriage, and that of Pius III who had died shortly after his enthronement at the Vatican. Their successor, Julius II, then expressed doubts about his own authority to provide this Dispensation, so it was delayed again until, in 1505, he was finally reported to have consented to it. Both in Spain and England this was immediately taken as sufficient to permit the formal betrothal of the young couple, notwithstanding such feelings as they themselves are known to have expressed about it. The subsequent wedding, however, was again delayed by doubts about the validity (in the absence of written confirmation of the Pope's consent) of this Dispensation and further rancorous negotiations, until Henry VII died in 1509.[9] Thus, only after his own accession at the age of 18, as King Henry VIII, did he feel free to resolve his personal doubts by accepting the advice of his Privy Council and thus rescue the hapless Catherine by making her the new Queen of England two months later. Sadly for both of them, that was not to be the last of this troublesome matter (see pp. 107–8 and 111 below).

Once safely crowned and married, Henry set about exploiting the advantages that his father's far-sighted and prudent reforms had bequeathed to him. Handsome, athletic and well educated, he could claim the admiration and respect of his own subjects and foreign dignitaries alike by providing an idealised portrait of a young Renaissance Prince in his own person. Equipped, moreover, with a Privy Council that continued to be led by distinguished churchmen who could be relied upon to retain the approval of the Vatican, and that contained lawyers who could be trusted to uphold and enforce the English common law in his own and his subjects' interests, he could feel free to devote his energies to updating and consolidating the reputation of his own Court with little regard to increased costs to his Exchequer. In this, as an accomplished horseman, archer, musician and dancer, he led the way himself, thereby transforming life at Court into a constant round of hunting, tilts and jousts by day, with prize-givings, plays, disguisings and dancing to follow them at night.

That he viewed these activities as matters of deliberate policy and not just as high-spirited expressions of youthful self-indulgence and extravagance, may be judged by the fact that he instructed those members of his household employed as Kings of Arms, Heralds and Pursuivants at the College of Arms to make and preserve records of them in their library; and it is to these, frequently illuminated, manuscript records that we owe most of what we know about these festivities today.[10]

Beyond that, Henry was strong enough minded to reserve time to further his own political interests by remaining in close touch with the actions taken by his Council in the name of the King in Parliament, to be sure that no conflict was arising between them. This was soon to prove necessary, following the election to his Privy Council of one of the Court's chaplains, Thomas Wolsey, in 1509.

Although only a butcher's son in Ipswich, young Thomas had been regarded as precocious enough to be encouraged to seek preferment as a scholar at Magdalen College, Oxford, where (propelled as much by his own ambitions as by his academic abilities) he elected to follow a clerical career. Thereafter, his promotion was meteoric. Summoned to Court as a chaplain in 1507, he was invited to join the Privy Council two years later and promoted to the Deanery of Hereford when only thirty-four. Within a year he had become Dean of Lincoln, then Bishop in 1514 and then Archbishop of York. Within the English Church, that was as far as he could go while William Wareham remained Archbishop of Canterbury.

Although that might be supposed to have sufficed for most ambitious young careerists of humble origins, for Wolsey it still did not, for what obsessed him most was a craving for power, in its political and financial senses, which had long since overtaken any theological interests that he may have entertained while still a Fellow of Magdalen College, Oxford; and the road to that lay first in obtaining promotion within the Church to the rank of Cardinal and then, with the King's assistance, to becoming Pope.

The first of these coveted ambitions was fulfilled in 1515 when he received his Cardinal's red hat; but in the second, despite two spirited attempts in 1521 and again in 1523, he was to be disappointed. From that time onwards, however, the powers already delegated to him by his English master and sovereign had begun to seem threatening to Henry rather than helpful, a fact that was to lead inexorably towards a downfall from grace and favour that was to be as swift as his earlier rise to power had been spectacular (see Plate X, No. 13).[11]

Perhaps the best summary of them available to us today was that provided by Shakespeare in his tightly condensed and foreshortened dramatisation of these events in Act III, Scene 2, of his *King Henry VIII* written in 1613. Placed as it is there between that of Catherine of Aragon's defence of her own cause in the divorce proceedings begun against her by the mighty Cardinal on the King's behalf, and its subsequent referral to Rome in Scene 1, and that of the Coronation of Anne Boleyn at the start of Act IV, Scene 2 succeeds in depicting for its audiences not only the many charges brought by members of the Privy Council against Wolsey, but a deeply touching account of his own recognition of their likely consequences, followed up by his subsequent confession and expressions of repentance offered to Thomas Cromwell in its closing lines.

What had brought Wolsey to this pass was his single-minded pursuit of power and wealth at the expense of the Church's most pressing need to find a leader willing to champion the cause of reform within its own ranks. He had himself consistently ignored the growing chorus of protest and complaint about absentees among holders of benefices at all levels in the Church who, while delegating the duties incumbent upon them to others, continued to cream off the financial rewards for their personal aggrandisement. Even more offensive to many laymen was the fact that when clergy were accused of breaches of the common law, they seemed able to escape prosecution by claiming protection from the Vatican.[12] More serious, however, than these increasingly frequent and more blatant abuses of privilege, was the widely held belief that leading churchmen were failing to address the need for doctrinal reform. This was centred upon the nature and quality of faith and belief with a view to bringing them more closely into line with recent scholarly thought and pronouncements on the one hand, and with the rapidly expanding horizons of sixteenth century life on the other.

When, therefore, these home-grown rumblings of discontent were supplemented by the more serious eruptions that accompanied the protests and actions of Martin Luther in Augsburg in 1526, and by William Tyndale's publication in Flanders of his translation of the New Testament into English in 1525, both King and Cardinal were taken by surprise and became alarmed enough to take steps to try to prevent news of the former and copies of the latter being imported into England; for, as they had already begun to discuss how and when to open divorce proceedings that would clear the way for the King to embark upon a second marriage offering better prospects of securing a male heir to the English throne, the last thing they wanted was to strain their cordial relationship with the Papacy.[13]

A time had thus come for the game of cat and mouse that Henry had thus far been content to play with his overweening Cardinal-Archbishop and Lord Chancellor, to end. He thus set

PLATE I

No. 1 Aerial View of the Colosseum, Rome.

No. 2 The Martyrdom of St. Ignatius.

PLATE II

Female athletes as depicted in the mosaic flooring of the 'Hall of the Ten Maidens' in the imperial villa at Piazza Armerina, Sicily.

No. 3 Competitors engaged in games (upper register).

PLATE III

No. 4 Prize-winners awaiting their awards.

PLATE IV

No. 5 North aisle of Syracuse Cathedral incorporating the Doric columns of the
Greek Temple on the same site.

PLATE V

No. 6 Coptic cross superimposed on a column of the hypostyle in the Temple of
Isis at Philae, Egypt.

PLATE VI

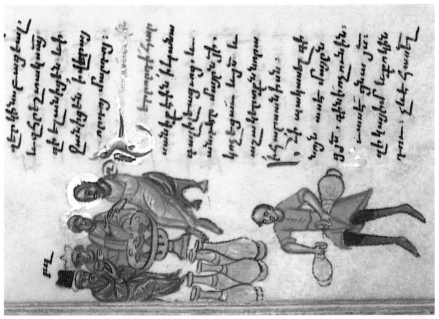

No. 8 Transformation of water into wine at the wedding feast at Cana in Galilee.

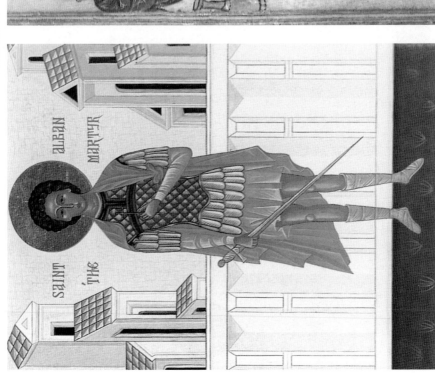

No. 7 Ikon of St. Alban, British protomartyr.

PLATE VII

No. 9 The 'Green', or 'Wild' Man as represented in a roof-boss in Warmington Church, Cambridgeshire.

PLATE VIII

No. 10 'Death and a Woman' by Swiss painter, Hans Baldung Grien. Reproduced by courtesy of Oeffentliche Kunstsammlung Basel, Kunstmuseum and Oeffentliche Kunstsammlung Basel, Martin Bühler.

No. 11 The Tudor Guildhall, Much Wenlock, Shropshire.

PLATE IX

No. 12 A replica of John Cabot's *Matthew*, 1997.

PLATE X

No. 13 Cardinal Thomas Wolsey, artist unknown, c. 1520. Reproduced by courtesy
of the National Portrait Gallery, London.

PLATE XI

No. 14 Reconstruction of the Chapter House, Wenlock Priory before
its dissolution in 1538.

No. 15 South wall of the Chapter House at Wenlock Priory as it is today.

PLATE XII

No. 16 Entry of Elizabeth I into the City of London, 1559.

PLATE XIII

Reconstruction of the Rose Theatre, Southwark by C. Watter Hodges.

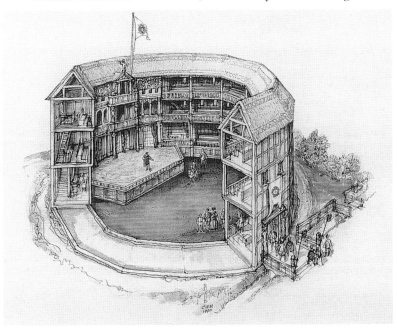

No. 17 As originally built in 1587.

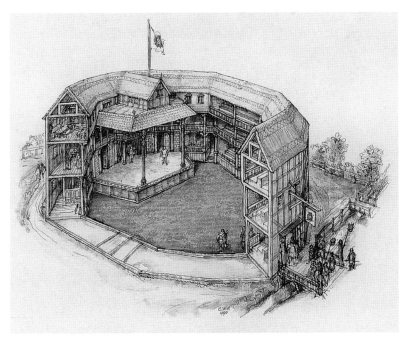

No. 18 As it appeared after the enlargement of the auditorium and the alterations
to the stage in 1593.

PLATE XIV

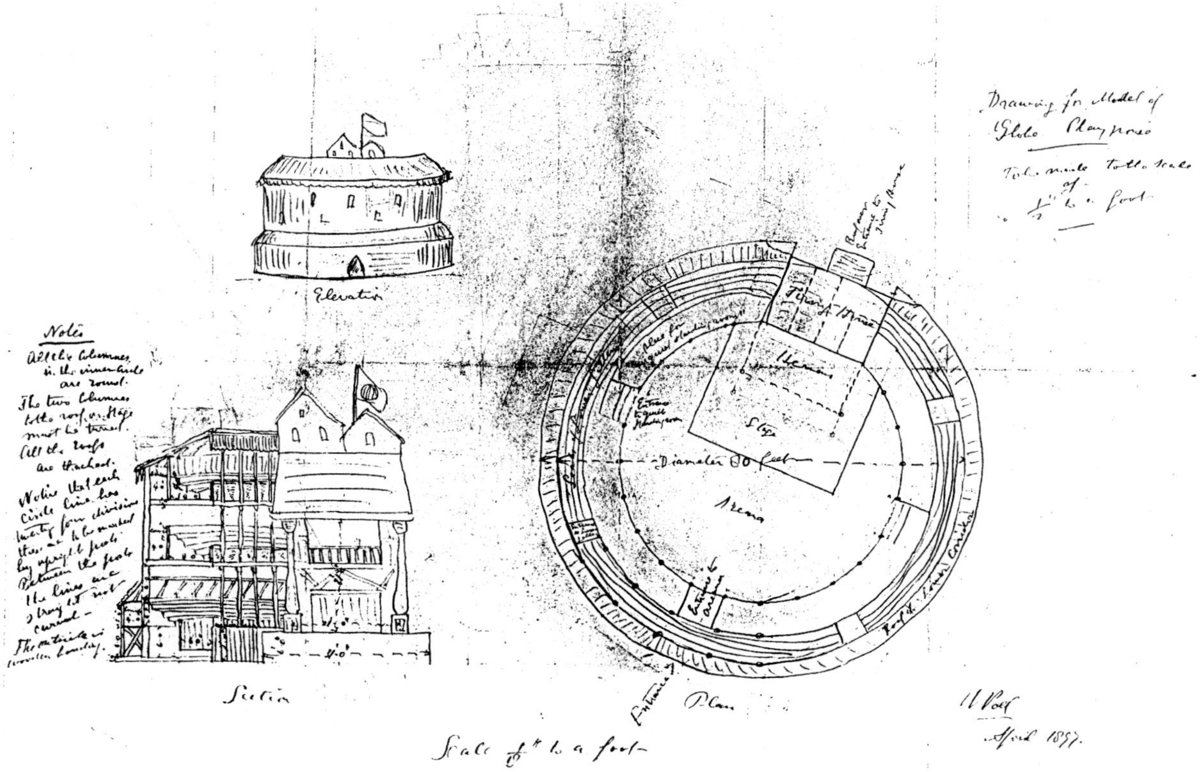

No. 19 William Poel's reconstruction of the Globe Playhouse, 1897.

PLATE XV

No. 20 The *Vieux Colombier* Theatre in Paris as renovated by Jacques Copeau for use by his *Companie des Quinzes*, 1919.

PLATE XVI

The Drama Studio in the Wills Memorial Building, Bristol University, opened in 1951.

No. 21 Its architect Richard Southern, explains the several types of theatre that can be set up in it to members of the Consultative Committee on Drama.

No. 22 An audience taking its seats for a performance in this Studio Theatre as set up in its Arena style, 1951.

about recovering control over all major affairs of state, both at home and abroad, into his own hands, but his efforts to stop surreptitiously imported printed copies of Tyndale's English version of the New Testament reaching evangelically-minded readers proved to be ineffectual.

No action was taken, however, to interfere with these English translations of stories lifted from both the Old and New Testaments for annual presentation in Corpus Christi plays and other religious drama habitually performed on major Calendar Feast Days and public holidays.[14] The most probable reason for this lay in the fact that all of these translations had been made from the Latin Bible as authorised by the Vatican (together with the licences required for their performance) in all countries within Western Christendom; but, by the mid-1520s, many of its civic sponsors and promoters in England must have begun to notice the storm-clouds gathering on the horizon to threaten its continuance.

Drama at Court, by marked contrast, had developed and expanded in several new directions, attributable at first to the initiatives promoted by Henry VII (see p. 104 above) and thereafter to the personal interest displayed towards them by Henry VIII. What is significant about these extensions of theatrical activity is that most of them were derived from Graeco-Roman sources and precedents already well advanced at several Italian courts, rather than from those already set up by the Roman Catholic Church during the fourteenth and fifteenth centuries. Most of them, moreover, were scripted to appeal to literate and academically-minded audiences.

Henry VII had recognised that any court seeking acceptance as that of a national state of Imperial potential needed to be seen to be possessed of a company of actors skilled enough in their art to complement that of its musicians on all festive and ceremonial occasions. Provision was thus made, in revisions to his own Household Order Book, for the establishment of a company of six players, privileged to wear the royal livery and licensed to travel and perform throughout the kingdom when not needed at Court. Henry VIII later extended this number from six to eight. While it would be anachronistic to describe these players as 'professionals' in our own, commercial sense of that word, it must have become apparent to them from the gratuities they received after performances in provincial towns and cities, that a road lay open towards acquisition of that status once the Church could be persuaded to withdraw its continuing refusal to recognise them as Christian communicants working within a profession at least as reputable and worthy of respect as that of musicians.[15]

Prospects for play-makers, however, improved faster and more firmly during the reign of Henry VII and the first two decades of Henry VIII's. While most of them continued to owe their licences to their status as priests, the creative and imaginative opportunities open to them in schools, choir-schools and at Court began to overtake those still offered to them in the service of the Church in provincial cities on its major Calendar Feast Days. Thus Henry Medwall, as private chaplain to the Lord Chancellor, could safely set pen to paper when writing *Fulgens and Lucres* I and II in 1497, in the knowledge that this play was required to entertain guests at Lambeth Palace that would include not only the Spanish and Flemish Ambassadors, but many influential English representatives of the King's Privy Council (see p. 99 above). Another extended Moral Interlude, *Nature* (again scripted in two parts), followed a year or two later. Both of these plays appeared in printed editions within the next twenty years.

A near contemporary of his, John Skelton, had likewise attracted attention as a scholar of distinction. After graduating from Cambridge University *c.* 1484, he taught Latin and Rhetoric at Oxford where his reputation brought him to the notice of the royal family. By 1499 he had moved to London to become tutor to Prince Henry (then only six years old) teaching him (as he was later to claim) to spell and to introduce him 'to the Muses Nine'.

His first play, *Nigromansir* (The Necromancer), was written for performance at Court in 1504 but has since been lost. His second, *Virtue*, has also been lost, but his third *Magnyfycence*, written *c.* 1515, survived to be printed *c.* 1530. While all three plays were cast within the familiar mould of a Moral Interlude, in *Magnyfycence* the traditional theological frame is stretched to allude unmistakably to topical, political issues, if less overtly than Medwall had chosen to do in *Fulgens and Lucres*.

By that time Roman plays were starting to be revived and presented by boys, not only at St. Paul's and Eton College but by students within the London law schools at the Inns of Court; and by 1520 news of these strikingly *avant-garde* productions had sufficed for invitations to be issued for some of them to be revived as repeat performances, given at Court, and at the private residences of such notable figures as Cardinal Wolsey and Thomas More. In such households as these, interest in the comedies of Plautus and Terence was extending to include some of the tragedies of Seneca and an acquaintance with Roman dramatic theory as formulated by Horace in his *Ars Poetica*; while at Oxford and Cambridge students were already being exposed not only to Aristotle's *Rhetoric* but to plays by Aristophanes and Euripides, either in Greek or in Latin translations.[16]

Meanwhile a younger generation of play-makers, including John Heywood, John Rastell, William Cornish and John Rightwise, all of whom were school or choir masters, was transforming the characters in their Moral Interludes from abstract personifications into recognisably contemporary human portraits of familiar figures drawn from village life who owed as much to Terence and Plautus as to Chaucer and Lydgate.[17] In this respect, the titles of Heywood's early plays speak for themselves. These start with *The Pardoner and the Friar, the Curate, Neighbour Pratte* (1519); next, *Johan Johan the husband, Tib his Wife and Sir John the Priest* and *The Four P's* (1520); and *The Play of the Weather* (1528).[18] None of these plays, however, was as satirically explicit in its political criticism as John Roo's (or Rho's) *Lord Governance and Lady Public Weal*, for this play (now lost or deliberately destroyed) so incensed Cardinal Wolsey when he saw it at Gray's Inn at Christmas 1526/7 that he confiscated Roo's chain of office as a sergeant-at-law, ordered his arrest and imprisonment and then reprimanded the student actors for their connivance in performing it (see *EES* I, pp. 236–7).

The contemporary historian, Edward Hall, regarded this incident as worthy of record in his *Chronicle*.[19] He also records performance of another explicitly political Moral Interlude (scripted this time in Latin and presented by boys) at Court in 1529, shortly before Henry VIII decided to ask the Papal Legate and Nuncio (Cardinals Wolsey and Campeggio) to open divorce proceedings against his Queen on grounds that the earlier Papal Dispensation of 1502 respecting consanguinity was invalid (see *EES* I, p. 238, and pp. 105–6 above). In these circumstances it seems strange that no evidence should have survived to suggest that either the King or his Council interfered in any way, or at any time, with the traditional performances of religious plays as presented annually on public holidays in the streets and open spaces of large provincial towns and cities considering that most of these plays, as has already been remarked (p. 109 above), were scripted from stories narrated in both the Old and New Testaments translated into English and acted by both priests and laymen. We must again recall, however, that all of these translations were made from the Latin Bible as authorised, and licensed for performance by the Vatican for nearly two hundred years; but by the mid-1520s, with storm-clouds gathering around the heads of Martin Luther and William Tyndale in Germany, and even that of Wolsey (for different reasons) in England, many of the civic sponsors and promoters of religious drama must have begun to entertain forebodings about the likelihood of its continuance for much longer.

Divorce proceedings were at last begun in May 1529, before a Consistory Court set up in the Hall of the Dominican Priory at Blackfriars within the City of London; but they were brought to an abrupt conclusion by the Papal Nuncio, Cardinal Campeggio who, in July, decided to support Queen Catherine's appeal to remove them out of English jurisdiction into that of the Pope in Rome.[20]

For his part, the King, on recognising that this could at best only result in further procrastination and delay, reacted angrily by first dismissing Wolsey from all his offices at Court and by deciding then that this matter would not be brought to its conclusion by the Pope in Rome, but in London by the King in Parliament.

In making this decision, Henry acted with alacrity and firmness by taking back ultimate control of all subsequent events into his own hands. After using the summer months to sound out the degree of support he could count on from Parliament, and to inform himself about the problems that had arisen from Wolsey's neglect of all ecclesiastical reform, he summoned Parliament to meet on 3rd November 1529. In doing so, it was to become the first of the seven sessions convened between then and 1536 which were subsequently to become known as 'The Reformation Parliament'.[21]

During the first of these sessions, members were only asked to approve measures directed against the most notorious of those abuses of power and privilege that had previously been connived at and committed by the English clergy. Since all of these measures commanded wide support throughout the country, they were quickly translated into law before this session was prorogued on 17th December in time for the forthcoming Christmas festivities.

These could then begin in the knowledge that a clear warning had been issued to the Pope that the King of England expected a quick and favourable decision respecting his divorce, and that notice had been given to all churchmen at home to bring their houses into line with English law as revised under the new Statutes, or to find Parliament doing it for them instead.

It may or it may not be significant that for the first time during the twenty years since Henry VIII had ascended the throne, no plays were performed at Court that year.

VII

DEATH SENTENCES AND
REPRIEVES, 1530–60

WHEN the second session of the 'Reformation Parliament' opened in January 1531, all forms of religious drama that had been born, nurtured and brought to full maturity within the Roman Catholic Church were already in danger of dying on their feet for lack of any injection of fresh creative initiatives since the end of the fifteenth century.

The events of the next eighteen months did nothing to dispel the bleakness of this outlook, while some of them suggested that it would become still bleaker rather than brighter. Of the latter, the first was a tersely-worded decision taken by the Town Council in Ipswich early in 1531:

'Corpus Christi play for ever taken away. Corpus Christi play laide aside for ever by order.' (See *EES* I. i, pp. 62n.2 and 62, and *Med Stage*, ii, p. 372)

As worded, this decision leaves several question marks floating over it. Why was it taken? It had already been 'laide aside' on five previous occasions between 1513 and 1519. Why? Possibly because insufficient funds were available to meet the costs of production? Yet why 'for ever by order' in 1531? Possibly in response to the disgrace and dismissal of Cardinal Wolsey from all the offices he held at Court? Was this then used as an excuse to rid the Town Council of all future obligations to fund performances?

No answers to these questions are ever likely to be definitive beyond the known facts that:

1 no evidence survives to suggest that the plays were ever revived;

113

2 the prompt-copies of the texts were either lost or suppressed; and

3 Parliament and Convocation at Canterbury had agreed to the King becoming 'Head of the Church in England as far as the word of God allows', instead of the Pope in Rome.

It was certainly in the light of this decision that the Mayor and his Council at Chester took it upon themselves in the spring of 1532 to order their Town Clerk, William Newhall, to delete all references to Papal jurisdiction over the conduct of audiences in the Proclamation advertising the forthcoming performances of the Chester Cycle in the following Whitsun week. A transcription of the entire text of this Proclamation together with Newhall's deletions is provided in *EES* I, Appendix D, pp. 340–7.

Within a month of these events in Ipswich and Chester, William Wareham, Archbishop of Canterbury for the past thirty years, died. To succeed him, Henry VIII nominated Thomas Cranmer, who had recently returned from Germany and who enjoyed his confidence; and when no opposition was encountered (John Fisher alone excepted) he was formally consecrated on 30th March 1533.[1]

It thus fell to Cranmer to deal with the situation that arose when it became known that Anne Boleyn was pregnant. Before the year was out, Henry had decided to marry her in secret and in March to persuade Parliament to pass an Act restraining all future appeals to the Papacy in Rome.

In doing this, Henry had effectively withdrawn all future jurisdiction over the government of the Church in England out of the hands of Rome and into his own, while leaving it to the Lords Spiritual assembled in Convocation to settle all future disputes respecting divine law and interpretations of scripture.

Once armed with this decision, Cranmer then brought Convocation to agree, in May of that year, that Catherine of Aragon's marriage to Henry VIII was contrary to divine law. With that done, he then obtained the King's permission to resume her trial (which had been adjourned and referred to Rome since 1529) in England. It opened on 10th May, but when Catherine refused to appear before the Court, he brought it to a swift conclusion two weeks later with a verdict in the King's favour and an assurance that his secret marriage to Anne Boleyn was valid.

With all obstacles thus removed, Anne was received into London on 31st May with a 'Coronation Triumph' of traditional street pageants, scripted on this occasion by Nicholas Udall and John Leland, and then crowned as the new Queen of England on 1st June. If this welcome was less lavish than that which had greeted Catherine of Aragon twenty-eight years earlier, it was noticeably more classical in its complementary allusions and visual imagery (see *EES* I, pp. 80–1 and 90–1).

With that achieved, it might seem that Henry had won his protracted four-year battle with Pope Clement VII to secure a male heir for himself and the nation, but when Clement responded four months later by issuing his own sentence of 'the greater excommunication' upon the King, it became clear that only the battleground had shifted. For by setting those of his subjects who chose to retain their allegiance to Rome, in point of Christian faith and doctrine, in conflict with what the Vatican continued to regard as the upstart, 'heretical' government hierarchy in London, he was effectively inviting them to open a campaign of civil disobedience in England while assuring them (on as-yet uncontested grounds) of support and practical assistance from all the Catholic Kings within the self-styled 'Holy Roman Empire'.

Here, the King again proclaimed himself to be his own man in ignoring these threats and by calling upon Parliament to confirm in Statutes 'the submission of the clergy to his own authority', already granted by Convocation in 1532, the 'Restraint of Annates' (i.e. taxes payable to Rome) of the same year, and the 'Restraint of Appeals' of 1533 and—as a final gesture of defiance—an Act of Supremacy in 1534.

With the passing of that Act, the time had finally come for decisions to be reached on the future of religious drama in England, together with that of the monastic establishments which had trained and protected most of its play-makers and many of its actors for the past five hundred years.

To formulate policies to deal both with this and with other educational aspects of the severance of all relationships with the Papacy, Henry decided to delegate his authority to a rising star within his Privy Council, Thomas Cromwell (see *EES* II, Plate III, No. 3).[2] It thus fell to him to advise the King on the future, not only of plays of Roman Catholic origin and doctrinal content, but also that of all monastic foundations, including those established primarily for the education of the young and their preparation for careers in the Church, the Judiciary and other positions of influence in the government of the country. These embraced virtually all the University Colleges at Oxford and Cambridge, as well as most of the collegiate schools like Winchester and Eton, thus bringing their future into question.

To this end, Cromwell set about organising a series of formal 'visitations' to the smaller Monastic foundations (like priories, friaries and nunneries) in 1535/6, to be followed later by others to the larger abbeys and minsters, with a view to discovering what degree of local resistance might be anticipated to their closure and to compile an audit of their lands, wealth and possessions.

Some time in that same year, Sir Richard Morrison sent a letter to the King attacking the Roman Catholic Church for its systematic indoctrination of youth in schools and . . .

'. . . played in plays before the ignorant people, sung in minstrels' songs and books in English . . . '

He follows this up with an equally outspoken attack on such dangerously anarchic folk plays as that of . . .

'Robin Hood, Maid Marion, Friar Tuck wherein beside the lewdness and ribaldry that is there opened to the people disobedience also to your officers is taught. . . .'

Such plays, he claims, are 'commonly performed upon Holy Days in most places of your Realm'. This then leads him to the core of his argument:

'How much better is it that those plays should be forbidden and deleted, and others devised to set forth and declare lively, before the people's eyes the abomination and wickedness of the Bishop of Rome, monks, friars, nuns and such like, and open to them the obedience that your subjects, by God's and man's laws, owe unto your Majesty.'

He concludes this argument by claiming that:

'Into the common people things sooner enter by the eyes than that they hear . . . '[3]

This was a sentiment with which Shakespeare found himself still able to agree when writing *Coriolanus* some seventy years later when Volumnia reminds her son that in times of crisis,

116

'Action is eloquence, and the eyes of th'ignorant
More learned than the ears . . . ' (III.2, 76–7)

The importance of Sir Richard's letter lies partly in the evidence it provides of the direction in which the most ardent of Protestant Reformers were moving and partly in its being the first to suggest that, in future, all English drama should be made subject to State censorship.

What is certain, however, is that Cromwell and Cranmer acted instantly upon this advice—with or without the King's permission—by recruiting John Bale, a sometime Carmelite friar who had renounced his vows and married (then resident as a parish priest in Thorndon, Suffolk) to write and perform polemical plays of the kind recommended by Morrison in his letter to the King. Payments begin to be recorded to 'John Bale and his fellows' in Cromwell's Household Accounts in 1536 and continue thereafter until 1540 when Bale felt it expedient to flee to Germany.[4]

Two other events arising between 1535 and 1537 merit attention here since they serve to illustrate the tide of feeling that was also growing at this time on the other side of this widening religious divide. The first was the arrest, trial and execution in 1535 of John Fisher, Bishop of Rochester since 1504, and Sir Thomas More, the most illustrious literary figure in England at that time. Fisher had been the only bishop who refused to support the submission of the clergy to Convocation's agreement to replacing the Pope's authority over the Church in England with the King's in 1532. More had likewise resigned his office as Lord Chancellor for the same reason, and when both of them refused to accept the Act of Supremacy in 1534 they met their deaths as traitors who had elected to remain loyal to their faith.[5]

The second was an Order from the King to the Justices in York (c. 1536/7) obliging them to arrest and imprison papists who wrote and performed religious Interludes.

'And whereas we understand by certain report the late evil and seditious rising in our ancient city of York, at the acting of a religious interlude of St. Thomas the Apostle, made in the said city on the 23rd of August now past; and whereas we have been credibly informed that the said rising was owing to the seditious conduct of certain papists who took part in preparing for the said interlude, we will and require you that from henceforward ye do your utmost to prevent and hinder any such commotion in future.'

117

In its conclusion, this Order explains the King's reasons for taking this action:

'And for this ye have my warrant for apprehending and putting in prison any papists who shall, in performing interludes which are founded on any portions of the Old or New Testament, say or make use of any language which may tend to excite those who are beholding the same to any breach of the peace.'6

Between them, the four items cited above suffice to confirm that even before the dissolution of the larger monasteries began in 1538, the politicising of English drama had already transformed all overtly religious drama into a dangerous form of 'game' or 'play' carrying far more serious consequences for all participants when the 'earnest' behind them was explicitly spelt out in performance than had ever been thought of before—a contention to be confirmed during the final decade of the King's reign.

Before Cromwell proceeded to dissolve the larger monasteries in 1538, he briefed his commissioners to minimise resistance by offering compensation to the senior clergy in the form of pensions, benefices and other sweeteners to be deducted from the financial gains that would accrue to the Crown from its seizure of monastic lands, buildings, rents, libraries and other possessions. Some monasteries situated within large urban areas like Chester, Gloucester, Bristol and Westminster were to be spared pending decisions on their use as cathedrals in future.

Of the 850 monasteries known to exist in England when Henry VIII became king in 1509, 300 had been listed as smaller houses in the *Valor Ecclesiasticus* audit of 1535; and by 1538 some 250 of these had already reverted into the possession of the Crown. What remains astonishing to us today is that the seizure of the remaining 600 larger houses should have been completed within the next two years, and then sold off or rented out to eager bidders from among the English nobility and landed gentry with so little resistance.

These changes in the lifestyle of the English countryside, however, were large enough to enforce not only substantial legal changes in the judiciary system, but to encourage the most ardent of Protestant reformers to reinforce them by embarking on an iconoclastic attack upon all visual representations of scripture that could be branded as symbols of Roman Catholic superstition and idolatry. With the leading ripped off the roofs of Abbey churches, stained-glass windows were smashed, frescoes ripped out or smothered behind coats of whitewash. This vandalism, reminiscent of that of the seventh and eighth centuries in both eastern and western Christendom (see pp. 18–19 above), was then carried over into surviving parish churches all over the country, but especially in southern and eastern counties where Lutheran support was at its strongest. (See Frontispiece, and Plate XI, Nos. 14 and 15, together with accompanying Notes to Illustrations.) Within this climate of opinion, what hope was there left for the survival of those fully animated biblical personifications resurrected annually in the streets of Hereford, Shrewsbury, Coventry, York, Carlisle and elsewhere in processions and plays celebrating the Feast of Corpus Christi and many saints' days?

In 1540 it must have seemed to the promoters and actors of these religious plays that a death sentence would follow shortly; but, if so, they were given cause to think again when it became known that the King had decided that Cromwell (now Earl of Essex) had overreached himself in his support of the English Lutherans and that, like Wolsey before him, he could be dispensed with once he had delivered all former monastic revenues into the hands of the Crown. Left unprotected by the master he had striven to please, he was arrested by his enemies among the Privy Council on 10th June within Parliament itself, stripped of his possessions, convicted of treason and beheaded at Tyburn on 28th July.[7]

Most historians have chosen to interpret this abrupt change of heart to the fluctuations that were afflicting the King's conscience at this time, together with his efforts to secure a male heir by frequent changes in his marital status. If so, he was called upon in 1541 to clarify and define his own stance in matters of religion following the arrest of at least two small groups of outspokenly Protestant polemical play-makers and actors in London and Salisbury. Both groups were imprisoned and questioned, and those found guilty of heresy burned at the stake as recorded by John Foxe in his *Acts and Memorials* or the *Book of Martyrs*.[8] Urged both by Convocation and his own Privy Council to define and confirm his views concerning his authority over matters relating to the interpretation of doctrine within the Church of England, he returned to Parliament with his instructions. Parliament then duly obliged him by giving statutory form to 'An Act for the Advancement of True Religion, and for the Abolition of the Contrary' (*Statutes*, iii, p. 894, para. 7).

Since this Act has already been quoted at length in *English Professional Theatre* (pp. 23–5), only its principal provisions need be repeated here. Having established in its preambles that the purpose of this Act was . . .

'. . . to take away, purge and cleanse . . . His Highness's Realm . . . of all such books, writings, sermons, disputations, arguments, ballads, plays . . . with all the causes, instruments and means of the same . . .'

that could be classified as heretical, seditious or both, it then proceeds to exempt the writing and performance of . . .

'. . . songs, plays and enterludes, to be used and exercised within this Realm and other of the King's dominions, for the rebutting and reproaching of vices, and the setting forth of virtue: so always the said songs, plays or enterludes *meddle not with interpretations of scripture contrary to the doctrine set forth, or to be set forth,* by the King's Majesty . . .' (the italics are mine)

Yet within the next two years this Act proved itself to have been too vaguely worded (at least respecting those words here placed in italics) to meet its intended purpose, for theatrical problems arose both in Cambridge University and in London between February and May of 1545 that were regarded as serious enough to warrant action.

At Cambridge, it was a small group of dons and students at Christ's College who provoked the trouble by deciding to celebrate Shrove Tuesday by performing a violently anti-Catholic polemical play. Described as 'a tragedy', it had been written by the German play-maker and author, Thomas Kirchmayer (c. 1538) and translated into English, presumably by John Bale before he fled to Germany in 1540, under the title of *Pammachius*. When news of this performance in the Hall of Christ's College in 1545 reached the Chancellor (Stephen Gardiner, Bishop of Winchester and a Privy Councillor) from an outraged junior fellow, he wrote at once to the Vice-Chancellor, Matthew Parker, describing it as 'so pestiferous as were intolerable' and instructing him to enquire how it had been allowed to be produced. From there this row escalated to embrace the Fellows, Heads of Houses and some of the student actors, together with some of the local residents on the one hand, and members of the Privy Council on the other. In the course of the ensuing depositions and correspondence, it becomes clear that what the Chancellor most feared was that the King might see fit to punish the whole university by withdrawing the Colleges' privileges reserved to them when their former monastic status was in question—especially their many endowments.

However, when it became clear that no riots or breaches of the peace had accompanied this performance, either within the University or among the townsmen, the Chancellor concluded the affair with a very stern rebuke to the Vice-Chancellor. Writing to him on 18th May, Gardiner begins his letter as follows:

'Your own men deride your own affairs in your precincts. Indeed they guaranteed the truth of this with ostentation in the tragedy of *Pammachius* when, while [*possibly* because] you were looking on and dithering, after they deservedly hissed the bishop of Rome from the stage, they forced off all the doctors with the same authority by jeering.'

He concludes this letter with a bitter commentary on the general laxity, selfishness and indiscipline among those in positions of authority within the University and by contrasting this with the state of affairs at Oxford and by a personal reminder of the vulnerability of his own continuance in his high office of Vice-Chancellor.

'Nothing of this kind happens among the Oxonians, and someone has said to me that there would be more suitable administration at your university if the vice-chancellor were chosen by decision of the Chancellor alone, according to their [i.e. Oxford's] example.'[9]

The trouble in London that provoked the issue of a Proclamation from Guildhall in February of that year and an Order of the Court of Aldermen two months later are less clearly defined. The Proclamation, issued on the King's behalf, offers three reasons of which the first is said to be:

'Forasmuch as by reason and occasion of the manifold and sundry Enterludes and Common Plays that now of late days have been by divers and sundry persons more commonly and busily set forth and played [than] heretofore has been accustomed in divers and many suspicious, dark and inconvenient places of this our most dread and most benign sovereign Lord the King's City and Chamber of London, wherein no plays ought to be played.'

The second is that these performances take place on 'Sundays and other Holy days in the time of Evensong and other Divine Service'. And the third is a charge that was later to become almost perennial, namely the corruption of youth coupled with absenteeism from divine service and, on working days, from their normal occupations.

In consequence,

'no manner of person or persons from henceforth, of whatever estate, degree or condition he or they be of, presume or take upon him or them at any time hereafter to play or set forth, or cause to be played, any manner of Enterlude or common play within any manner of place or places in this His Grace's said City'

other than the private residences of

'noblemen, or of the Lord Mayor, Sheriffs or Aldermen . . . or else in the houses of gentlemen, or of the substantial and said commoners or head parishioners . . . '

Further exceptions are allowed for performances given

'in the open streets as in time past it hath been used and accustomed'

and for those given

'in the Common Halls of the Companies, Fellowships or Brotherhoods of the same City.'[10]

The Proclamation concludes with the imposition of a ban on the advertising of forthcoming performances by means of playbills stuck on walls or otherwise displayed in public places.

The subsequent Order of the Court of Aldermen passed two months later seeks only to reinforce the ban on bill-posting by instructing its members 'to cause the same bills to be pulled down and the setters up to be attached and commit unto Ward', any unauthorised persons caught undertaking to perform interludes or plays within their wards, 'there to remain until they shall find sureties that they shall no more so use themselves'.[11]

While both of these Orders were clearly issued in an endeavour to support the 'Act for the Advancement of True Religion and the Abolition of the Contrary' within the City of London, by preventing public performances of provocative polemical plays, they fail to answer the question of who the actors of all these 'Common Plays and Enterludes' were. While many of them may well have been literate monks and friars recently dismissed from their former abbeys and priories and in search of an alternative artistic occupation, others must more certainly have been those household servants, maintained by the nobility and by many members of the landed gentry, as quasi-professional actors still licensed to travel beyond the boundaries of their local domains to supplement their income by seeking new audiences wherever they could find them.

What, therefore, the fortunate survival of these and other documents establishes for us is that these troupes of nomadic entertainers had already gained a firm enough foothold among civic audiences to support their hole-and-corner economy while attempting to gain public recognition as professionals in their own right, and by popular acclaim. When compared with this rapid growth in the number of plays, comedies and interludes that were being frequently performed in London, however, surviving records of the entertainments provided at Court during the final decades of Henry's reign are strikingly thin. While Masques continue to figure among them on a regular basis, all texts and descriptions of them have vanished. Nor is there any record of plays being commissioned from named play-makers, or of performances by schoolboys being imported as revivals for presentation at Court.

In 1545 the King thought it necessary to enlarge his own household by creating a new office within it responsible for organising and supervising all such entertainments as were to be provided at Court, indoors and at night. This was to be called 'The Revels Office' and based within the buildings formerly occupied by the Dominican monks at Blackfriars, now described as the Royal Wardrobe. A Royal Patent was accordingly issued on 11th March appointing Sir Thomas Carwarden as Henry's first 'Master of Games, Revels and Masks' with a Sergeant and a Yeoman as his assistants (see *EES* I, pp. 275–9).

I suspect myself that this decision was taken as a direct sequel and extension of the Proclamation issued from Guildhall in the King's name on 6th February (see pp. 121–2 above) setting out the conditions that were to govern all theatrical performances in London in future; in other words, specifically to preserve the King's prerogative to protect all such privileges in that respect as were still to pertain to his own, and to other noble households licensed by him, to maintain private companies of players.

This explanation at least accords with his own interpretations as set out in his *Acts for True Religion* (see p. 120 above). The likelihood, however, of his personal interpretation of that Act outlasting his own reign, when considered in conjunction with such interpretations as his successors might choose to place on *The Acts of Supremacy* of 1535, were already slim. For where Henry had chosen to restrict his religious reforms to the seizure of the monasteries between 1536 and 1540, together with the compiling of parish registers in 1538, and provision of Cranmer's authorised version of the Bible in English in 1539, he had also decided to avoid interference with the conduct of services in parish churches and to leave their richly endowed Chantry and Guild Chapels, their vestments, altars and organs virtually untouched. The temptation, therefore, to settle all such unfinished business when the King died in 1547 was already great.

Since Prince Edward was only nine when his father died, a Council of Regency had already been prepared to assume responsibility for the government of the Realm; this was to be led by his uncle, Edward Seymour, Earl of Hertford and Duke of Somerset, as Lord Protector while the young king was still a minor. As Somerset was widely known to be a supporter of more radical Protestant reform than Henry VIII had proved to be during the last four years of his reign, it thus became inevitable that Parliament would soon be called upon to make statutory provision for further, far-reaching reforms. These began at once with attacks on the forms of worship still permitted in many parish churches and on the maintenance of chantries, guild chapels and those religious fraternities endowed by wealthy parishioners for pious purposes that had been spared following the dissolution of the monasteries and the dismissal and execution of Thomas Cromwell in 1540.

Between 1547 and 1548, all chantries, chapels and religious guilds were swept away under the Chantries Act of 1547; Henry VIII's Act for the Advancement of True Religion was revoked, and an Act for the Uniformity of Service and Administration of the Sacraments had replaced the saying or singing of mass by substituting Archbishop Cranmer's first *Book of Common Prayer* in January of 1549.[12] The last of these changes became legally enforceable by Whitsun, and within the clauses of that Act it became an indictable offence for anyone who,

'. . . in any enterludes, plays, songs, rhymes or by other open words [to] declare or speak anything in the derogation, depraving or despising of the same book [i.e. Common Prayer] . . . '

Thus, from then onwards, anyone found guilty became liable to a fine of £10 for the first offence; for the second, a fine of £20; with forfeiture of goods and life imprisonment for any further repetition.

An even greater threat, however, had overtaken the continuance of religious drama derived from Roman Catholic sources in the passing of the Chantries Act of 1547, which had abolished not only those guilds founded to promote and finance theatrical celebration of the Feast of Corpus Christi, but celebration of the Feast itself, together with other Calendar holidays that had come to be regarded as superstitious or idolatrous.

Confronted with this, the City Council in Hereford decided on 18th December 1548 to follow the example set in Ipswich in 1531 to 'set aside for ever' its customary procession and accompanying Cycle of plays. It was accordingly recorded in the Council's 'Great Black Book' that,

'Forasmuch as there was before this time divers Corporations of Artificers, crafts and occupations in the said City who were bound by their grants of their Corporations yearly to bring forth and set forward divers pageants of ancient histories in the procession in the said City upon the Day and Feast of Corpus Christi which now is omitted and surceased. Wherefore it is agreed . . .'.

This entry then proceeds to set out in detail how in future each craft guild is to direct its former production funds to assist with the upkeep and maintenance of the city (see Plate VIII, No. 11).[13]

York City Council also took stock of its situation under the Chantries Act but responded to it less drastically: while deciding to authorise production of its own Corpus Christi Cycle that year, it demanded that its three plays devoted to the Death, Assumption and Coronation of the Virgin Mary should not be performed.[14] As this decision appears to have satisfied everyone in positions of authority and, since performance provoked no disturbance of the peace, it was repeated in 1549 but, for reasons unexplained, the Council decided in 1550 that the whole Cycle was 'to be spared' and 'not to be played that year'.

In London, however, the Government appears to have been more alarmed at this time by the theatrical situation developing in the capital than by such relatively occasional performances by local amateurs as those persisting in York, Chester, Coventry and other provincial cities;[15] for there, between August 1549 and April 1551, two Proclamations were issued in the King's name, the first of which begins by spelling out the reasons for its issue:

'Forasmuch as a great number of those that be Common Players of Enterludes and Plays, as well within the City of London as elsewhere within this realm, do for the most part play such Enterludes as contain matter tending to sedition and condemning of sundry good orders and laws where upon are grown and daily are like to grow and ensue, much disquiet, division, tumults and uproars in this realm . . . '.

To prevent this, all performances, whether given in public or in private performance-spaces, were to be banned for the next three months.[16]

The second of these two Proclamations is far more restrictive in its intentions, for not only does it bring printers and booksellers within its provisions for the first time, along with players of Enterludes, but it also obliges all actors to acquire written licences from the Privy Council before presuming to perform any plays in English anywhere in the country. Printers and booksellers are likewise required to obtain written licences from either the King himself or, failing that, six members of the Privy Council, before either importing books printed in English from abroad or printing and selling books themselves.[17]

All these measures were clearly put in place in an attempt to control the spread of opinions regarded by the new Protestant establishment as either seditious or heretical in the wake of the many changes in religious observance that the Lord Protector and his colleagues had placed so rapidly on the Statute Book between 1547 and 1549. They are just as clearly indicative, moreover, of a growing awareness within government circles of the power already acquired by the stage to inflame and subvert public opinion which had arisen from the ambiguity surrounding the Church's powers of censorship following the passing of the Act of Supremacy and the excommunication of Henry VIII.

The danger of this situation could not have been more succinctly summed up than it was by Stephen Gardiner in a letter to a fellow member of the Privy Council, Sir William Paget, on 5th February 1547, warning him that while he, as Bishop of Winchester, was arranging for a Requiem Mass to be held in Southwark for the dead King, he had been told that a company of players was proposing to perform a play simultaneously, 'to try who shall have the most resort: they in game or I in earnest . . .'

and urging him to ask the Lord Protector to ban it.[18]

It was within this climate of opinion that Thomas Cranmer decided to accord asylum to one of John Calvin's most ardent and able disciples, Martin Bucer who, after having established his headquarters among French Huguenots in Strasbourg, was facing threats of arrest. On his arrival in England in 1549, it was Cranmer who obtained the vacant Chair of Divinity for him at Cambridge.

It was there that he wrote his influential book, *De Regno Christi* (Christ's Kingdom), a chapter of which is entitled 'De Honestis Ludis' (On the Propriety of Plays) and of which a translation is to be found in Volume II (2) of *Early English Stages* under Appendix C, pp. 329–31.

Bucer, like Calvin, was well enough read in both Greek and Latin to have adopted a liberal-minded approach towards drama and theatre. Rather than wishing to suppress them, he sought instead to support both plays and acting that could be justified as advancing instruction in the articles of Christian faith as interpreted by Calvin: so, to this end, he advocated that:

'. . . in order that Christ's people may profit from religious comedies and tragedies, men will have to be appointed to the task of preventing any comedy or tragedy which they have not seen beforehand and decided should be acted: they must be men both outstanding in their knowledge of this kind of literature and also of established and constant zeal for Christ's Kingdom.'

This advice reached the King in the form of a New Year's gift in 1551 when Bucer presented him with a copy of his book. In its essence, this advice resembles that advanced by the Vatican two hundred years earlier when licensing religious plays for performance as an integral feature of the celebration of the Feast of Corpus Christi; but it also echoes (or incorporates) the advice offered to Henry VIII by Sir Richard Morrison in 1535 (see p. 116 above) and improves upon it by providing a mechanism for the imposition of a form of politically motivated stage-censorship enforced by the State to correspond with the situation that was currently facing the King and his Council when issuing their Proclamation in April 1551, 'for the reformation of vagabonds, tellers of news, sowers of seditious rumours, players, and printers without licence and divers other disordered persons'. Since, however, Bucer died later that year and as Edward followed him eighteen months later, neither of them saw this advice given statutory form. It is thus ironic that when it was finally adopted in August 1553 by Mary I, it would at once be applied in directions diametrically opposite to those intended by its author.

Before Mary Tudor could succeed her stepbrother as Queen, however, a *coup d'état* intended by the Duke of Somerset's successor as Lord Protector (John Dudley, Duke of Northumberland) to preserve a Protestant succession by replacing Edward VI with his own daughter-in-law, Lady Jane Grey, had first to be aborted. Within two weeks this coup collapsed, leaving Northumberland's and Mary's roles reversed and with the former finding himself a prisoner in the Tower of London and the latter being welcomed into London on 3rd August as Queen Mary I.[19]

For the many Catholics who, like the new Queen herself, had remained loyal to the old faith, despite all the revolutionary changes that had overtaken its observances in England during the past twenty years, the reprieve thus suddenly offered to them can only have seemed to be predestined by Divine Providence. David Loades, when assessing the impact of this situation on the country as a whole, has summed it up with such admirable clarity and precision in *Revolution in Religion: the English Reformation, 1530–1570* as to oblige me to quote from it here:

'Considering the magnitude of the revolution and the venerable nature of the customs which had been overturned, the effectiveness of the Edwardian Reformation at the parochial level was remarkable. Compliance was reluctant and far from universal, but the great majority of church-wardens and incumbents did more or less as they were ordered. It was, however, very largely a negative revolution.'[20]

He then proceeds to explain this by adding:

'There were certainly more Protestants in England in 1553 than there had been in 1547, but the main protagonists of change, such as Archbishop Cranmer, were the first to admit that they had not really converted the people of England to a new piety.'[21]

The reprieve offered to Catholics by Mary and her new Privy Council included restoration of the mass, together with other liturgical rituals, including those associated with the Feast of Corpus Christi and its accompanying religious plays.

In most parish churches, however, it was to prove far harder to repair or replace the damage done to them by the iconoclastic vandals amongst Protestant extremists following the passing of the Chantries Act in 1547. As had been the case with the monasteries when they were dissolved, their endowments had been seized by the Crown; their vestments, plate and ornaments had been sold off; and all imagery considered by the King's commissioners to be superstitious or idolatrous such as statuary, stained glass and frescoes, smashed or buried under whitewash. Brighter prospects had dawned, however, for the recovery of organs, altars, roodscreens and, above all, for church music.[22]

While it can thus be said that Mary's accession to the throne as Supreme Head of the Church in England was generally welcomed throughout the nation, it nevertheless encountered stubborn resistance both in London and its adjoining counties, from convinced evangelistic reformers including recent converts to Lutheran and Calvinist beliefs.

As a result, Mary thought it essential to retain personal control over those powers of censorship that had been imposed upon all play-makers, actors, printers and booksellers by Edward VI in his Proclamation of 1551 (see pp. 125–6 above). This she made clear in the Proclamation that she issued on 18th August within a fortnight of her arrival in London. It opens soothingly with an appeal for tolerance and patience:

'First: Her Majesty being presently by the only goodness of God settled in her just possession of the imperial crown of this realm and other dominions thereunto belonging, can not now hide that religion (which God and the world knoweth she hath ever professed from her infancy hitherto) which as Her Majesty is minded to observe and maintain for herself by God's Grace during her time and would be glad the same were of all her subjects quietly and charitably embraced.'[23]

In its subsequent provisions, however, which seek to combine those made by Edward VI in his Proclamation of 1551 respecting plays and play-makers, with those set out in her father's *Act for the Promotion of True Religion and the Abolition of the Contrary* of 1543 (which Edward had revoked in 1549 when substituting his own *Act for the Uniformity of Service and Administration of the Sacraments*),

Mary's first Proclamation becomes more uncompromising in its tone and more widespread in its aims.

'And furthermore, for as much as it is well known, that sedition and false rumours have been nourished and maintained in this realm by the subtlety and malice of some evil disposed persons, which take upon them without sufficient authority to preach, and to interpret the Word of God after their own brain in churches and other places both public and private. And also by playing of Interludes and printing false fond books, ballads, rhymes and other lewd treatises in the English tongue, concerning doctrine in matters now in question and controversy, touching the high points and mysteries of the Christian religion: which books, ballads, rhymes and treatises are chiefly by the Printers and Stationers set out to sale to her Grace's subjects, of an evil zeal for lucre and covetous of vile gain.'

This Proclamation concludes by extending its provisions outwards from players, play-makers, printers and booksellers to embrace preachers, teachers and all self-appointed interpreters of scripture:

'Her Highness therefore straightly chargeth and commandeth all and every her said subjects, of whatsoever state, condition, or degree they be, that none of them presume from henceforth to preach, or by way of reading in churches, or other public or private places (except in schools and universities) to interpret or teach any scriptures, or any manner points of doctrine concerning religion. Neither also to print any books, matter, ballad, rhyme, interlude, process or treatise, nor to play any interlude, except they have Her Grace's special licence in writing for the same upon pain to incur Her Highness's indignation and displeasure.' (See *EES* II.i, pp. 69–70 and *English Professional Theatre*, pp. 40–1.)

All might yet have been well, following this attempt to achieve a generally acceptable settlement of religious belief and practice in England, but that was not to be. For once Mary had taken it upon herself (as much in loyalty to her Spanish mother as in seeking support from Catholic states) to propose a marriage to Philip II of Spain, popular opinion in England of her real intentions began to turn against her.[24] Yet notwithstanding the popular agitation that arose in Essex, Kent, Wales and some Midland counties during the following months, she persisted (with an obstinacy and determination characteristic of her father) in bringing this proposal to a conclusion by marrying Philip in Winchester Cathedral on 25th July 1554.

Thus where civic authorities in Coventry, Chester, Carlisle, York, Lincoln and even London itself could now safely resume performances of religious plays to celebrate the Feast of Corpus Christi and other traditional Calendar Holidays, no such tolerance was likely to be accorded to polemical plays regarded as heretical, seditious and both written and performed with a view to provoking public disturbances. Arrests, imprisonment and executions of actors and play-makers found guilty of so doing were thus just as certain to resume.[25] And this they continued to do for the next three years until Mary died without a son or daughter to succeed her, and her consort King Philip II had returned to Spain.

Thus, when Mary I was succeeded by her Protestant stepsister, the Princess Elizabeth, a large question mark returned to hang over the reprieve that Mary had granted to the remaining promoters of all religious drama still ineradicably branded with unmistakably Roman Catholic parentage.

Another such question mark, however, had also moved into the foreground during the two decades between Elizabeth's birth in 1533 and her accession in 1558, concerning the future of *all* theatrical activity in England. This was the apparent inability of Tudor governments, whether of Protestant or Roman Catholic persuasion, to stop the writing and performance of religious plays deliberately scripted to subvert legally licensed expressions of religious opinion in order to provoke breaches of the peace (with ensuing brawls and riots in public places) both in London and in the provinces.

Solutions to both of these questions thus awaited Elizabeth's attention as soon after her Coronation as she had appointed a new Privy Council to assist her, and to arrange for the first Parliament of her reign to be called into session to approve statutory action. In the circumstances, however, it is likely that both of these questions were eclipsed in her subjects' minds by the fact that this twenty-five-year-old Princess was yet another woman and—in the eyes of staunch Catholics, a bastard at that—usurping a throne which long-standing tradition had proclaimed to be rightfully occupied by a man. Yet, at that time, her immediate heir seemed to be both another woman and a Roman Catholic, Mary, Queen of Scots. Who then would she marry both to provide herself with a male heir and to retain her inheritance within Protestant hands?

VIII

DEATH AND
TRANSFIGURATION,
1560–80

T HE coining of the catch-phrase, 'If you want to be a leader of men, you must cultivate an image' is usually attributed to Napoleon; but to the young Princess Elizabeth it must already have seemed self-evident as she reflected on the political and religious situations that confronted her when being escorted through the streets of London on her way to her Coronation as Queen Elizabeth I in 1558. If it was not, then the author, devisers and actors of the pageant theatres that punctuated her progress through the city had taken great care to spell it out to her, both verbally and visually, in a sequence of striking images designed to contrast good government with bad.[1]

These pageants were prepared on a scale that rivalled those mounted for Catherine of Aragon in 1501, both in their cost and in the content of their emblematic narrative (see Chapter 6, pp. 101–3 above).[2] On recognising the theatricality of the welcome that was awaiting her, Elizabeth at once decided to enter into the spirit of the occasion as a principal participant. This she did by causing the procession to halt whenever she felt that she needed time to offer a considered personal response to the greetings and advice given to her by the actors in each pageant (see Plate XII, No. 16).

On leaving the Tower of London her procession entered the city at Aldgate and moved on into Fenchurch Street where it was greeted by an instrumental fanfare from a scaffold, richly draped, in the centre of which stood a child who delivered a speech of welcome. Having listened attentively, Elizabeth thanked the child and the citizens assembled round this platform before moving on into Gracechurch Street where an elaborate pageant was erected across the street above a triple-arched gateway. This consisted of three platforms rising one above the other on the lowest of which sat Henry VII and his wife Elizabeth enthroned, respectively, within a red and white rose. From these roses branches sprang upwards to support the second platform containing actors costumed to represent Henry VIII and Ann Boleyn; and from there a single branch of the same red and white roses linked the second to the third platform containing a single figure dressed to represent Queen Elizabeth I herself.

The whole pageant, decked out as it was with red and white roses, depicted 'the uniting of the houses of Lancastre and Yorke'. After listening to another child orator who made verbally explicit the message of union, conjoined with peace and concord, expressed in the visual imagery of this pageant, Elizabeth replied by promising to 'do her whole endeavour for the continued preservation of concord, as the pageant did import' (see *EES* I, p. 72).

David Bergeron, in his splendidly detailed account of this Royal Entry in *English Civic Pageantry, 1558–1642*, remarks that at this point in her progress Elizabeth was having so much difficulty in making herself audible above the cheers from the crowds that she despatched representatives ahead of her to all the ensuing pageants 'to require the people to be silent for her majestie was disposed to heare all that shold be said unto her'.[3]

From there, she moved on to the Great Conduit in Cornhill where she was presented with another emblematic tableau, 'The Seat of Worthy Government'. This took the form of a second triple-gated archway surmounted by another image of the Queen, supported by actors representing 'Pure Religion, Love of Subjects, Wisdom and Justice' with each of them treading the corresponding Vice under their feet. In this case the Vices chosen are as significant to the meaning of this pageant as the Virtues. Here, 'Pure Religion' is contrasted with 'Superstition and Ignorance'; 'Love of Subjects' with 'Rebellion and Insolence'; 'Wisdom' with 'Folly and Vainglory'; 'Justice' with 'Adultation and Bribery'. Again, a child-actor is here employed to spell out verbally the message, implicit in the personification of the Virtues and Vices, presented visually, with verses.

One advantage of adopting this technique was to enable the Queen to be given a personal copy of these verses for her retention. In this case she is reported to have replied saying: 'I have taken notice of your good meaning toward mee, and will endeavour to Answere your several expectations'.[4]

133

From Cornhill, the procession passed into Cheapside to be greeted by a pageant graced by eight children personifying the Beatitudes (or blessings), as recorded in St. Matthew's Gospel, but here applied to the Queen by a ninth child-orator acting as their spokesman.[5] Both the Standard and the Cross in Cheapside had been freshly decorated. Passing on through lines of City Councillors the procession was brought to a halt on approaching St. Paul's Cathedral to allow the city's Recorder, Randulph Chomley, to present a gift of 1,000 marks in gold coin from the Mayor and Aldermen to the Queen together with their greetings. Her extemporary reply, as recorded by Richard Mulcaster in his printed version of the day's proceedings, is worth quoting in full since nothing could better convey her ability to rise to an occasion by transforming herself from the status of a privileged spectator into that of the leading actor:

'I thank my lord maior, his brethren, and you all. And wheras your request is that I should continue your good ladie and quene, be ye ensured, that I will be as good unto you, as ever quene was to her people. No wille in me can lacke, neither doe I trust shall there lacke any power. And persuade yourselves, that for the safetie and quietness of you all, I will not spare, if need be to spend my blood, God thank you all.'[6]

Charged with heartfelt emotion as this response is, its cadences and vocabulary prefigure the use that was, thirty years later, to be put to the English language by Marlowe, Peele, Greene and Shakespeare on the stages of the Theater, the Curtain and the Rose. One need hardly add that this speech was rapturously received.

Before leaving Cheapside the procession halted again at the Little Conduit to witness a fourth pageant, 'of square proportion' on which two mountains, with a cave between them, had been constructed. One of these hills symbolised a decayed Commonwealth (*Ruinosa Respublica*) barren of all vegetation other than a withered, leafless tree; the other represented a flourishing Commonwealth (*Respublica bene instituta*) 'fayre, freshe, grene, and beautifull, the grounds therof full of flowres and beawtie'. This hill too was topped by a tree. Placards hung from both of these trees, the former specifying the Vices that had reduced the Commonwealth to a desert, and the latter extolling 'Fear of God, A wise prince, Learned rulers, Obedience to officers, Obedient subjects, Lovers of the Commonweal, Virtue rewarded, Vice chastened'. Under the leafless tree *sat* a boy dressed as a peasant in rags; under the fruitful tree *stood* a boy, smartly if soberly dressed.[7]

Neither of these lads appears to have been called upon to speak; for this was where the cave placed between the two hills came into its own. This cave housed Father Time and his daughter, Truth, who was to verbalise the visual symbolism of this pageant in her speech. As the Queen approached, Time emerged from this cave. Dressed as an old man and equipped with his habitual scythe, he was accompanied by a child 'cladde in whyte silke', who represented his daughter, Truth, carrying a copy of the English Bible. It was then left to her to address the Queen from the top of the prosperous Commonwealth with verses interpreting the visual message offered to her within this elaborate tableau before descending to present her with the Bible.

I believe David Bergeron to have been right in regarding this pageant as intended to mark the dramatic climax of this elaborate sequence of theatrical 'shows' by dismissing the mistakes made during the two previous reigns through the emblematic use of the barren mountain when contrasted with the promise symbolised by equating her arrival on the English throne with the paradise garden.[8] This impression is confirmed by Elizabeth's response to it when the Bible was lowered from the hilltop to the street into the hands of Sir John Parrot, to be presented to her. Her response was theatrically impeccable:

'As sone as she had received the booke,' Mulcaster records, she 'Kyssed it, and with both her handes held up the same (*i.e. to public view*), and so laid it upon her brest, with great thankes to the citie therfore.'[9]

For all that, this remains a drama both scripted and theatrically represented in a style forged within that of the Corpus Christi Cycles and Morality Plays written during the years of Papal jurisdiction which remained intelligible to both illiterate and literate hearers and spectators alike. This was a style, moreover, that playmakers and actors, seeking to earn a living as quasi-professionals within the secular theatre of that time, would continue to employ to attract audiences who were still broadly accustomed to the use of metaphor, oblique allusion, distancing of time and place, and the endowment of abstract personifications with concrete actuality throughout the young Queen's reign (see pp. 159–63 below).

The last Act, as it were, of the shows prepared for her within the city of London consisted of a short address followed by two more spectacular street pageants.

When passing the churchyard of St. Paul's Cathedral, she stopped to listen to an oration, delivered in Latin, by a boy from the adjacent school. Since Rhetoric had figured so prominently and for so long in that school's curriculum, it seems probable that the other boys engaged as orators in these pageants were recruited either from St. Paul's School or other schools within the city's precincts (see Chapter 6, p. 104 above).

Moving on from there into Fleet Street, two more pageants claimed the Queen's attention, the first at the Conduit and the second at Temple Bar. The former consisted of a three-tiered stage, crowned by a single palm tree beneath which sat 'Deborah, the judge and restorer of the house of Israel'. On the platform below her sat six figures—two noblemen, two bishops and two commoners. All seven of these figures were dressed in parliamentary robes, with Deborah holding a sceptre. This pageant thus associated Deborah and her advisers with the English Queen in Parliament. Below them on the platform closest to street level sat yet another child holding the verses needed to explain this device to the crowd assembled around it. These verses remind the audience of Deborah's achievements in times of both war and peace:

> 'In war she, through gods aide, did put her foes to flight
> And with the dint of swords the band of bondage brast [burst].
> In peace she, through gods aide, did alway mainteine right
> And judged Israel till forty yeres were past.'[10]

The final entertainment at Temple Bar where she would leave the city, was valedictory. Presented to her by the city's two legendary giants, Grotmagot the Albione and Corineus the Briton (now better known as Gog and Magog), it endeavoured to summarise the meaning and intent of all the earlier pageants she had seen in verses that ended with a cordial expression of the city's wishes for her future years as their Queen:

> 'Live long, and as longe raigne, adourning thy countrie
> With vertues, and maintein thy people's hope of thee.'[11]

Professor Bergeron's assessment of that afternoon's initial meeting between the young Queen, escorted by her Privy Councillors on the one hand and those subjects whose futures she would be expected to determine on the other hand, is so cogent as to warrant quotation here:

'From Fenchurch Street to Temple Bar the sovereign has moved through the city amid the shouts and acclamations of London's citizens; it has indeed been a theatrical experience of the highest sort with actors, stage properties, music, audience, and honoured guest joining for one great entertainment. The dramatist has sounded the theme of unity, warned about the need for virtue to drive out vice and error, called for the Word of Truth to be the guiding presence for a fruitful Kingdom, given us a concrete example of a sterile and arid Kingdom. And Deborah who judged Israel for over forty years becomes something of a prototype of Elizabeth.'[12]

This idea of images to accord with political, religious and social situations as each arose was a message that the new Queen took to her heart, and exploited with consummate success through the rest of her reign by presenting herself to her subjects, as occasion appeared to demand, in a long sequence of theatrical icons starting out as Deborah and moving on from that to a much-yearned-for substitute for the recently exiled Virgin Mary, and from there to such figures from classical mythology as Iris, Astrea and Minerva.[13] In so doing, she succeeded in protecting her own freedom of action while enhancing the respect, affection and admiration of her subjects through the next forty-five years of an often perilous reign.

At their outset, the questions demanding her immediate attention were threefold: the first being a religious settlement calculated to satisfy the majority of both her Protestant subjects and those who still remained faithful to Papal obedience and beliefs. Second only to that were new measures to control the writing, publication and performance of deliberately subversive stage-plays. The third, and undoubtedly the most eagerly debated topic among all her subjects, was whom she would choose to marry to provide the Kingdom with an heir.

To resolve the first and second of these problems, two Proclamations were swiftly issued in her name by her Privy Council in May and June of 1559. The first of these was used to restore to the Statute Book Edward VI's 'Act of Uniformity of Common Prayer and Divine Service in Church and the use of the Sacraments' in a revised form; but it retained a reminder to play-makers and actors that anything said 'in derogation, depraving or despising of the

Book of Common Prayer' would be punished with heavy fines (see *EES* II. 1, p. 75, and pp. 124–6 above). It also sought to define in clearer detail those duties delegated to all members of the judiciary ranging from Lords Lieutenant in the shires to Mayors, Justices of the Peace and Magistrates, for ensuring that no play or interlude was acted without written licence. The second Proclamation reinforced these provisions by establishing, through letters patent, Ecclesiastical Commissions within the archdioceses of Canterbury and York to assist the Privy Council with the licensing of printed books and plays, and by giving 'special charge to her nobility and gentlemen, as they profess to obey and regard her Majesty, to take good order in this behalf with their servants being players, that this Her Majesty's commandment may be duly kept and obeyed'.[14] As a further conciliatory measure, when re-affirming the Act of Supremacy, she sought to secure a comprehensive acceptance of it by declining to receive for herself the full title of Supreme Head of the Church, preferring 'Supreme Governor' and concluding with the words *etcetera, etcetera*.[15]

With these measures taken, Elizabeth appears to have adopted a *laissez-faire* stance towards both the conduct of worship in churches and the continuance of such amateur performances of religious plays directly linked to Calendar Holidays as her newly established Ecclesiastical Commissions were prepared to authorise. This solution was one that might well have sufficed to meet the situation confronting her in this respect during the early years of her reign; but as both she and her subjects were to learn within a decade of her accession, it was not one that was likely to withstand well-organised attack from zealous reformers on either side of the religious divide.

In the meantime, however, there was no reason why entertainments at Court should not proceed along already familiar lines at all major Calendar Festivals, and this they duly did with sequences of Disguisings organised by the Master of the Revels from within the Court itself, and an intermittent supply of Moral Interludes of Protestant persuasion imported from neighbouring schools, or prepared in advance by the Queen's own company of players (or those of her courtiers) and chosen from among those that had already been successfully presented to public audiences.

An element of novelty and surprise was offered in the names of a new and able group of play-makers that included William Wager, Richard Edwards, George Gascoigne and Ulpian Fulwell, and another derived from the growing number of revivals of classical plays performed in the university colleges at Oxford and Cambridge and at London's law schools at the Inns of Court.

Of these the most notable was the first neo-classical tragedy modelled on Seneca's, to be written and performed in England— *Gorboduc*, or *Ferrex and Porrex*. Scripted by Thomas Norton and Thomas Sackville, both of whom were members of Parliament, it was acted by students at the Inner Temple during their Christmas festivities in 1561/2 and promptly transferred to Court for a repeat performance before the Queen on 18th January 1562. Despite the protection offered by its classical form (complete with Choruses) and the distancing of the stage action into a legendary Britain of remote antiquity, the play's moral message (or 'earnest') is transparently aimed at the Queen and her Councillors and is as explicitly topical as was John Bale's *Kyng Johan* some thirty years earlier (see *EES* III.i, pp. 228-9). This is spelt out in the fifth Act, when the Duke of Albany (a newcomer to the scene) unexpectedly returns to Scotland (Albion)—just as Mary, Queen of Scots, had done in 1561—and threatens to invade England (Brutayne) to settle the question of the succession there by seizing the throne for herself (see *EES* III.i, pp. 242-8).

Within the next eight years, this theatrical fiction had become a contemporary reality, with Mary a refugee on English soil 'in honourable custody' but known to be plotting with Philip II of Spain and Pope Pius V in Rome to restore Roman Catholicism to both England and Scotland by recourse to an invasion, led by Spanish troops in the Netherlands, to be followed by a Spanish marriage.

At this point, it becomes obligatory to embark upon a digression into the politics of this decade if readers are to understand why the death sentence, first pronounced upon public performances of Corpus Christi plays by the Reformation Parliament of 1531-6 and the subsequent Chantries Act of 1548, had finally to be carried into effect in the 1570s. Without further apology therefore, I will now endeavour to sketch in the sequence of melodramatic events that made this inevitable by returning to those affairs of state that confronted Elizabeth and her Council after their initial conciliatory settlement of their immediate religious problems.

First among these was a resolution of the diplomatic disputes with France occasioned by the late Queen Mary I's surrender of Calais: the second pertained to her own marriage prospects and her subjects' hopes for a male heir to secure a Protestant succession— as, indeed, she and her courtiers had been so outspokenly reminded by the performance of Norton's and Sackville's *Gorboduc* on 18th

January 1562. Where the first of these questions became bogged down in protracted and acrimonious negotiations, the second was answered by Elizabeth's own precipitate action in letting her heart be ruled by her eyes. These had fallen on the Master of the Horse, Robert Dudley, who had escorted her litter throughout her triumphal entry into London in 1558. This is understandable, given his youthful good looks and athletic bearing on the one hand, and remembering on the other that she was still a young woman addicted (as her father had been) to hunting, music, dancing and theatrical entertainments. Yet it was nevertheless imprudent (to say the least of it) to engage in so open a flirtation with a man who was known to have befriended her during the reign of her step-sister and whom she knew to be already married; for, in London, Dudley's constant attendance upon her at Court was likely to be viewed in terms of neglect of his wife, Amy Robsart, in distant Warwickshire, giving rumour-mongers fodder enough to transform this liaison into one of scandalous proportions.

At that time, however, the fact was that Elizabeth—again like her father before her—having entrusted the tiresome tasks of attending to the affairs of her realm to her Privy Council, had decided to enjoy herself. This was excusable while she continued to command the respect and affection of most of her subjects and while her Council could protect her from threats from abroad; but when John Knox left Geneva to return to Scotland in May of 1559 in the expectation that English support could be relied upon when rousing his fellow countrymen to expel their French oppressors, that situation changed dramatically.[16] From then on, both Elizabeth and her Council found themselves propelled into an immediate sequence of diplomatic exchanges that involved secrecy, duplicity and outright lying in efforts to contain the spectre of wars in Scotland and in France, and to answer a proposal of marriage from the young Earl of Arran.

These emergencies had the advantage of exposing Elizabeth to the actualities of her situation (as spelt out in political terms) before crisis point was reached in her relationship with Robert Dudley, who was already considered by many members of her Council to be a man on the make and a double-dealer. This arrived on 11th September when news reached the Court that his wife, Amy Robsart, had been found dead at the foot of a staircase in her own home.

The Coroner brought in a verdict of 'accidental death', but the scandal-mongers were swift to pounce on other explanations. Was it suicide, provoked by shame, neglect and depression? Or was it murder? Had she been pushed? If so, by whom? Her husband? To open a path to his own aggrandisement?

None of these questions has ever been answered definitively, but between them they served to tarnish Dudley's reputation, both at home and abroad, beyond redemption. Moreover, they jolted Elizabeth into letting her intellect recover control over her emotions, thereby enabling her to recognise that while she could still enjoy his company, it would no longer be in the role of an emotionally susceptible young woman but in that of an accomplished actress using her power over him to protect herself against unwanted suitors wished upon her by councillors.

With the Treaty of Edinburgh signed between the Scots and the French in July of 1560, the former were free to press home their advantage by remodelling their Parliament on Protestant lines and by urging Elizabeth to marry the Earl of Arran with a view to uniting the two kingdoms into a single Protestant Empire of Great Britain; but, by December, Mary's husband Francis II of France was dead and Scottish euphoria evaporated as it became clear that Mary, on reaching her majority, had no option but to return to Scotland as Queen in her own right. This she did in August 1561.[17]

This made it inevitable that these two northern kingdoms would become a stage for a battle of wits to be played out between two women rulers of sharply contrasted emotional and intellectual qualities that was certain to attract attention from all crowned heads in continental Europe; for, while Elizabeth remained unmarried and Mary a widow, these two cousins and neighbours—the former branded by ardent Catholics as a heretic and a bastard, and the latter already loudly blasted by John Knox's trumpets in Geneva and Edinburgh as an image of Anti-Christ incarnate—were certain to focus all eyes and ears upon their every move as icons of the most glamorous and glittering terrestrial prize available to any suitor. Here, as Elizabeth knew well, her rival possessed a trump card that had yet to be played, for it only needed Papal support to transform what still remained domestic rivalry into an international crusade that would set the whole of Europe ablaze. Thus, no sooner had Mary landed at Leith than urgent diplomatic efforts, of a kind familiar to us in the Middle East today, began to be made by them and their councillors to arrange a meeting between them in the hope that, as cousins and neighbours, they could reconcile their differences with a settlement of the succession to the English throne heading the lists; but sadly the fates thought otherwise and this was not to be.

141

At least four attempts were made to arrange a meeting between 1561 and 1565 but all of them had to be cancelled or postponed for one pressing reason or another.[18] In a vain attempt to secure the last of these, Elizabeth even offered to sacrifice her precious Dudley as a prospective husband for Mary, having first secured his election to her Privy Council and then ennobling him as Earl of Leicester; but Mary had by then acquired self-confidence enough to decide for herself how best to retain control over her own Kingdom, and to marry Henry Stuart, Lord Darnley, the young son of the Earl of Lennox.[19]

This was a brilliant move and a *coup de théâtre*, since it was one that Elizabeth could not resist. As both a Scot and a Protestant, he was allowed to return to Edinburgh in February 1565.[20] Once there, by swiftly captivating Mary with his good looks, their marriage had become a *fait accompli* by July; and, with that, all such trust and cordiality as remained between these rival queens faded beyond recall.

Having thus recovered her independence in all future dealings with her cousin in England, Mary began scheming to recover control over her own and her country's future. Catastrophically for herself, however, she chose to let her emotions govern her judgement (just as her English cousin had done in 1558) in the steps she took to achieve this. Her first, fatal, blunder was to dismiss her doubtless irksome but scrupulously loyal secretary, William Maitland, and replace him with an obscure Italian musician in her retinue of household servants of whom she had become especially fond—David Riccio.[21] The folly of this action at once outraged her Scottish nobles and supplied her jealous young husband with grounds for suspecting her motives, precipitating an avalanche of melodramatic events culminating in her transformation from undisputed Queen of Scotland into a pathetic prisoner charged with both murder and adultery.

This particular sequence of events has been made so familiar to everyone acquainted not only with official histories of these years but, more recently, in countless novels, operas, plays, films and television dramas, for only a brief summary of them to be needed here.

When, by January 1561, it was known that Mary was pregnant, Darnley had come to feel himself so spurned and isolated as to be ready to conspire with a posse of the Scottish nobility (led by James, Earl of Bothwell) to rid themselves of the arrogant upstart Riccio. On the night of 9th March, they entered Holyrood Palace, burst in upon the Queen when at supper with her 'David', stabbed him fifty-six times and dumped him in a pauper's grave.[22]

Mary at once retaliated by having his corpse exhumed and reburied in the Royal Chapel; effected a reconciliation with her husband; proceeded to inform Elizabeth of her pregnancy and invited her to become a godmother. Elizabeth accepted and, represented by the Earl of Bedford as her proxy, loaded her new godson, James Stuart, with a golden font for his christening in December 1566.[23]

It thus seemed that some semblance of stability had been restored to Anglo-Scottish relationships, but it soon became apparent that such optimism had been misplaced after Mary had again yielded to the emotional side of her nature by accepting the overtures of the rugged, ruthless and ambitious Earl of Bothwell. This too is understandable, given the sickly constitution of her first husband and the reputedly indeterminate sexual orientation of her second, for her feelings about Bothwell, whom she knew to be already married, were governed for the first time by passion; but this could hardly excuse her rashness in abandoning herself to him since this was almost certain to lead on to her connivance in the method chosen to dispose of her husband.

In January 1567, when Darnley was recovering from smallpox in Glasgow, Bothwell persuaded her to lure him back to a small suburban house in Kirk O'Fields near Edinburgh to resume their relationship as husband and wife and to share in the upbringing of their young son James. Three months later, the weak-willed invalid duly entered the trap that had been set for him. Once there, Mary kept up this pretence for a day or two, but on the night of Sunday 9th February she excused herself to attend a wedding masque at Holyrood, promising to return after it had ended. This she failed to do, and shortly after midnight a violent explosion was heard in Edinburgh that carried the house in Kirk O'Fields, and Darnley with it, high into the night sky. When his corpse was found next day in a neighbouring garden, it was said that he had been strangled.[24]

Accusing fingers were immediately pointed at both Bothwell and Mary, and expressions of outrage flooded in from at home and abroad, but no action followed. Somehow they managed to contain this situation by living apart for the next six weeks. Then, on 24th April, Bothwell kidnapped Mary on her return from Stirling to Edinburgh and removed her to the fortress of Dunbar. Within the next three weeks he had opened divorce proceedings against his innocent wife—preferring the prospect of a crown to that of marital fidelity—and on 15 May he and Mary were married as protestants in Edinburgh, 'by the same church,' as J. E. Neale puts it, 'as a few days earlier had pronounced Bothwell an adulterer and granted his wife a divorce on that ground'.[25]

By then, such was the resulting anger in Scotland that within a month Bothwell found himself forced to flee to Norway, leaving Mary to be arrested and brought back to Edinburgh as a prisoner. From there she was swiftly transferred to an island castle in the middle of Loch Leven for greater security to await trial for complicity in Darnley's murder and to force her to surrender her son James into the care of a Regent.[26]

The Earl of Murray came thus to be recalled from self-imposed exile to rule Scotland in her son's name during his minority. What no one there could have expected was that Elizabeth would defy her own Privy Council in England by offering to assume the role of a mediator between them and their hapless Queen.

The diplomatic consultations that followed this unexpected invitation sufficed to give Mary time to plan an escape that could both release her from her fears of a judicial hearing that would conclude in a death sentence in Scotland, and carry her across the Solway Firth into England as a refugee from persecution. This remains a familiar story today.

This she effected in May 1568 and was at once placed 'in honourable custody', at first in Carlisle and then in Bolton Castle, under the guardianship of Sir Francis Knollys.[27] Elizabeth could thus regard this as an ultimate success to all her scheming to regain control over her rival in determining who would succeed her on her own throne. Mary, however, at once resumed her own plans to enlist support both from dissident Catholic nobles in the north of England and through correspondence with her Catholic friends in Spain and in Rome.[28]

The upshot of this was that within a year of seeking asylum in England she had persuaded the Earls of Northumberland and Westmoreland, together with Lord Leonard Dacres, to enlist their tenantry to help them to recover her freedom, which would then be followed by a Spanish invasion launched from the Netherlands.

By 14th November 1569, these rebels had entered Durham Cathedral, burnt all Protestant service books and homilies, restored its altars and stoups of Holy Water together with Mass; but Mary had already been moved south to Coventry before they captured Hartlepool and Barnard Castle. These events provided the rumourmongers with a field day but, when the promised Spanish support from the Netherlands failed to arrive, enthusiasm for this rebellion fizzled out among the rebels thus forcing their leaders to flee north across the Scottish border, leaving Lord Dacres and his tenant militia to engage Elizabeth's army on 19th February 1570 in a final confrontation that ended in their rout.[29]

Elizabeth and her Council revenged themselves by executing at least eight hundred of them as an example to others tempted to engage in seditious conduct; but, warned by John Knox of the long-threatened Papal excommunication that was to follow in May—branding the Queen as an arch-heretic and releasing her subjects from their allegiance—the savagery of this action becomes understandable.[30] Pope Pius V's action had both stripped Elizabeth of her rightful tenure of her throne and offered advance absolution to anyone who succeeded in assassinating her.

This brings this lengthy digression into the politics of a decade that had outstripped, in its long sequences of melodramatic incidents, any scenario that either amateur or professional actors could offer at that time to public audiences on public stages, to a timely end; for what the Pope's intervention did achieve was to alert Elizabeth and her Council to the need to place the country on a wartime footing that must include measures to strengthen control over all future performances of polemically subversive plays. We can thus return to the death sentence that had hung over all Corpus Christi plays (and other, overtly religious, drama of Catholic parentage) for more than twenty years but which had thus far failed to be put into effect.

The first warning of what was so soon to follow was delivered by the Dean of York to the Lord Mayor and his brethren on 24th March 1568, in response to a decision announced five weeks earlier by the City Council on 13th February:

'... that instead of Corpus Christi play this year, the Creed play shall be played. And the same to be provided for and brought forth by the oversight and order of the Chamberlains.'[31] (Spelling and punctuation have here been modernised)

Preparations were to begin at once by recovering

'... the Original or Register [i.e. *the prompt-copy*] of the said Creed play to be gotten of the master of St. Thomas's Hospital who have the custody thereof.'

The next step was to search out

145

'. . . expert and meet players . . . for the cunning handling of the said play: then, every of them to have their parts fair written and delivered to them (in time) so they may have leisure to con [*learn*] every one his part. And the said Chamberlains further to see all manner the pageant's playing gear and necessaries to be provided in a readiness: And, as occasion shall require to ask, advise and aid aboute the same.'[32]

Since the Creed Play had not been performed for at least twenty years, one of the individuals thus asked for advice may have been Matthew Hutton, Dean of York and newly appointed as a member of the Ecclesiastical Commission for the North. Or, alerted by the news of these preparations, Dean Hutton may himself have asked the Lord Mayor to see a copy of the script. Either way, he sent his considered response to the text of this play, expressing his own doubts about the wisdom of proceeding with it:

'*Salute in Christo*, My most humble duty remembered I have perused the books that your Lordship with your brethren sent me; and, as I find many things that I much like because of the antiquity, so I see many things that I cannot allow because they be disagreeing from the sincerity of the Gospel, the which things, if they should either be altogether cancelled, or altered into other matter, the whole drift of the play should be altered; and therefore I dare not put my pen unto it, because I want [*lack*] both skill and leisure to ammend it, though in goodwill I assure you—if I were worthy to give your Lordship and your right worshipful counsel surely mine advice should be that it should not be played. For though it was plausible 40 years ago [i.e. before the Reformation Parliament of 1531–6], and would now also of the ignorant sort be well liked, yet now in this happy time of the Gospel, I know the learned will mislike it, and how the State will bear with it I know not. Thus, being bold to utter my opinion unto your Lordship, . . . etc. etc.'[33]

On receipt of this letter the City Council met again on 30th March and, although the Dean had gone out of his way to avoid outright prohibition of the proposed performance, they decided among themselves '. . . to have no play this year and the books of the Creed to be delivered in again'.[34]

It was perhaps just as well that the Council had heeded this friendly warning, for, before this performance could have been presented to public audiences on Corpus Christi Day, Mary, the recently deposed Queen of Scots, had arrived in England and been placed in honourable custody as a penniless refugee at Bolton Castle—a turn of events that was to precipitate the Northern Rebellion in 1569 that was to be shortly followed up by the excommunication of Elizabeth in 1570 (see pp. 144–5 above).

The catalyst that was inexorably to lead on to the Privy Council's decision to suppress all future performances of Corpus Christi plays was the unmasking of a second conspiracy in November of 1571 involving Mary herself, the Catholic Duke of Norfolk and the Spanish Ambassador, together with a Florentine banker, Roberto Ridolfi, who was employed by the Pope as his London agent. Known as the Ridolfi Plot, its objective was to persuade the Duke of Norfolk to marry Mary and, with help from Spanish troops, to restore both England and then Scotland to Roman Catholicism.[35]

When Parliament next met in May 1572, it found itself under intense pressure from bishops, nobles and commons alike to persuade Elizabeth to sign death warrants for high treason for both Norfolk and Mary. Norfolk was executed on 2nd June, but Elizabeth vetoed the death warrant prepared for Mary. Instead, she remained a prisoner and a continuing source of anxiety to the Queen herself, her Council and her subjects for the next fifteen years, and it was within this context that the decision was finally taken to let the great axe of state fall on all remaining performances of religious plays of Roman Catholic provenance in the course of the next four years.

Action towards this end began within four weeks of Norfolk's execution when Parliament revised its existing Act for the Punishment of Vagabonds on 29th June 1572. Although these revisions were excused under cover of clarifying the existing situation,

'. . . And for the full expressing what person and persons shall be intended within this branch [Clause 5] to be Rogues, vagabonds and Sturdy Beggars . . . '

—they were just as clearly intended in their effect to be tightly restrictive; for, not only did they bring actors and other nomadic entertainers more firmly within this Act's embrace, but they withdrew the right to maintain a company of travelling players from the whole of the English squirearchy below the rank of Baron.[36]

Having thus drastically curtailed the number of professional acting companies officially entitled to perform plays in London, the Privy Council (working through its Ecclesiastical Commission in the North) next turned its attention to the amateur players in the City of York where its Paternoster play had been performed on Corpus Christi Day in June 1572. Between then and 30th July, the Lord Mayor received a request from the Archbishop to see

'. . . a copy of the Books of the Paternoster play: whereupon it is now agreed by these presents that his Grace shall have a true copy of all the said books even as they were played this year.'

In November of that same year another letter was received by the Lord Mayor, this time from the Archbishop and the Dean together with four other members of the Queen's Commissioners:

'Whereas there hath been heretofore a very rude and barbarous custom maintained in this City, and in no other City or town of the Realm to our knowledge that yearly upon St. Thomas's Day before Christmas, two disguised persons called Yule and Yule's Wife should ride through the City very indecently and uncomely drawing great concourses of people after them to gaze, often times committing other enormities; foreasmuch as the said disguised riding and concourse aforesaid, besides other inconveniences, tendeth also to the prophaning of that day appointed to holy uses, and also withdraweth great multitudes of people from divine service and Sermons, we have thought good by these presents to will and require you—and nevertheless in the Queen's Majesty's name by virtue of her High Commission for causes ecclesiastical within the province of York to us and others directed straightly to charge and command you—that ye take order that no such riding of Yule and Yule's Wife be from henceforth attempted or used.'[37]

For good measure, this order is to be placed in the City's Record Books and observed annually thereafter.

As no records survive of any attempt to revive the Corpus Christi Cycle in York after 1569, we must assume that these prompt-books, like those of the Creed and Paternoster plays, had also been taken into the Archbishop's custody and not returned, for in July 1575 the City Council decided to try to recover them when it was agreed

'. . . that before Michaelmas next Mr. Allyn, Mr. Maskewe (Aldermen); Mr. Robert Brooke and Mr. Andrew Trewe shall go and require of my Lord Archbishop his Grace all such ye play-books as pertain this City now in his Grace's Custody, and that his Grace will appoint two or three sufficiently learned to correct the same wherein, by the law of this Realm, they are to be reformed . . .'[38]

A final attempt seems to have been made to resume performances of the Corpus Christi Cycle in 1579 but it failed.[39]

The death-throes of Chester's Whitsun Plays between 1571 and 1575 followed a similar, hesitant and erratic pattern to those in York; but one, nevertheless, which differs from it in the more spirited defence of them offered under the succeeding mayoralties of Mr. John Hankey and Sir John Savage—doubtless in the city's commercial interests but at great personal risk to themselves.

By 1571–2 it was known that the Bishop of Chester was of one mind with the Archbishops of York and Canterbury in thinking that performances ought not to be given, but Mayor Hankey (backed by his Council and the Craft Guilds responsible for presenting them) decided to risk their displeasure by authorising the plays to proceed. Not surprisingly, it is recorded in the Mayor's List that 'the Whitsun plays were played this year to the dislike of many'.[40]

Encouraged by this relatively mild response, the City Council decided yet again to allow performances to be given in 1572/3.[41] This time, however, the Archbishop of York intervened by issuing an Inhibition intended to stop them, but mysteriously it arrived in Chester too late for any action to be taken to effect it. This warning was heeded in 1573/4 when performance of the Whitsun plays was 'forborne':[42] but when Hankey was succeeded as Mayor by Sir John Savage in 1574/5, the Council decided by thirty-three votes to twelve,

'. . . that at midsummer next [the Whitsun plays] should be played and set forth in such order and sort as they have been accustomed with such correction and amendment as shall be thought convenient by the Mayor . . .'[43]

This time, however, the risks taken by the City Council in flouting the warnings that had previously been set out in letters and Inhibitions received from the Archbishop of York and the Lord President of the Queen's Council in the north in earlier years proved to be greater than they were prepared to accept.

The plays were duly performed that summer, seemingly without interference, but there was a price to be paid for this in the autumn. Perhaps fearing that to arrest the Mayor while still in office for seditious conduct (or even high treason) might only serve to spark off trouble among both the actors responsible for these popular performances and the local audiences who had flocked into the city to enjoy them, the Lord President of the Council delayed taking action for four months. Then, on the day on which Sir John Savage was due to surrender his office as Mayor to his successor (Mr. Henry Hardware), following the latter's election, he pounced.[44]

A Pursuivant was despatched to arrest Sir John as he, together with the Aldermen and Councillors, having completed their business, were leaving the City Hall, by which time Sir John could no longer claim to be the Queen's representative in the city. Savage was then conveyed immediately to London for questioning before the Privy Council. Similar writs for contempt were served on John Hankey (his predecessor as Mayor) and to several other citizens and players to be answered at a later date.

Writing to Henry Hardware (his successor as Mayor) on 10th November, Savage tells him that:

'... it hath been informed to the Privy Council that I caused the plays last at Chester to be set forward only of my self which yourselves do know the contrary. And that they were by common assembly appointed as remaineth in the Record for the easing of and qualifying all controversies grown about the same, I am most heartily to desire you to send me a Certificate, under your hands and Seal of the City, to testify that the same plays were set forward as well by the Counsel of the City as for the commonwealth of the same, whereby their honours may be the better satisfied thereof; and hoping thereby to reduce all such matters quiet as are risen now against me and Mr. Hankey whom you must make mention of in the Certificate as well as myself which, I pray you may be sent me with as much convenient speed as is possible ... '[45]

This letter was duly presented to the City Council on 21st November and the Certificate requested was then drafted, sealed and despatched that same day. It is so worded as to discharge both Savage and Hankey of all blame for proceeding to authorise performances on their own initiative, and insists that these decisions were

'... severally done by the assent, consent, goodwill and agreement of the Aldermen, Sheriffs, Sheriffs peers and Common Council of the said City ... '

It concludes by stating that all correspondence relating to it, together with the Certificate itself, is to be recorded verbatim in the city's Minute Book. The Council then followed this up by issuing a Proclamation that same day to inform all citizens of these proceedings.[46]

On receipt of this Certificate, the Privy Council appears to have released Savage and to have dropped all charges brought against Mayor Hankey and others in the belief that the City Council would never again dare to risk reviving these 'popish plays'.

Instead, through the agency of its Court of High Commission in the North, it transferred its attention to the town of Wakefield where, in 1576,

'. . . upon intelligence given to the said Commission that it is meant and purposed that in the town of Wakefield shall be played in Whitsun week next, or thereabouts, a play commonly called Corpus Christi play which hath been heretofore used there. . . . '

The Commissioners, instead of demanding to see the play-books and then retaining them as had been the case in York, or issuing Inhibitions as in Chester, decreed that a letter be sent to the Bailiffs, Burgesses and other inhabitants informing them that this performance could proceed *provided* that

'. . . no pageant be used or set forth wherein the Majesty of God the Father, God the Son or God the Holy Ghost, or administration of the Sacraments of Baptism, or of the Lord's Supper be counterfeited or represented, or anything played which tends to the maintenance of superstition and idolatory, or which be contrary to the laws of God or the Realm.'[47]

These instructions effectively censored performance of the Wakefield Cycle out of existence both in 1576 and thereafter.

The 'softly, softly' approach, so evidently adopted by Elizabeth and her Council towards the suppression of overtly religious plays in all these northern towns and cities, bears witness to the continuing sensitivity of the government and its agents to the risks of stirring up more trouble among Catholic recusants while Mary Queen of Scots remained a prisoner and rallying point for another rebellion.

Surviving records from Coventry and Lincoln, and from such remote citadels as Kendal and Carlisle, fail to supply us with exact dates for their suppression, but government action already taken in York, Chester and Wakefield makes it virtually certain that any serious effort to revive them after 1576 would become ever more half-hearted and infrequent. We must thus conclude that by then a great era of religious drama, embracing communities in all walks of life that had endured for three centuries and proved itself to be the most vital bonding factor in the nation's educational and social fabric throughout that time, had reached its appointed end: *Requiescat in Pace.*

*   *   *

While it is both right and proper to lament the passing of all things that had once been great, like those

'Bare ruined choirs where late the sweet birds sang'

—as Shakespeare was later to describe the medieval monasteries that had given birth to religious drama (see Frontispiece and Sonnet LXXIII), it is also appropriate to recall the message delivered within the Introit for Mass on Easter morning by the angel guarding Christ's sepulchre to the three mourners approaching the tomb to embalm the crucified corpse they thought lay within it:

> *Quem quaeritis in sepulchro, o Christicolae?*
> *Jesum Nazarenum crucifixum, o caelicolae.*
> *Non est hic, surrexit sicut praedixerat,*
> *Ite, nuntiate quia surrexit. Alleluia!*

for this had been devised (*c.* 975) to celebrate transfiguration (see Ch. 2, pp. 21–3 above). We should then recall that within the same decade that had witnessed the final death throes of amateur religious drama in England—devised and presented as festive celebrations of Calendar holy days by local communities—Elizabethan audiences were participating in a similar transfiguration of their own theatrical horizons into much broader ones brought into being by small companies of professional players with the assistance of merchant-entrepreneurs.

By 1570, Corpus Christi drama and its several offshoots was already moribund, having been dying on its feet for the past half-century (see Chapters 6 and 7 above), yielding all the creative energy that it had once possessed to those companies of players privately maintained by the nobility and gentry, and to the young poets whom they had commissioned to provide them with their repertoires of domestic moral interludes and other topical and satirical plays. It was these actors, moreover, who (since at least the 1540s) had been besieging inn-keepers and wealthy merchants in London, and the Mayors and Aldermen of provincial towns and cities, to lease out such performance spaces to them as lay under their control.

A time had thus come for someone to explore the possibility of setting this haphazard situation onto a more orderly and convenient footing for everyone directly concerned; and between 1567 and 1577 this was brought to its triumphant fruition. Here, the facts can, once again, speak for themselves.

In 1567 the first property in London to be acquired for conversion into a playhouse for public use since Roman times was 'the court or yard . . . belonging to' a farmhouse called the Red Lion in Middlesex, about a mile east of Aldgate near the recreational area known as Mile End which was still used for City Musters and other pastimes. This land was bought by John Brayne, a London grocer, who then hired two master carpenters—William Sylvester and John Reynolds—to build the playhouse and the stage respectively.[48]

This example was then followed between 1568 and 1575 by the owners of four inns, all of which were situated within the city walls. Three of these were in Gracechurch Street: the Bel-Savage, the Cross Keys and the Bell. The fourth was the Bull near Bishopsgate.[49]

By 1576 John Brayne had entered into another contract—this time with James Burbage, a joiner by trade and leader of the Earl of Leicester's company of players—to erect a free-standing purpose-built playhouse on land rented from the ground landlord, Giles Allen, within the boundaries of the dissolved Priory at Holy-well in the north-eastern suburb of Shoreditch. They named it The Theater.[50]

Their example was immediately copied by two other landowners and entrepreneurs of whose names little is known. The first of these playhouses was situated a mile to the south of London Bridge in the County of Surrey in the suburb of Newington and known as Newington Butts; the second, named likewise after the land on which it stood, was the Curtain which was a near-neighbour of the Theater in Shoreditch. Both were in business by 1577.[51]

To this reckoning of seven public playhouses, we must also add the opening of the first 'private' playhouse in London which had been leased and adapted for such use from two large rooms knocked into one in what had once been the buttery of the Dominican Priory at Blackfriars and which—ironically—lay immediately below the Great Hall (or Refectory) in which Queen Catherine of Aragon had first faced the divorce proceedings brought against her in 1529 (see Ch. 6, p. 112 and n. 20, p. 195 below). This project was the brain-child of Richard Farrant, Master of the choristers of the Royal Chapel at Windsor Castle and deputy to the Master of the Chapel Royal in London, William Hunnis.

Such unprecedented provision of performance spaces for regular as opposed to occasional use in London within so short a time span impels us to ask why this was thought to be so necessary and desirable as to justify the substantial, and largely speculative, capital investment required to fund a total of five conversions of existing buildings and the erection of four new ones.

Here, the only acceptable answer that fully meets these facts is the pressure exerted on the rapidly expanding numbers of professional acting companies drawn into visiting London on a regular basis by the size and eagerness of the audiences awaiting their performances in a capital city that was also expanding rapidly; for as these companies came to rely upon these audiences to maintain them and their families in their chosen profession, their top priority became the need to acquire personal control over the admission fees levied for attending their performances.

This contention is supported in part by the Privy Council's decision to call on Parliament in 1572 to restrict the number of companies licensed to perform in London (see p. 147 above) and in part by the Queen's unilateral decision to honour the Earl of Leicester's company with the unprecedented award in 1574 of a Patent to perform anywhere within her Kingdom to which they were themselves willing to travel and, more specifically, in London.

This singular Royal Patent is significant enough in its contents and wording to warrant quotation in full since not only does it supply us with the names of all the actors that comprised that fortunate company, but also with two names closely linked with two of the custom-built playhouses built in London in 1576 and 1577:

'*Pro Iacobo Burbage et aliis de licencia speciali*

Elizabeth by the grace of God, Queen of England, &c. To all justices, mayors, sheriffs, bailiffs, head constables, under constables, and all other our officers and ministers greeting. Know ye that we of our especial grace, certain knowledge, and mere motion have

licensed and authorised, and by these presents do license and
authorise, our loving subjects James Burbage, John Perkin, John
Laneham, William Johnson, and Robert Wilson, servants to our
trusty and well beloved cousin and counsellor the Earl of Leicester,
to use, exercise, and occupy the art and faculty of playing comedies,
tragedies, interludes, stage plays, and such other like as they have
already used and studied, or hereafter shall use and study, as well
for the recreation of our loving subjects, as for our solace and pleasure when we shall think good to see them; as also to use and occupy
all such instruments as they have already practised, or hereafter
shall practise, for and during our pleasure. And the said comedies,
tragedies, interludes, and stage plays, together with their music, to
show, publish, exercise, and occupy to their best commodity during
all the term aforesaid, as well within our City of London and liberties of the same, as also within the liberties and freedoms of any our
cities, towns, boroughs, &c. whatsoever as without the same,
throughout our realm of England. Willing and commanding you
and every of you, as ye tender our pleasure, to permit and suffer
them herein without any your lets, hindrance or molestation during
the term aforesaid, any act, statute, proclamation, or commandment
heretofore made, or hereafter to be made, to the contrary notwithstanding. Provided that the same comedies, tragedies, interludes,
and stage plays be, by the Master of our Revels for the time being
before seen and allowed, and that the same be not published, or
shown in the time of common prayer, or in the time of great and
common plague in our said City of London. In witness whereof &c.
Witness our self at Westminster the xth day of May.'52

Inclusion of the phrase used to justify the issue of this patent—'. . .
as well for the recreation of our loving subjects, as for our solace
and pleasure when we shall think good to see them . . . '—while
appearing to be generously intended, is more likely to have been so
worded as to protect the traditional prerogative of the nobility to
maintain personal companies of players from the rising tide of
clamour for the abolition of all plays and playing from Protestant
extremists in their sermons and printed denunciations of both.

Other companies invited to present plays at Court between 1574
and 1578 were those of the Earls of Sussex (four times) and Warwick (three times), and that of Lord Howard of Effingham (twice),
so we must presume that their need to prepare their plays in performances before public audiences (along with that of the Earl of
Leicester) took precedence over all others for regular access to the

three custom-built playhouses that were being erected in London during those years.[53] Records survive of some of the plays that these companies held in their respective repertoires when they were invited to present them at Court; but, sadly, all of these texts have long since been lost or destroyed.[54]

Reverting now to the Queen's Patent awarded to the Earl of Leicester in 1574, we must take a closer look at the wording of its concluding sentence (see p. 155 above). This makes it clear that use of this document is only granted on condition that all

'comedies, tragedies, interludes, and stage plays be, by the Master of the Revels for the time being before seen and allowed, and that the same be not published, or shown in the time of common prayer, or in the time of great and common plague in our said City of London . . .'

At Guildhall, however, the issue of this Patent was regarded as provocative enough to warrant an angry and intemperately worded response. This took the form of an Act of Common Council for the regulation of all theatrical performances within the City of London passed on 6th December that same year.

It starts by branding plays and playhouses as a prime source of sexual promiscuity and the corruption of young minds, and then goes on to blame them for providing the Almighty with cause enough to punish London's residents with visitations of the plague for supporting them. To prevent recurrence of this, the Act states that:

'. . . from henceforth no play, comedy, tragedy or enterlude, nor public show (*i.e. prize-fights, jugglers and tumblers*) shall be openly played or showed within the liberties of the City, wherein any lewd words, examples or doings of any unchastity, sedition, nor suchlike unfit and uncomely matter, upon pain of imprisonment by the space of fourteen days of all persons offending in any such playing or showings, and £5 for every such offence.'[55]

The next clause is aimed at the owners and managers of the performance spaces within the city walls and insists that

'. . . no Innkeeper, Tavern Keeper nor other person whatsoever within the liberties of this City shall openly show or play, nor cause or suffer to be showed or played within the house, yard, or any other place . . . any play, enterlude, comedy, tragedy, matter or show, which not be first perused and allowed in such order and form, and by such persons as by the Lord Mayor and Court of Aldermen for the time being shall be appointed, nor shall suffer to be interlaced, added, mingled or uttered in . . . any other matter than such as shall be first perused and allowed as is above said . . . '56

This clause effectively dispenses with the authority of the Master of the Revels within the city's precincts and seems clearly to have been intended to ward off the threat seen to be posed in the Patent awarded to Leicester's company of players by members of the Privy Council, to usurp the city's jealously guarded jurisdiction over its own affairs. It ends by making disciplinary provisions to reinforce the conditions already imposed on those Innkeepers, Tavern-keepers and other property owners licensed to lease out their premises as performance spaces for plays by binding them to the City Chamberlain to provide bonds or other sureties that would be forfeited to the City Treasury in the event of any breach of the terms of their contracts.57

In its subsequent paragraphs the authors of this Act then added a stealth-tax of an undisclosed but variable amount upon these same leaseholders. This took the form of an enforced, charitable donation

'. . . to be paid to the use of the poor in hospitals of the City, or of the poor of the City visited with sickness, by the discretion of the said Lord Mayor and Aldermen for the time being on the one party, and such person so to be licensed or permitted in the other party, shall be agreed. . . . '58

This tax was almost certainly calculated as a percentage of the profits from performances and seems likely to have been introduced as a softener to appease Puritan resistance to this Act, since this tax was still in force some thirty years later (see *English Professional Theatre*, pp. 90–1).

As might be expected, however, a let-out clause is provided in the final paragraph to exempt the devisers of this tax, and other citizens of consequence residing within the city who chose to invite licensed companies of actors to perform plays to celebrate festive occasions within their own homes, from payment of this tax. This reads as follows:

'Provided alway that this Act (otherwise than touching the publishing [?*inclusion*] of unchaste, seditious and unmeet matters) shall not extend to any plays, en[terludes], comedies, tragedies, or shows to be played or showed in the private house, dwelling, or lodging of any nobleman, citizen or gentleman, which shall or will then have the same there so played or showed in his presence for the festivity of any marriage, assembly of friends, or other like cause without public or common collection of money of the Auditory or beholders thereof, reserving always to the Lord Mayor and Aldermen for the time being the judgement and construction according to equity what shall be counted such a playing or show-ing in a private place, anything else in this Act to the contrary notwithstanding.'[59]

As a response to the Privy Council's connivance in the Queen's award of a Royal Patent authorising the Earl of Leicester's players to perform plays both within the City of London and elsewhere wherever and whenever they wished to do so, the measures taken by Guildhall within this Act of Common Council amounted, if not to an outright declaration of war, then to an unmistakable warning that any further trespassing upon the city's own powers of jurisdiction would not be acceptable.

Here, the weakness of the Court's position lay in the widespread disrespect into which the Revels Office had itself fallen since its Master, Sir Thomas Benger, had ceased to exercise his own duties within it and passed them over to his Clerk, Thomas Blagrave. By 1575, Blagrave was finding himself besieged by creditors, many of whom had waited for up to five years or more to obtain settlement of their bills, and so overburdened by trying to handle his Master's duties as well as his own, that he appealed to the Lord Treasurer (formerly William Cecil, but now Lord Burghley) for help. This plan was answered by the setting up of an internal enquiry to review the organisation and administration of the office;[60] no changes were made, however, until Benger died in 1577.

With the need to appoint a new Master by then an imperative, Burghley moved swiftly to recommend root-and-branch reforms and to appoint Edmund Tilney as a replacement for Benger. As an interim measure, a Patent was issued bearing Tilney's name in July 1579, backdated to March 1578 which was to be followed up with a second Patent incorporating all the new reforms. This was finally ready for issue in December 1581.

Tilney's new Patent authorised him

'... or his sufficient deputy or deputies to warn, command and appoint in all places within our Realm of England, as well within franchises and liberties as without, all and every player with their play-makers either belonging to any noblemen or otherwise bearing the name or names or using the faculty of play-makers or players of Comedies, Tragedies, Enterludes, or what other shows soever from time to time, and at all times to appear before him with all such plays, Tragedies, Comedies, or shows as they shall have in readiness, or mean to set forth, and then to present and recite before our said Servant or his sufficient deputy whom we ordain and appoint and authorise by these presents of all such shows, plays, players, together with their playing places, to order reform, authorise and put down, as shall be thought meet or unmeet unto himself or his said deputy on that behalf . . . '61

This Patent concludes by granting powers to the Master to punish any offending players or play-makers at his own discretion. It also sets the scene for the triumphal transfiguration of what had once been a largely amateur, community-organised and heavily subsidised form of drama and theatre of Roman Catholic, evangelistic and morally instructive religious content, into fully-fledged professional and commercialised forms of satirical, romantic, historical and tragic dramatic literature and theatrical experiences which had already won wide popular support from audiences prepared to pay to see and hear them.

With three custom-built suburban playhouses already sited and erected in London outside the jurisdiction of the City Fathers at Guildhall and within that of the less puritanically minded County Magistrates in Middlesex and Surrey, and with a fourth—the Rose—shortly to be built in Southwark (close to the existing bull- and bear-baiting arenas) in 1587 by Philip Henslowe and his actor-son-in-law, Edward Alleyn, it only needed the arrival of Thomas Kyd, Christopher Marlowe and William Shakespeare to complete this transformation with sequences of plays that would set the town talking about them for years to come (see Plate XIII, Nos. 17 and 18).62

The principal reason explaining the relative ease with which this metamorphosis was accomplished lies in the fact that, despite the noticeable difference in the subject matter treated on the stage since the banishment of 'all matters concerning Scripture and Religion now in question', the visual iconography and methodology of theatrical representation used in the staging of these new plays had not. This was largely dictated by the playhouse owners and acting companies who had acquired licences to perform in them and who preferred familiarity to novelty when deciding how to build and equip them. Caring little about the niceties of neo-classical theory that had spread from schools, universities and law schools to graduates in positions of influence at Court, they opted to use the simple, largely wooden, triple-tiered auditoria already standing in London as their models for their new playhouses.[63]

With that task completed, they then instructed their carpenters to build a platform stage to be set up within them, either adjacent to the sunlit end of the rectangular yard or to be contained within the corresponding angles of the polygonal arena.[64]

Behind this platform, provision was to be made within the galleried wall of the auditorium adjacent to it to accommodate the needs of the actors, musicians, fencers and tumblers who were to use it. These had to include a dressing-room (or tiring house) for the actors and other entertainers at platform level; room for musicians (or as a supplementary acting or seating area) in the gallery immediately above it; and a hut at roof level from which to fly a flag to advertise performances, to house such artillery as might be needed in performances, and to place a trumpeter to silence spectators before a play began.[65]

With these basic requirements met, provision still had to be made for sufficient space within the tiring house at platform level to contain the scenic gear needed for that day's play and at ground level below both the tiring-house and the platform itself to store such other gear as was known to be needed in performances of other plays. It remained the responsibility of the acting companies who leased these playhouses to supply both these scenic items and their own costumes. The platform, and the first gallery to which it adjoined, had thus to be raised high enough above ground level both to provide spectators standing in the yard surrounding it with a clear view of the stage action, and to allow access to the platform from below and vice versa.

This scenic gear (often referred to as 'devices'), as we know from stage directions in plays written between 1573 and 1577, as also from a long inventory drawn up by Henslowe and Alleyn of such items as were stored at the Rose in 1598,[66] normally included tables, chairs, a bed, a throne, city walls, a mountain, a cave, an arbour and single trees—all of which were still familiar from recent use in Corpus Christi plays and civic pageants (see *EES* II.1, Plates XXI to XXVI and *EES* III.1, Chapters IV to VI).

With these basic requirements met, play-makers and actors alike could retain the freedom to call upon their own and their audiences' imaginations, both to assist in locating stage-action and to facilitate extensions of the timespan represented within the play far beyond that of the two-to-three-hour traffic of actual performance. This freedom, moreover, could be extended to permit play-makers so to order the subject matter of some plays as to allow it to be presented in two or three parts on different days as would be the case with George Whetstone's *I & II Promos and Cassandra* (1578), Marlowe's *Tamburlaine the Great* (1588) and Shakespeare's *King Henry VI* (1592).[67]

All that was needed to achieve this fluid, yet sustained, style of theatrical representation, was for those items of scenic gear prescribed in the stage directions for use in that play to be pushed, carried or wheeled onto the platform as required in the text, and likewise to be withdrawn at the end of that scene. In short, while the play scripts performed in the new playhouses were notably more secular in their content, the method adopted to combine a strong storyline with comic, heroic or tragic incidents interlaced within it, continued to resemble that already made familiar to audiences in earlier Saint Plays, Moralities and biblical histories.

One further aspect of the legacy inherited from medieval play-makers and their methods of play production that had thus safely been bestowed upon the professional and commercialised theatres of Elizabethan London during the 1570s remains to be considered here. That is the need of those acting companies still licensed to travel into the provinces to supplement their annual incomes whenever use of their London bases was denied to them by closure during Lent, or on account of frequent epidemics of plague in summer months.[68]

Given the void created there by the suppression of all amateur religious drama, however, a ready market existed for the repertoires of plays that these companies had already performed in London, even if attendance had to be paid for. Notice, however, must here be taken of the fact that human beings have always needed to externalise their instincts through art—as in the caves of Lascaux in prehistoric times, or as in the Athenian tragedies of Aeschylus and the satyr plays of Aristophanes during the fifth century BC. It was thus only to be expected that any attempt to stifle it, such as that championed by the Protestant hierarchy in Elizabethan England, would provoke a corresponding reaction from those citizens whom the Ecclesiastical Commission for the North had so recently deprived of their own theatrical means to meet this need.

It should not occasion us much surprise, therefore, that visits from London-based companies of actors should have been welcomed into distant provincial market towns and larger cities as eagerly as they found themselves to be; but as no custom-built playhouses existed in provincial towns and cities, travelling companies had to use their licences (received from the Master of the Revels) to solicit local Mayors to allow them to perform their plays in such Guild or Moot Halls, Inns or vacant Chantries as could be leased from their owners for that purpose for as many consecutive days as the size of the resident population would sustain. Since permission to use such premises on a temporary basis still rested in secular hands, this normally proved easy to obtain on acceptance of three provisos: the first was each company's ability to supply the Mayor with a document containing the names of its members and that of its patron signed by the Master of the Revels on the Privy Council's behalf; the second was that the Mayor and Councillors, together with their guests, should be given a free preview of the play (or plays) proposed for performance during the visit. This came to be known as 'the Mayor's play', rewarded with a standard gratuity after this performance. The third was that the leader of the company would reimburse the Council for the costs of any alterations or damage done to the premises during their occupancy of it.

Given acceptance of these arrangements, it quickly became possible for these nomadic companies of players to set up touring circuits that covered the whole country from Canterbury to Bristol and Bridgwater in the south; from there northward via Gloucester and Shrewsbury to Chester and York in the north, returning to London via Coventry and Oxford, or Lincoln and Cambridge, with several small towns visited *en route* for one-night stands. This was a situation that was to remain virtually unchanged for another sixty years.[69]

Yet while this form of nomadic existence enabled these actors to sustain their professional status and domestic economy year by year, it must be remembered that it obliged them to continue to adopt an approach to the staging of all their plays that was flexible enough to make performance possible in a wide variety of performance spaces that lacked many of the standard features and fittings of the custom-built playhouses in London. In that context, moreover, they were also forced to include the logistics of transporting themselves, their costumes and such stage furniture as they were unlikely to be able to borrow or hire locally, over long distances on roads that could be unreliable in bad weather and sometimes dangerous.

Improvisation thus had to become a constant factor in their thinking, making it desirable to carry painted hangings (instead of heavy three-dimensional scenic items like mountains, caves and arbours) and to hang labels inscribed with place names like 'Athens', 'Dover' or 'Verona' somewhere above the platform stage.[70] Having thus mastered these problems created by the actors' need to rationalise the difficulties that habitually confronted them when touring in the provinces, the London-based companies could legitimately start to regard themselves as financially secure in their chosen profession.

Prosperity beckoned as anonymity started to be replaced by that swelling bubble of 'reputation' which we describe today as 'celebrity status'; and, following the creation of the Queen's own company of players in 1583, actors could start to strut in lavishly tailored costumes (constructed and stored within their own wardrobes) with heads held high in city streets as recognisable members of a respected profession, and laugh off the strictures levelled against them by puritanically-minded pamphleteers, and by jealous preachers when comparing the size of audiences flocking to fill playhouses to their own, often thinly attended congregations.[71]

With that said, let us conclude this extended survey of *Early English Stages* with a brief, retrospective look at a company of respectable artisans aspiring to gain recognition as professional actors during the late 1560s and early 1570s, since this has been offered to us by William Shakespeare in his gentle parody of the casting meeting of a play which its actors assume to have been listed for possible transfer to Court, and which brings us as close to Elizabethan actors at work as we are ever likely to get.

This is provided in Act I, Scene 2, of *A Midsummer Night's Dream* which received its first performance in 1595. This is a scene in which Shakespeare himself looks back at the conditions that had confronted the founder-members of his own company—James Burbage, a carpenter by trade and father of the more celebrated Richard and Cuthbert—when embarking upon his speculative decision to build The Theater in 1576.

The scene opens on a company of six actors including its manager, Peter Quince (in whose house it is set) assembling for their first encounter with a play newly acquired for them to perform. Five of them are respectable artisans who have graduated from earlier apprenticeships as members of City Companies, Guilds or

Mysteries. The sixth is a tinker: and all of them are aspiring to receive recognition as professional actors in the near future should this play be selected for performance at Court before Queen Elizabeth I and an audience that was as influential as it was sophisticated. All of them, moreover, are here engaged in trying both to externalise the content of this play into theatrical images drawn from their own experience of life as they know it, and to match them to such mimetic skills as each of them regards himself to be possessed.

As a scene that continues to provide both its readers and audiences today with a portrait-in-words that reflects the vanity, tempered by insecurity, and the optimism accompanied by doubt, that was then, and remains endemic to all actors and directors worthy of that name, it thus merits quotation here—interspersed with selected annotations from the prompt-copy of my own production of this play for the Bath Festival in 1951.

Peter Quince, a carpenter:	Is all our company here?
Nick Bottom, a weaver:	You were best call them generally, man by man, according to the scrip(*t*).
Quince:	Here is the scroll of every man's name, which is thought fit through all Athens to play in our interlude before the Duke and the Duchess, on his wedding-day at night.
Bottom:	First, good Peter Quince, say what the play treats on: then read the names of the actors; and so grow to a point.
Quince:	Marry, our play is, *The most lamentable comedy, and most cruel death of Pyramus and Thisby.*
Bottom:	A very good piece of work, I assure you, and a merry. Now, good Peter Quince, call forth your actors by the scroll. Masters, spread yourselves. (*They sit down*)
Quince:	Answer as I call you. Nick Bottom, the weaver.
Bottom:	Ready. Name you what part I am for— and proceed.
Quince:	You, Nick Bottom, are set down for Pyramus.
Bottom:	What is Pyramus? A lover, or a tyrant?

164

| Quince: | A lover, that kills himself most gallant for love. |
| Bottom: | That will ask some tears in the true performing of it. If I do it, let the audience look to their eyes; I will move storms; I will condole in some measure: yet my chief humour is for a tyrant. |

As Bottom then demonstrates his histrionic abilities at length, regardless of his companions still waiting to learn what roles they are to play, he slowly becomes aware of their irritation and grudgingly allows Quince to proceed with the casting.

Quince:	Francis Flute the bellows mender?
Flute:	Here, Peter Quince.
Quince:	Flute, you must take Thisby on you.
Flute:	What is Thisby? A wand'ring Knight?
Quince:	It is the lady that Pyramus must love.
Flute:	Nay, faith, let me not play a woman; I have a beard coming.
Quince:	That's all one: you shall play it in a mask, and you may speak as small as you will (i.e. *falsetto*).
Bottom:	And I may hide my face, let me play Thisby too. I'll speak in a monstrous little voice,—'Thisne, Thisne . . .'

Quince, who by then is becoming impatient with Bottom's attempts to steal attention, cuts both of them short.

Quince:	No, no; you must play Pyramus; and Flute, you Thisby.
Bottom:	Well, proceed.
Quince:	Robin Starveling, the tailor?
Starveling:	Here, Peter Quince.
Quince:	Robin Starveling. You must play Thisby's mother. Tom Snout, the tinker?
Snout:	Here, Peter Quince.
Quince:	You, Pyramus' father. Myself, Thisby's father. Snug, the joiner? (*He indicates*

	his presence). You the lion's part. And, I hope, there is a play fitted.
Snug:	Have you the lion's part written? Pray you, if it be, give it to me, for I am slow of study.
Quince:	You may do it extempore, for it is nothing but roaring.
Bottom:	Let me play the lion too: I will roar, that will make the Duke say, 'Let him roar again, let him roar again'!
Quince:	(*Gently dismissing this suggestion.*) And you should do it too terribly, you would fright the Duchess and the ladies, and that were enough to hang us all.
All:	That would hang us, every mother's son!

When Bottom again intervenes with another plea to double as the lion, Quince finally loses patience with him and resorts to flattery to shut him up.

Quince:	You can play no part but Pyramus: for Pyramus is a sweet-faced man; a proper man as one shall see on a summer's day; a most lovely, gentleman-like man: therefore, you must needs play Pyramus.

This handsome tribute, however, far from silencing this ebullient actor, only encourages him to deflect everyone's attention to his own costume.

Bottom:	Well, I will undertake it. What beard were I best to play it in.
Quince:	(*Exasperated.*) Why, what you will!

Quince then winds up this meeting by discharging the business of distributing the scripts containing their respective lines and cues to these actors; urges them to learn them 'by tomorrow night' before meeting again next day to begin rehearsing the play; and ends it by promising to compile a list himself of all the stage properties that will be required in its staging. Bottom, however, still tries to have the last word.

Bottom: We *will* meet: and there we may rehearse most obscenely and courageously. Take pains: be perfect: adieu.

But Quince is too experienced a company manager and play director to let him get away with that. He thus concludes this scene by reminding them of where they are to meet next day.

Quince: At the Duke's oak we meet.

EXEUNT

It now only remains for me to supply an 'Epilogue' that can explain the summary dismissal of all lingering memories of medieval methods of play construction and theatrical representation that these Elizabethan actors, and their Jacobean and Carolean successors, had managed to salvage from the past, and to carry forward for another half-century until they were snuffed out by the civil war that overtook the country in 1642.

Beyond that, this Epilogue will also try to trace the furtive, but steady, revival of interest in those memories by antiquarian men of letters that began during the eighteenth century and then accelerated throughout the nineteenth century to a point that has enabled us in our own times to stage whole cycles of Corpus Christi plays in York, Chester, Wakefield, Coventry, Lincoln and Cornwall, together with many surviving Morality plays, Saint plays and shorter Moral Interludes in other places, for twentieth century audiences to hear, see and assess for themselves.

EPILOGUE: ZENITH, ECLIPSE
AND RESURRECTION

THE action taken by Elizabeth I and her Privy Council in seizing control over all aspects of theatrical activity both in London and the provinces between 1572 and 1581 (see p. 147 above) had proved to be strikingly effective, notwithstanding the protests levelled against it by churchmen and by the Lord Mayor and Aldermen at Guildhall in London.

Both had claimed, correctly, that those aspects of the jurisdiction over plays, players and performance spaces which had formerly been delegated to them, had been arbitrarily removed by stealth—more especially under cover of the Royal Patent awarded to Edmund Tilney in 1581—and usurped into the hands of the Crown; but by then it was too late for a government that was already preoccupied by the mounting threat of an imminent invasion of England by Spanish and other Catholic powers in continental Europe to be willing to take much notice of them.

In the fifteen years that remained of the Queen's reign, following the execution of Mary Queen of Scots in 1587 (see *EES* I, Plate XXV, No. 38) and Sir Francis Drake's defeat of the Spanish Armada in 1588, only two breaches of government regulations respecting theatrical activities in London were regarded as serious enough to warrant punitive action; and, as responsibility for both of them could be squarely directed at the actors, they had no one to blame but themselves for the further tightening of the restrictions already contained within their licences that were imposed upon them by the Privy Council in 1589 and 1597 respectively.[1]

By March 1603, when Elizabeth died, theatrical life in London had thus been successfully transferred out of the hands of some fifty small groups of nomadic 'Players of Interludes' who in 1558 had claimed the right (as household servants of members of the aristocracy and landed gentry) to present their plays to public audiences in whatever performance spaces they could rent from their owners, into those of three companies of professional actors recognised as such by the Privy Council and licensed to present their plays on a regular basis in a custom-built playhouse of its own.

Yet, despite the radical nature of all these administrative changes in the regulation of theatrical life in London that had been effected within the first forty years of Elizabeth's reign, the approaches adopted to play-construction and theatrical representation by the company managers and playhouse owners had remained consistently conservative. This is principally attributable to the actors' continuing need to retain the loyalty of the widest range of spectators willing to pay to see and hear performances of plays presented within a style that remained familiar to them and which the acting companies could afford to finance from their slender production resources. Times change, however, and when they do, public tastes change with them.

As the sixteenth century drew to its close, the Queen was nearing her seventieth birthday; and, as rumour hardened into belief that she had finally made up her mind to nominate her own godson and kinsman, King James VI of Scotland, as her successor, the nature of the impending changes that would shortly affect the whole kingdom became a central topic of correspondence, conversation and gossip within all ranks of English society.

It thus soon became clear that while most of the nobility and gentry would welcome release from fifty years of subjection to a woman ruler, many of her subjects in humbler walks of life were starting to reflect on what changes this might bring with it for them.

Where all literary and theatrical matters were concerned, speculation inevitably centred on the gulf that had slowly begun to declare itself throughout the last century between academic enthusiasm for Renaissance adherence to the proprieties of neoclassical theory and practice on the one hand, and the preference that continued to be voiced by the illiterate majority of the population for their own inherited and traditional manners of linguistic and theatrical expression (see Chapter 8, pp. 159–61 above). Thus, when the last of the Tudor sovereigns handed over the reins of power to the first of the Stuarts in March 1603, the stage was set for a long fight to determine which of these two rival factions within English society would emerge as the victor in the literary and theatrical wars that were to occupy most of the seventeenth century.

The battle-lines along which these wars were to be fought were sketched in with surprising speed during the first two years of the new reign. Threefold in number, the first of them was set in place by James I himself within three months of his arrival in England when, in May 1603, he decided to remove all remaining uncertainties still threatening the future of the three adult and the two boy companies of actors licensed to perform regularly in London in three public theatres and two 'private' ones by transferring all five of them into the service of the Royal Households.[2]

The second resulted from Queen Anne's decision a year later to commission a Masque for presentation at Court on Twelfth Night, 1604/5. Its libretto was to be supplied by Ben Jonson and to contain a role in which she could herself participate as a performer. The stage setting was to be devised by Inigo Jones who she recalled from her father's Court in Denmark for this purpose. Entitled *The Masque of Blackness*, this entertainment surprised its Court audience by exposing it to its first encounter with realistically painted changeable stage scenery, depicted in receding perspective and set out behind a proscenium arch that concealed the elaborate and costly machinery needed to effect these changes of scene from public view.

The third of these battle-lines was defined by Ben Jonson when opting to champion the cause of the avant-garde himself by refusing all offers to collaborate with other play-makers in supplying scripts to company and playhouse managers that he could not claim to be his own unaided work. Presumptuous and arrogant as this stance may have seemed to be at that time, he saw it as the only sure way open to playwrights who sought to acquire recognition within sophisticated society as 'men of letters' in their own right. It was on this account that in 1604 he had chosen to publish his own contributions to the civic pageantry commissioned jointly from Thomas Dekker and himself, to welcome King James into London under the grandiloquent title of *The Magnificent Entertainment*, ignoring all the texts and scenic devices provided by Dekker (see *EES* II.i, Plate XII, Nos 15 and 16).[3]

With the gap separating the tastes and preferences of the fashionable Jacobean intelligentsia from those of less sophisticated theatre-goers thus clearly established within the first three years of Stuart rule, it was certain to widen after 1609 when James took it upon himself to dispense with further assistance from Parliament and to govern by decree.

New patents were issued to provide his younger children—Prince Charles, Duke of York, and the Princess Elizabeth—with companies of their own in 1608 and 1611 respectively.[4] Yet another patent had been used to license the Queen's company to open a new playhouse in Clerkenwell—the Red Bull—in 1605/6; and in 1608, following the suppression of the company of boy-actors known as that of the Queens Revels for infringements of their licence, use of the private playhouse at Blackfriars was allowed to revert to its original owners—the King's company of adult players—to supplement their occupation of the Globe with one that had been designed to protect its patrons from the weather throughout the winter months.[5] Private playhouses, moreover, also offered their patrons a much more intimate actor–audience relationship, thus justifying their owners and managers in raising their charges for admission to between three and five times those levied in the public theatres. The inevitable result of the imposition of so steep a price differential, however, was to endow the private playhouses with a degree of exclusiveness grounded on relative wealth, taste and accompanying social snobbery.

I suspect myself that these changes in English political and social attitudes to the theatre may have sufficed to persuade Shakespeare, in or around 1611/12, that a time had come for him to retire from life as lived in London and in touring the provinces as an active member of the King's Men, to New Place in his native Stratford-upon-Avon which he had bought in 1597.[6] What is more certain is that his retirement cleared the way for Ben Jonson to succeed him as the undisputed leader of the rising generation of aspiring English playwrights. This was a situation that he exploited to the full by writing three of his most moralistic and satirical 'Humours' comedies—The Alchemist; Epicoene, or The Silent Woman; and Bartholomew Fair—and a second, explicitly neo-classical tragedy, Cataline, his Conspiracy, together with six glittering Court masques between 1609 and 1613 and by publishing all of his own plays, masques and poems in a single, folio edition which he described as his Works in 1614.

In doing this, he staked out his claim for recognition as 'a man of letters' and was duly rewarded as such three years later on receiving a pension from the King, together with a laureate's wreath and the award of honorary graduate status from both Oxford and Cambridge Universities; and when he died in 1637 he was succeeded as Laureate by another dramatist, William Davenant.

In the meantime, however, another theatrical battle had begun.

Throughout the first half of King James's reign, all the royal companies of actors had continued to enjoy the privilege he had bestowed upon them under their patents of touring the provinces without serious let or hindrance; but, from 1615 onwards, official attitudes towards touring players had begun to harden. Much of the blame for this undoubtedly lay with the actors as exemplified in their failure to pick up the bill for repairing damage done to civic buildings loaned or hired out to them as performance venues, and in travelling under suspect patents that appeared to have been duplicated or forged.[7] They could also be accused by their ecclesiastical and mercantile opponents of being carriers of plague to provincial towns and cities in summer months in years when their London playhouses had been closed on that account. As a result, complaints had by then begun to reach the Privy Council.

By 1617 we know that the Council (and more especially the Master of the Revels on the Council's behalf) had recognised the need to respond to these complaints by authorising local Mayors and Magistrates to arrest any players suspected or accused of such offences and to return them to London for questioning.[8]

It was within this context that in April 1624 such questions reached a crisis point when the Princess Elizabeth's company (then led by Francis Wambus) arrived in Norwich and, on presenting his licence to the Mayor, was refused permission to perform his plays in the city. On finding himself thus denied what he regarded as his company's 'right' under his patent, he defied the Mayor by insisting that '. . . he would make trial what he might do by the King's authority; for he said he would play'.[9] He then promptly set up hand-written playbills on the gates of the White Horse Inn advertising his company's intention of performing 'an excellent new comedy called *The Spanish Contract* there on 26 April 'at one of the clock', that afternoon.

On receiving a copy of this poster that same morning, the Mayor sent one of his officers to instruct Wambus to appear 'before him and other Justices of the Peace'. This Wambus refused to do, saying:

'. . . he would play, whatsoever had been said to the contrary, and accused the mayor to his face that he condemned [i.e. *countermanded*] the King's authority.'

The Mayor then countered by ordering his immediate arrest and imprisonment.

When released a month later Wambus was allowed to return to

London to discuss his predicament with the Master of the Revels, Sir Henry Herbert. Having duly done so, he returned to Norwich in September in the expectation that he would receive financial compensation both for his company's inability to perform in Norwich and for his own, wrongful imprisonment; but he failed to get it. He thus left Norwich in the knowledge that, from thenceforth, a Royal Patent would no longer suffice to guarantee his own, or any other company's, right to perform

'within any Town Halls, Moot Halls, Guild Halls, School Houses, or other convenient places within the liberty and freedom of . . . any City, University, Town or Borough whatsoever within [the King's] Realms and Dominions.'[10]

We must admire Francis Wambus and his fellow actors for the courage they displayed in defending what they had been given good reason to suppose was their right to perform their plays in the provinces, when unable to do so in London, in order to maintain themselves and their families in their chosen profession; but we must also recognise that it was the abuses already made of their patents by other royal companies which persuaded the Privy Council to downgrade the authority of royal patents in the way that they chose to do in this case. What elevates this incident, however, into a test case was, sadly, its inevitable consequence; for when the Princess Elizabeth's company emerged as the losers— notwithstanding their appeal to the Privy Council—Mayors and Magistrates in other towns and cities, were at liberty thereafter to refuse permission to all actors who sought to perform in '. . . convenient places within the liberty and freedom . . . ' of their own town or city. The normal formula adopted, as a matter of courtesy, was to offer them a small gratuity that sufficed to cover their travelling expenses in exchange for their agreement 'not to play'.[11]

When James VI and I died in 1625, to be succeeded by his even more despotically-minded son, Charles I, the more extreme Protestant churchmen (who regarded all actors as Satan's ambassadors) and their allies amongst elected members of Parliament and the Judiciary were inevitably encouraged, as news of the precedent set in Norwich spread to other towns and cities, to adopt the same course of action. As they did so during the next fifteen years, the tone of the wording, used in civic Account Books to record payments of these gratuities, changes into one of contempt: the once respected royal companies of professional actors became nicknamed 'royal slaves' and, instead of receiving a reward for their agreement 'not to play', are given this gratuity 'to rid them out of this town'.[12]

When Parliament was next in a position to interest itself in theatrical matters, it intervened decisively by bringing not only these provincial disputes, but all plays and play-acting in London to an end on 2nd September 1642, with an Ordinance so worded as to correspond with

'... the distracted estate of England threatened with a cloud of blood by a civil war ... to avert the wrath of God.'[13]

Civil war and the radical political, religious and constitutional changes that accompanied it between 1642 and 1660, finally served to destroy the fundamental medieval belief that play-acting was a recreational 'game', through participation in which it became possible to instruct largely illiterate audiences in the 'earnest', or serious, philosophical and moral issues of family life. The greatest loss to accompany it was that of a wholly popular (or community-based) franchise for *the legitimacy* of dramatic art as accepted by both Church and State alike and within society at large. Public playhouses reopened in Britain after the restoration of the monarchy in 1660, but only in London and for the amusement and solace of coterie audiences restricted to those literate and moneyed men and women with leisure time on their hands.

Second only to that was the loss of an emblematic stage that had thrived on audience participation in making the most use of every individual listener's and spectator's imaginative powers of picking up relevant contemporary allusions from direct, verbal address and from conventionally accepted emblematic scenic representations of time and place on open, platform stages, whether in open-air locations or within walls and protected under a roof from all weathers.

When playhouses and acting were re-licensed in London in the 1660s, neither their patrons nor their managers thought it important to try to reawaken interest of the labouring classes in English society, either in London or in the provinces, to the delights of theatre-going as both a pleasurable and an educative force in the bonding of society at large.

What is curious about this situation is the contradiction in terms contained within the principles that governed the licences issued by the Lord Chamberlain authorising two companies of players to be formed to rehearse and present plays before public audiences in London in order to prepare themselves to bring plays to Court for the entertainment of King Charles II and his brother James, Duke of York, when required to do so, for this in itself was a reversion to precedents set by Elizabethan governments and inherited without significant change by both James I and Charles I, despite their absolutist aspirations. Yet by contrast both Charles II and his brother (together with most members of the royal households) who returned to London in 1660 had spent their years of exile in Paris where Italianate principles of neo-classicism concerning dramatic theory, play construction and verisimilitude in theatrical representation had already become firmly established as the order of the day. It is thus scarcely surprising that on the Court's return to their own capital city, the architects and theatre managers whom the King commissioned under Elizabethan and Jacobean statutes to build London's two new playhouses and to assemble two new companies of players to rehearse a repertoire of plays before public audiences for their own recreation when called to Court at Whitehall, Hampton Court or Greenwich, should also have been instructed to follow Parisian fashions without paying any serious attention to the populist tastes and wishes of their own subjects both in London and in the provinces who had been denied any theatrical entertainment for the better part of twenty years.

This gulf was too large to bridge. As a result, dramatic art, from being the property of the whole nation prior to the Civil War, dwindled into becoming the toy of the aristocracy and those literate and fashion-conscious citizens with both money and leisure enough to wish to keep up with neo-classical avant-garde taste, scandal and spectacular displays of pictorial illusion, song and dance. These concerns, however, go far beyond my own in the preparation of this book and have, in any case, already been fully documented elsewhere.[14] Nevertheless, what these radical changes of approach and attitude do spell out for us is that moment in time which marks the final eclipse of all aspects of medieval traditions of dramaturgy and theatrical representation on English stages for the next two hundred years.

If recognition of this is itself a twentieth-century phenomenon (which it is), and if no serious attempt has thus far been made to classify which aspects of medieval and early Tudor dramaturgy survived into the succeeding eras and which did not, then the most powerful inhibiting factor against any such attempt has been the magnetic attraction of a single English dramatic poet who, since his death in 1616 and the subsequent publication of the prompt-copies of all his plays in 1623 has come to acquire worldwide renown:

William Shakespeare. For, although so little biographical material survives to help us to chart his career, and although he himself saw fit to withhold publication of more than half of his thirty-eight plays during his own lifetime, he emerged after the resumption of professional play-acting in London in the 1660s to smother all aspects of early Tudor and medieval theatrical life under the broad mantle of his own poetic and dramatic genius, together with that of a select few of his Elizabethan and Jacobean contemporaries.[15]

As a result of these improvisatory changes, Shakespeare began to emerge as the most enduring of all earlier English play-makers and the one whose scenarios and title roles proved to be the most easily adaptable to suit post-Restoration literary, theatrical and musical tastes. *A Midsummer Night's Dream* and *The Tempest* were transformed into operas with help from Matthew Locke and Henry Purcell. Sir William Davenant added female confidantes for both Lady Macbeth and Lady MacDuff to the cast list of *Macbeth*, and provided Hecate with a company of flying, singing and dancing witches together with spectacular scenes and machines to endow their entrances and exits with the semblance of appearances and disappearances from either heaven or hell. *Antony and Cleopatra* re-emerged as Dryden's *All for Love*, set in a single location instead of forty-two scenes oscillating between Rome, Messina, Athens, Syria and Egypt on land and at sea; and before the seventeenth century reached its end, Naham Tate had provided *King Lear* with a happy ending, and in that state it stayed until after the Napoleonic Wars.[16] By contrast, *The Merchant of Venice*, as handled by seventeenth- and eighteenth-century adapters, was debased into becoming a vehicle for a comic Shylock.

Equipped with hindsight, it is easy for us to understand how and why this should have happened, for where it was one thing for Charles II to license two playhouses to reopen in London, it was quite another for their managers to acquire a repertoire of plays and operas in English that conformed to the standards of play construction and pictorial verisimilitude set by the *Académie Française* in the 1630s and now required by their patrons in London. They had also to overcome the problems caused not only by the acute shortage of trained boy-actors with good singing voices to play female roles, but also by their need to substitute pictorial verisimilitude of the kind pioneered in Jacobean and Caroline Court masques for the emblematic methods of scenic representation formerly adopted in the public playhouses.

This they did by adopting the precedent long set in France, Italy and Spain of recruiting women to play female roles, but the question of supplying a large repertoire of plays and operas in the new mode took far longer to answer. Initially, they tried to meet it by reviving the best-remembered plays from the years before the Civil War that were still readily accessible in printed editions, and then proceeding to adapt them to conform with fashionable taste by versifying them and excising sub-plots where possible, and also by enlarging the female roles and adding new ones to the original cast lists. Thus, what Sir William Davenant, Thomas Killigrew and John Dryden began doing during the 1660s continued to be done by their successors through the rest of the seventeenth century and beyond.

Nevertheless, even while these persistent vulgarisations of Shakespeare's plays were accelerating, a start was being made to restore the integrity of the originals to help posterity to reach its own conclusions about them. Led by Francis Rowe and Dr. Johnson during the eighteenth century, and followed by Dyce, Hazlitt, Lamb and Malone during the early decades of the nineteenth century, scholars and theatre critics succeeded between them in offering—at least to readers—a steady stream of texts, restored as closely as was possible at that time, to the original quarto and folio texts that were already in print by 1623 for comparison and reappraisal.

Gothic Romanticism, as pioneered in Britain by Horace Walpole, Wordsworth, Coleridge and Walter Scott through the latter part of this same period, served also to stimulate many architects, philologists, archivists and other scholars to carry this research work farther afield into areas of local history (surviving only as manuscripts in public and private libraries) nationwide. These included many Tudor and medieval plays, account books and other records of stage history that had been seemingly consigned to oblivion under the weight of Shakespeare's shadow for the past two hundred years. As the nineteenth century progressed, so these long-forgotten records of plays, players and play-makers began to become available again to a wider public in printed books published under the auspices of the Early English Text Society, the Percy Society (dealing principally with those relating to the north of England) and the miscellaneous publications of many local archaeological societies (together with sundry literary and philosophical societies) county by county.

From these many and varied sources, sufficient information had become available for serious thought to be given once again to the legacy that Shakespeare and his fellow actors and play-makers had received from some four hundred years of medieval and early Tudor creative dramatic experiment and achievement, and to how much of that they succeeded in bequeathing to their immediate successors. In 1888, however, the discovery in the library of the University of Utrecht at Leiden of Arneld van Buchel's copy of Johannes de Witt's sketch of the interior of the Swan Playhouse made during his visit to London in 1596, ignited the fuse already laid by more than a century of collective scholarly research and already pointing directly towards practical experiments in the staging of Shakespeare's plays on open, platform stages with little other than curtains, a few pillars and such simple stage furniture as was demanded by the texts to locate the stage action (see *EES* II, Pt. 1, Plate VIII, No. 11).

In London these experiments were pioneered by William Poel, himself an actor, with the founding in 1894 of the Elizabethan Stage Society. Stripped as they were of spectacular, pictorially realistic stage scenery, they met with the contemptuous opposition of the leading professional actor-managers of the day—most notably Henry Irving and Herbert Beerbohm Tree—whose ridicule of this fledgling society's pretentious pronouncements and productions, far from dismissing them into limbo, served to attract a surprising degree of attention from dramatic critics (not least from Bernard Shaw); from devotees of English language and literature; and from many regular theatre-goers drawn to them as much from idle curiosity as for any other reason.

What seems to have struck everyone who attended these early experimental productions most forcefully was the restoration of continuity of action together with a marked reversion from lavish pictorial realism to the pre-eminence of the text with its accompanying verbal imagery and poetic diction, and the intimacy of the actor–audience relationships achieved within the restricted performance spaces available.

By 1897, Poel himself was sufficiently encouraged to embark on the making of a set of drawings for the reconstruction of the first Globe Playhouse (which had opened in 1598/9) with a view to raising funds to rebuild it in London, not only as a home-base for the Stage Society to rival Irving's 'Lyceum' and Tree's 'Her Majesty's' but as a national memorial to Britain's greatest poetic dramatist (Plate XIV, No. 19). In the event, as is now common knowledge, neither of these ambitious projections was to be realised in Poel's lifetime: both would have to wait for nearly another century to reach fulfilment. Coincidentally, however, Sam Wanamaker's and Theo Crosby's reconstruction of the second Globe Playhouse (rebuilt after a fire had destroyed the first, on an old foundation but described as 'fairer than before') was officially opened to the public by Queen Elizabeth II in June 1997, a hundred years after Poel had made his drawings (dated April 1897) which bear so many striking resemblances to the splendid building that now graces the South Bank of the River Thames a mile to the east of the National Theatre and adjacent to St. Mary Overy's Church (now Southwark Cathedral) where Shakespeare had himself served as a church warden for several years.

If, to date, these Shakespearean aspects of Poel's achievements in company with fellow-members of the late Victorian Stage Society have eclipsed all others for stage-historians, no less consequential to the fortunes of our own theatrical life throughout the past century were the logical extensions of these experiments into revivals of medieval and early Tudor plays, not only in London but throughout the country—once again under predominantly amateur auspices—stimulated in large measure by the publication in 1904 of Sir Edmund Chambers's *The Medieval Stage.*[17]

The first of these was Poel's production of *Everyman,* revived for the first time in four hundred years in 1901; but by far the most notorious was Nugent Monck's attempt in 1909 to stage the Passion Plays from the Middle English East Anglian Cycle known as *Ludus Coventriae* which was aborted when he was arrested on orders from the Lord Chamberlain and threatened with imprisonment for breaching the censorship (then under the control of his Office) banning representation of the Deity in any form on public stages in Britain. Following the end of the First World War a decade later, however, Monck set about converting a dilapidated building in Norwich into an Elizabethan-style 'private playhouse' to seat some two hundred and fifty spectators around an open platform stage which became known as the Maddermarket Theatre.

Warned off from attempting to revive any of the seven surviving epic Mystery Cycles dramatising the whole of biblical history from the Creation to Judgement Day by Monck's experience, amateur enthusiasts in many universities and schools during the two decades between the two world wars rose to the challenge he had issued to revive several of the surviving texts of shorter medieval and early Tudor Morality Plays and Moral Interludes from *Mankind* (c. 1495) to *Gammer Gurton's Needle* (c. 1555), culminating in Nevill Coghill's production of *Everyman* staged in the open air against the west front of Tewkesbury Abbey in the summer of 1936.[18]

A member of that company was Tyrone Guthrie who was so

179

impressed by its success that, a decade later (following the end of the Second World War) he decided to revive Sir David Lyndsay's *A Satire of the Three Estates* (first written and staged in 1540) at the second Edinburgh Festival of Music and Drama in 1948. To stage this scabrous attack on the privileges accorded to the Lords spiritual and temporal in King James V's Scotland, he chose the Assembly Hall which lacked all semblance of a proscenium arch but which offered a large platform that could be extended into the centre of the hall with spectators seated round it. When hailed by press critics and its audiences alike as the most innovative and exciting feature of this Festival, that reception sufficed in itself to secure the annual repetition of this production in all ensuing festivals for the next four years.

Whether or not this also sufficed to persuade the Lord Chamberlain to relax the ban his office had placed on the revival of any of the English Mystery Cycles forty years earlier may never be known, but the fact is that in 1951 E. Martin Browne, in collusion with T. S. Eliot, the City Council and the Cathedral Chapter of York, finally broke through it with a revival of the York Cycle, presented on a wide, open stage in the ruins of St. Mary's Abbey Church within the city of York itself. This too was greeted with an awed and rapturous reception from both the press and the public to match that accorded to Guthrie's revival of *A Satire of the Three Estates* three years earlier. Chester followed this example in 1952, then Coventry, Wakefield and Lincoln (claiming *Ludus Coventriae* as its own), and finally Cornwall with *Origo Mundi, Passio* and *Resurrectio,* presented by the Drama Department of Bristol University and staged on three successive days in the original earthwork arena built to contain these and other plays at St. Pirran's Round on the moors above Perranporth, as translated and directed by Dr. Neville Denny in 1969.

It would be as jingoistic and untrue to suggest that these ground-breaking experiments through the first half of the twentieth century in restoring recognition to the strength and resilience of medieval and early renaissance principles of play construction and theatrical representation to modern audiences were an exclusively British achievement, for on the continent of Europe efforts to promote it advanced just as steadily, if along rather different lines, in France, the Netherlands, Germany and Switzerland. There, however, the pioneering impetus sprang almost exclusively from the scholarly research pursued in universities and led by professors who were not only outstandingly fine scholars themselves, but who enjoyed advantages denied to their British fellow travellers;

for they were unfettered by the laws of censorship still governing the staging of religious plays in Britain through the first half of this century, and encouraged in their endeavours by the creative achievements of the Symbolist School of poets and dramatists led by Strindberg, Maeterlinck, Wedekind and Apollinaire at the turn of the nineteenth into the twentieth century, and by their Expressionist and Surrealist successors from the end of the First World War onwards. Behind them, moreover, they possessed at Oberamagau in Bavaria, a unique and still living example of an extended medieval Passion Play which had continued to be presented once in every ten years by local amateurs as a touchstone for the importance of their own research work and for such practical experiments as might flow from it.

Pride of place in strict point of time amongst this group of scholars must be accorded to three Frenchmen: J.-A.-A. Jusserand, L. Petit de Julleville and Gustave Cohen. Jusserand published his doctoral thesis on the history of the English theatre from the Norman Conquest to the accession of Elizabeth I in Lyon in 1878. Petit de Julleville followed this up with his far more ambitious 'History of the theatre in France' (with two volumes devoted to the Middle Ages) two years later. Cohen, whose interests were slanted more particularly towards the practical aspects of theatre history than the literary ones, then followed the publication of E. K. Chambers's *The Medieval Stage* in 1904, with his own *Histoire de la mise en scène dans le théâtre religieux français* in 1906.

After joining the staff of the Sorbonne, Cohen inspired a group of his students to help him to recover some of the long-forgotten arts and crafts of medieval play production that he had encountered and described in the preparation of his highly influential book. These early experiments came to an abrupt end with the outbreak of the First World War in 1914 but were resumed again soon after it ended. Within a decade, he and a younger group of students felt ready to present the fruits of their labours to public audiences and in 1933 created a society which they named *Les Théophileans*, a title borrowed from that of the first full-length play that they chose to revive, Rutebuef's *Le Mystère de Théophile*.[19] From then onwards they presented a richly varied repertoire of medieval plays to public audiences, including farces scripted by Adam de la Halle, and toured them widely in neighbouring countries both before and after the Second World War. Cohen himself felt forced in 1939/40 to quit the Sorbonne, removing himself to Canada where the example he had set in Europe was copied with the founding in the University of

Toronto of another group of players dedicated to the revival of medieval plays, the *Poculi Ludi Societas* (PLS Group) led by Professor Lyele.

Following closely upon this initiative, the decision taken by Alec Guinness, Tyrone Guthrie and Tanya Moisewitch to try to establish a Shakespeare Festival at Stratford, Ontario—at first under a circus tent and then in a custom-built playhouse equipped with a large platform stage—generated much wider general interest throughout the country and quickly developed into an annual summer event: and that in its turn led on to the publication of that majestic series, *Records of Early English Drama*, set up by Alexandra Johnson and her colleagues at Victoria College in the University of Toronto. Volume by volume, this has been regularly published year by year since 1979 assisted, as it has been since its inception, with substantial subsidies from the Canada Council.[20] Similar expressions of the vitality of ever-expanding twentieth-century interest in the revival of Shakespearean and pre-Shakespearean dramatic traditions spread to Australia with the founding in Sydney of the Elizabethan Theatre Trust under the direction of Hugh Hunt in 1954. In the USA reconstructions of Elizabethan-style public playhouses sprang up from coast to coast (at Ashland, Oregon; Minneapolis, Minnesota; San Diego, California; Cedar Springs in Utah; and at Stratford, Connecticut) which collectively led on to the building of a Japanese 'Globe Theatre' in Tokyo.[21]

Meantime, from the 1940s onwards, the publication of one revolutionary reappraisal of medieval and early renaissance drama after another provided scholars and theatrical practitioners alike with further factual information and well-informed opinion thitherto denied to them which forced them to submit all earlier judgements and assumptions to question and reassessment. Among the most notable of these books were Father H. C. Gardiner's *Mysteries' End* (1946), F. M. Salter's *Medieval Drama in Chester* (1953), Richard Southern's *The Medieval Theatre in the Round* (1957), M. D. Anderson's *Drama and Imagery in English Medieval Churches* (1963), Sandro Sticca's *The Latin Passion Play: its origins and development* (1970), and David Bergeron's *English Civic Pageantry* (1971). All of these books served to attract public interest in aspects of the religious, political, social, economic and aesthetic conditions which had occasioned the radical changes that had overtaken both play-making and play production during the latter half of the sixteenth century but which had escaped any serious attention before the outbreak of the Second World War.

Within the theatrical profession itself, academic enthusiasm and calls for release from the tyranny of the proscenium arch, together with all the pictorially realistic stage scenery behind it, came slowly to be shared by some of the younger actors, producers and company managers as the twentieth century advanced.

Their interest, however, was fuelled more directly by those economic exigencies occasioned in part by swiftly accelerating production costs but more particularly by the competition presented to them by the rapid rise in the popularity of realistic motion-picture photography as developed in cinemas between the 1890s and 1920, than out of academic curiosity. Yet, given the alternatives by then being offered by theatre historians and amateur enthusiasts alike, a tentative return to Elizabethan and earlier theatre practice began to seem attractive enough to warrant modest experiments on open stages. So did the alternatives offered in Scandinavia, France and the Low Countries by the work of the Symbolist poets and musicians, and by the Impressionist, Cubist and Surrealist painters; and by the end of the First World War, similar invitations to experiment were on offer from the Futurists in Italy, the Expressionists in Germany and from the Dadaists in Switzerland.

Pioneered in Britain by Gordon Craig, Harley Granville-Barker, Lillian Baylis and the many founders of the 'Little Theatre' movement: by Copean and Antoine, Cocteau and Artaud in France (see Plate XV, No. 20); by Max Reinhardt, Georg Kaiser and Bertolt Brecht in Germany; by Pirandello in Italy, Adolph Appia in Switzerland, and by Meyerhold in Russia, this revolution in both dramaturgical aspirations and theatrical practices had then already gone far by the end of the Second World War to catch up with the published writings of theatre historians and academically trained theatre critics and directors (see Plate XVI, Nos. 21 and 22).

In the first four volumes of *Early English Stages* I sought to combine the lessons learned from all these innovatory approaches to pre-Shakespearean theatre history with my own research and to add those derived from personal experience of a long catalogue of revivals of medieval, Tudor and Jacobean plays (including all the English Cycles of Mystery Plays together with several Saint Plays, Moral Interludes and a wide range of plays by Shakespeare's contemporaries) which I had either directed or seen in productions directed by others in Britain, North America and in continental Europe.

Thus, when taking the collective result of this sudden and

explosive rebirth of worldwide public interest in pre- and post-Reformation drama into account, it became difficult to exaggerate the radical nature of the changes that had overtaken both literary and theatrical approaches to Shakespearean drama and its antecedents in the course of a mere thirty years. Yet when taken together with what has since followed from these many achievements (including the Swan at Stratford), it has also become much easier to distinguish today between what Shakespeare and his contemporaries inherited from their predecessors and what they themselves succeeded in bequeathing to their successors. In doing that, moreover, it has also become easier to recognise what was lost or destroyed in the course of the many changes in both dramatic theory and practice that accompanied both the infiltration, via the English Court, of Italian Renaissance educational and artistic ideals into schools and universities and the impact of the Reformation throughout northern Europe.

This Epilogue is thus now offered to its readers as a first attempt to sort through the debris created by the cultural shock-waves occasioned in the first place by the invention of both printing and gunpowder during the latter half of the fifteenth century, and by the fall of Byzantium to the Turks, for with that came the return to the West of whole libraries of Greek and Hellenistic manuscripts in the ships of Venetian and Genoese merchant-adventurers.

These shocks to long-established medieval scholasticism and deeply-rooted patterns of feudal life were shortly to be followed up by the startling discoveries of maritime explorers that would open up new worlds across the Atlantic, Indian and Pacific Oceans, together with those relating to the sun, moon and planets revealed by Copernicus and Galileo. Further blows were administered by Martin Luther, King Henry VIII and John Calvin to all the previously accepted certainties of Roman Catholicism through the rest of the sixteenth century, bringing wars, schisms, persecutions and censorship in their wake.

Among the most notable losers in Tudor England as these shockwaves began to register their effects were Cardinal Wolsey, Queen Catherine of Aragon, Sir Thomas More, Archbishop Cranmer and, ultimately, Mary Queen of Scots. The prime beneficiaries, by marked contrast, were many members of an emergent middle class of bourgeois citizens comprising civil servants, lawyers, merchants, mariners and an influx of well-educated, continental European refugees seeking asylum from religious persecution whose ranks included wealthy bankers, skilled craftsmen and representatives of extreme, non-conformist, religious sects. What united them all as an identifiable new class was a shared ability to spot the cracks that were everywhere appearing in the old social fabric and then to exploit them to advance their own interests. For most of them this meant the aggrandisement of themselves and their families by seizing upon every new entrepreneurial venture that offered itself to view as the century grew older and the rush to 'get rich quick' accelerated.

Within a period of such rapid change, this blatant opportunism could not escape recognition for very long, and among the first to grasp its potential as an object for comic satire were the professional playhouse owners, play-makers and actors of Elizabethan London from the 1570s onwards. The xenophobia engendered by the alarming and widely unpopular influx of French, Dutch and Italian asylum-seekers sufficed to make them prime targets for comic caricature on public stages both in London and in provincial cities, but it would not be long before a posse of young dramatists, led by Ben Jonson, George Chapman, John Marston, Thomas Dekker and Thomas Middleton who, seeking to advance their own prospects, would embark upon exposing the pretensions, greed and hypocrisy of many native-born representatives of the recently enriched English middle class of bourgeois citizens. In singling out the lawyers, civil servants, merchants and other less creditable entrepreneurs already familiar to their audiences in daily life as the prime targets of their wit, they succeeded in releasing a rich vein of realistic situation comedies to add novelty and spice to the repertoires of the acting companies who paid them for their plays.

While certainly beneficial to the professional actors and writers in the short-term view, it remains open to question whether in the longer term this decision may also have served so to alienate the many habitual theatre-goers who saw themselves thus pilloried in these new plays as to persuade them to join the formidable ranks of lobbyists who were already clamouring for an end to all play-acting and the closure of all playhouses. Just such draconian action had been promulgated by the Privy Council in July 1597, following the staging of Ben Jonson's and Thomas Nashe's *The Isle of Dogs* at the Swan Playhouse; but, happily for posterity, this Order mysteriously lapsed within the next three months, so was thus delayed for another fifty years.

As the sixteenth century drew to its close, this already highly volatile situation was also about to be confronted by the death of

Queen Elizabeth I in 1603 and the accession of a Scottish King, whose own accent was thought to be as comic as those of the continental refugees already pilloried on public stages, yet who viewed himself both as the creator of a reunited Protestant empire of Great Britain and as the prospective reuniter of all Christendom for whom 'peace processes' must take precedence over all other questions of state, domestic and foreign.

That anything as transient and ephemeral, yet ultimately as educative and socially cohesive, as dramatic art should have survived so many of these seismic shocks for another forty years is itself something of a miracle. I recognise, therefore, when attempting to explain how and why this should have happened, that I can only offer to readers of this book initial guidelines or signposts to the directions most likely to lead their own enquiries towards definitive conclusions.

However, in offering them here as an Epilogue to the preceding four volumes of *Early English Stages*, I remain an optimist, my hope being that such guidelines may help to concentrate the attention of tomorrow's research students and habitual theatre-goers alike upon what aspects of this story may still be worth seeking to recover in the course of the next half-century.

Such students, if tempted to do this, should also be aware that they are themselves again living in an age when they are having to come to terms with the social, economic and aesthetic disturbances to the established social order occasioned in the first place by two world wars; in the second by the invention of radio, television and computers; and in the third by the rejection of so many of the cultural values respecting religion, marriage, the arts and even athletic activities that were formerly regarded as an integral part of our national heritage. All of them, moreover, will continue to experience the further pressures exerted by a much broader mix of ethnic and cultural influences in society, commercial greed and by the many uncertainties provoked by scientific progress in genetic engineering and the advent of the euro.

In reciting these commonplaces of contemporary journalism, I am here only seeking to reassure tomorrow's students of medieval, Tudor and early Stuart theatre history that they are in many ways far better prepared than any of their predecessors to tackle the task confronting them of providing their successors with a comprehensive and definitive account of what survived and what was lost during the hundred and fifty years that separate the plays of John Heywood and John Bale in the 1520s and 1530s from those that led up to the execution of King Charles I in 1649 and the restoration of play-acting together with the monarchy in 1660.

Such, then, is the purpose of this Epilogue. And so, to quote Ben Jonson, 'If you like it you may'.

NOTES AND SOURCES

Chapter I, pages 3–12. Calendar Festivals and the Legitimacy of Play-acting

1. For a more detailed account, see *EES* III, pp. 23–6.
2. Starting with threats, severance from Rome proceeded piecemeal taking four separate Acts of Parliament to complete: the Act of Restraint of Annates (retention of revenues due to the Pope) 1532; an Act of Restraint of Appeals (severing all judicial links) 1533; followed a year later by the Act for Dispensations, the Act of Supremacy and the Act for First Fruits and Tenths; and finally the Acts against the Authority of the Bishop of Rome in 1536. For further details see David Loades, *Revolution in Religion: the English Reformation, 1530–1570*, University of Wales Press, 1992; and Keith Randell, *Henry VIII and the English Reformation*, Hodder & Stoughton, 1993.
3. See E. K. Chambers, *The Medieval Stage*, Vol. 11, pp. 371–3.
4. See *EES* I, pp. 340–7.
5. See Glynne Wickham, *Theatre in Europe: a documentary history: English professional theatre, 1530–1660*, Cambridge University Press, 2001, pp. 20–1.
6. *Ibid.*, p. 21.
7. See *EES* I, pp. 116 and 240, and III.1, pp. 85–6, 168–9 and 241–3.
8. See *English Professional Theatre*, pp. 21–2.
9. See Keith Randell, *Henry VIII and the Reformation in England*, Hodder & Stoughton, 1993, pp. 61–87.
10. See *English Professional Theatre*, pp. 22–3.
11. *Ibid.*, pp. 25–9.
12. *Ibid*, pp. 23–4.
13. *Ibid*, p. 32.
14. See *EES* II.1, Appendix B, pp. 327–8.
15. See Chambers, *Medieval Stage*, ii, pp. 368–90; also *Records of Early English Drama*, 'Herefordshire and Worcestershire', ed. David N. Zausener, University of Toronto Press, 1990, pp. 110–20.
16. Change starts with the accession of the House of Tudor in 1485, after which the governments of King Henry VII and Henry VIII made it a key point of domestic policy to reduce the power of the barons by creating a civil service dependent upon royal patronage. The first step to this was to revise the Statutes of long-established schools like those at St. Paul's, Westminster and Eton; the next was to found new grammar schools throughout the country to supplement them. Henry Medwall's *I & II Fulgens & Lucres* (1497) is a polemical interlude contrasting the claims of inherited titles and wealth with those of merit earned in the service of the State where the latter rather than the former wins the offered prize of Lucres' hand in marriage. (See p. 99 above).
17. See *EES* III, pp. 355ff.

18. See Glynne Wickham, *A History of the Theatre*, Phaidon Press, 2nd edn., 1991; reprinted 1993, 1994 and 1996, pp. 141–2.

Chapter II, pages 13–29. Ecclesiastical Festivals and the Superimposition of Christian Festivals upon their Pagan Antecedents

1. It was on this account that Hrostwitha of Gandersheim was enabled, late in the eleventh century, to compose her six comedies in praise of virtuous women that subsequently became known as 'the Christian Terence'; see Richard Axton, *European Drama of the Early Middle Ages*, Hutchinson, 1974, pp. 26–9.
2. It was from this source that Venetian and Genoese merchant venturers rescued so many of these Greek manuscripts and brought them home to Italy shortly before the fall of Constantinople to the Turks in 1485.
3. For the Latin text see Chambers, *Medieval Stage*, i, pp. 95–6.
4. See R. H. Pinder Wilson, 'Islam and the Tide of Arab Conquest', in *The Dark Ages*, ed. David Talbot Rice, Thames & Hudson, 1965, pp. 53 *et seq.*
5. See Cyril Mango, 'Justinian and Theophilus: the origins of iconoclasm', in *The Dark Ages*, ed. David Talbot Rice, Thames & Hudson, 1965, pp. 109–11.
6. See Chambers, *Medieval Stage*, ii, pp. 306–9; and *EES* I, p. 158, and III, pp. 26–8 and 35.
7. See Axton, *op. cit.*, pp. 72, 78 and 107–8.
8. On the Anglo-Norman *Le Mystère d'Adam* (or *Jeu d'Adam*), see Axton, *op. cit.*, pp. 112–31.
9. See Axon, *op. cit.*, pp. 69–70 and 208, note 28.
10. Such are the *Ludus de Anti Christo* (the Play of Anti Christ) from Tegernsee in Bavaria (*c.* 1160) with its exceptionally large cast list and wide-ranging scenic locations; *Ludus Danielis* (the Play of Daniel) from Beauvais Cathedral School (*c.* 1100) with its many processions, sumptuous costumes and elaborate musical notation; and a group of plays of German origin about miracles effected by St. Nicholas all dating from the middle of the twelfth century. The most startling of all of these early plays is Hildegard of Bingen's *Ordo Virtutum* (*c.* 1155) which charts the struggle of some sixteen Virtues to rescue a soul from attack by a devil.

    Disparate as all these plays are both in their countries of origin and in their subject matter, their survival warns us that the example established by the dramatising of the liturgical offices on major Calendar Festivals late in the eleventh century was seized upon and exploited experimentally in more sophisticated and secularly-orientated circles during the twelfth century than has often been supposed. See *EES* III, pp. 34–41; on the *Ludus de Anti Christo* see J. Wright, *The Play of Anti Christ*, Pontifical Institute of Medieval Studies, Toronto, 1967; and on *Ludus Danielis* see Noah Greenberg, *The Play of Daniel*, edited with music for Oxford University Press, 1959; and on *Ordo Virtutem* see Axton, *op. cit.*, pp. 94–9.

11. See *EES* III, pp. 41–7.
12. *Ibid.*, pp. 128–31.
13. See Sandro Sticca, *The Latin Passion Play: its origins and development*, New York, 1970.

Chapter III, pages 30–43. Secular Festivals and their Accompanying Entertainments

1. See Chambers, *Medieval Stage*, i, pp. 99–145.
2. See Chapter 2, pp. 14–15 above.
3. See *EES* I, Chapter II, pp. 13–50.
4. See *EES* I, Plates II, IX and X.
5. *Ibid.*, Plates II to X.
6. See Henry Goldwell, *A Description of the Siege of the Fortress of Perfect Beauty*, London, 1581; reprinted by J. Nichols in *The Progresses and Public Processions of Queen Elizabeth*, 2nd edn., 1823.
7. See *EES* I, Chapters V, VI and VII, pp. 179–253.
8. See *EES* III, pp. 91–2; see also II.1, Plates XX to XXIII, and Vol 2, Plate XXX.
9. Such comic incidents have frequently been regarded by critics as intended to offer 'relief' from heavy-going scenes of exposition or tragic tension; 'comic relief' or 'earnest' relieved by 'games'. Closer reading of medieval religious plays, however—and more especially experience derived from production of them—strongly suggests that the reverse is closer to the intentions of these play-makers; a 'game' to set audiences at their ease through laughter in preparation for the serious message, or 'earnest' that is to follow.
10. See *EES* I, Chapter II, pp. 51–111; see also Chapter 6, pp. 98 and 102–3 below.
11. See *EES* I, pp. 75–228.
12. See *EES* II.i, pp. 100–2; and *EES* III.1, pp. 201–2.
13. See Chambers, *Medieval Stage*, pp. 99–145; Glynne Wickham, *The Medieval Theatre*, 3rd edn., Cambridge University Press, 1987, pp. 125–49; and *EES* III, pp. 48–61.

Chapter IV, pages 44–64. The Making of Religious Drama

1. Of these Latin words, *mimus* was the most closely defined by being restricted to action and by excluding speech; only when extended in Imperial Rome to *pantomimus* did it come to embrace dance and song. *Histrio* was likewise restricted in its use to define an actor or stage-player.

   The verb *ludo* and with it the nouns *ludus* and *lusio* were more often used in an athletic context than a histrionic one; but, with that said, both verb and nouns were loosely enough defined to allow them to be stretched to cover actors, players of games, instruments and other recreational pastimes.
2. By that time the number of Benedictine houses established in England already amounted to some twenty-five or possibly more.
3. See *EES* III, pp. 34–41, and Axton, *op. cit.*, pp. 77–88 and 112–30.

4. See Glynne Wickham, *The Medieval Theatre*, pp. 81–95.

5. See *EES* 1, pp. 181–5 and 266–7.

6. See *EES* 1, pp. 182–9.

7. See *EES* 1, p. 183.

8. On *De Clerico et Puella* (the student and the girl) see *English Moral Interludes*, ed. Glynne Wickham, J. M. Dent, 1972, pp. 195–203. On the plays of Jehan Bodel and Adam de la Halle, see Richard Axton, *European Drama of the Early Middle Ages*, Hutchinson & Co., 1974, pp. 131–58. For detailed discussions of the minstrel troupes and their repertoires, see *Medieval Stage* i, pp. 42–86, and Nicoll, *Masks, Mimes and Miracles*, pp. 151–68.

9. Among these must be included the many mercenary soldiers (*eques*: horsed knights and *miles*: infantry) who risked their lives in the pursuit of adventurous and often lucrative careers offered by a succession of Crusades and wars with France during the thirteenth and fourteenth centuries. From their ranks there emerged a class of knighted gentry and yeomen farmers rewarded for services rendered by noble patrons, and with the fruits of pillage and plunder acquired during these wars.

10. For a fuller account of this see Glynne Wickham, *The Medieval Theatre*, pp. 106–12.

11. On the reforms of Pope Innocent III and the subsequent licensing of translation of the scriptures out of Latin and into vernacular languages, see G. R. Owst, *Literature and Pulpit in Medieval England*; also Glynne Wickham, *The Medieval Theatre*, pp. 58–9.

12. On the early history of the Chester Cycle see F. M. Salter, *Medieval Drama in Chester*, Toronto University Press, 1955, pp. 34–41; also Chambers, *Medieval Stage*, ii, pp. 348–53.

13. See *EES* 1, pp. 16–30; also Richard Southern, *The Medieval Theatre in the Round*, 1957, and *The Cambridge Companion to Medieval English Theatre*, ed Richard Beadle, Cambridge University Press, 1994, pp. 240–3.

14. That some degree of rivalry existed between authors of plays devoted to the heroes of chivalric romance and those devoted to biblical and legendary figures is clear from a thirteenth-century French poem—the so-called *Passion des Jongleurs*—which castigates audiences who prefer to hear stories of Roland and Oliver rather than those about Christ's Passion and the Saints who followed his example. See Grace Frank, *The Medieval French Drama*, 1954, p. 125. See also Darryll Grantley, 'Saints' Plays', in *Cambridge Companion to Medieval English Theatre*, ed. Richard Beadle, 1994, pp. 265–89.

15. For a transcript of the Account Rolls of Selby Abbey, see *EES* 1, Appendix C, pp. 332–8.

16. See *EES* 1, p. 267. On 'Game' or 'Play' houses see *EES* II.2, pp. 30–63.

17. The Bailiff's Accounts for the town of Shrewsbury between 1467/8 and 1483/4 as transcribed for *Records of Early English Drama, Shropshire* by J. Alan B. Somerset, University of Toronto Press, 2 vols., 1994, Vol. 1, pp. 146–56. These illustrate this particular point and several others raised in this chapter with exceptional clarity. Quoted here are those entries which refer to the royal companies.

1467/8   '... tribus Ministralles domini Regis ... pro honestate ville—xxs.'

1473/4   '... quinque Minestralles ducis Glowcestrie pro honestate ville—xijs ivd.'

'... tribus Mimis sive histrionibus Regine pro honestate ville—xxs.'

1477/8   '... sex Ministralles ducis Gloucestrie ... pro honestate ville—xxs.'

1478/9   '... sex Ministrallibus domini Regis ... pro honestate ville—xxs.'

1483/4   '... sex histrionibus domini Regis pro honestate ville—xxs.'

Readers must decide for themselves how the Latin words 'Ministralles', 'Mimes' and 'Histriones' are here to be translated. Prior to 1450 Ministralles was normally used to describe 'players' in the sense of musicians (i.e. players of instruments). Thereafter it could be stretched to include 'players' in the sense of actors. What is more certain is that after 1460 the words 'mimes' and 'histriones' were both used specifically to distinguish actors from musicians. These particular records moreover establish that by 1477 the number of actors maintained in the King's company was six.

18. See Chambers, *Medieval Stage*, ii, pp. 362–3.

19. *Ibid.*, ii, pp. 365–85; also Glynne Wickham, *The Medieval Theatre*, pp. 128–43.

20. See Chambers, *Medieval Stage*, ii, p. 363.

Chapter V, pages 65–94. Visual and Economic Aspects of Play-production during the Middle Ages

1. See *Medieval Stage*, ii, pp. 306–9, and Axton, *op. cit.*, pp. 100–5.

2. See Chapter 2, p. 25 below and Chapter 5, p. 71 above.

3. See *Medieval Stage*, ii, pp. 118–23.

4. See *EES* I, pp. 292ff.

5. *Ibid.*, Chapter 4, pp. 112–76 and 291–302; see also *EES* II, Pt. 2, pp. 5–12.

6. See *Medieval Stage*, ii, pp. 118–19 and 379–82.

7. *Ibid.*, p. 380.

8. Ben Jonson's savagely satiric comedy *Bartholomew Fair*, commissioned by Philip Henslowe and Edward Alleyn to open the Hope Theatre in 1614, conveys a vivid picture of this fairground and of the crowds who still patronised it as late as that, including pupeteers and their audiences.

9. This image was powerful enough to endure into the seventeenth century where it finds expression in the names given by the Burbages to two of their playhouses—The Theatre (1675) and the Globe (1598/99). It also provided Shakespeare with the soliloquy given to Jaques in *As You Like It* beginning, 'All the world's a stage / And all the men and women merely players ...' (II.7, 138–65) and the Spanish playmaker, Calderón de la Barca, with the title of his fine play, *The Great Theatre of the World* (c. 1645).

10. See Glynne Wickham, *The Medieval Theatre*, Plates 10, 25 and 26. For the provision of smoke, flames, fireworks (squibs) and other pyrotechnic devices, including protective clothing, see Philip Butterworth, *Theatre of Fire: special effects in early English and Scottish theatre*, Society for Theatre Research, London, 1998, pp. 21–98.
11. See *EES* I, p. 131, and V. A. Kolve, *The Play called Corpus Christi*, Stanford University Press, 1966, pp. 57–100.
12. For the plays in this Cycle and the probable location of its performance, see *Medieval Stage*, ii, pp. 412–15.
13. *Ibid.*, pp. 416–22 and 433–5.
14. See *EES* III, Chapter 5, pp. 83–155; also Glynne Wickham, *A History of the Theatre*, Phaedon Press, 1992, Plate 8.
15. For examples see *Medieval Stage*, ii, pp. 340–1, 363–4, 368–9, 385 and 424.
16. See Kahrl, *Lincolnshire*, pp. 87–9, and *REED, Coventry*, pp. 27–8.
17. For examples see:

    sub (1) *REED, York*, pp. 8 and 694 (translation); pp. 28–30 and 713–15 (translation); for Beverley, see *Medieval Stage*, ii, p. 339.
    sub (2) *REED, York*, pp. 10–12 and 697–8 (translation); also pp. 15 and 701 (translation).
    sub (3) *EES* I, pp. 341–7 and *Medieval Stage*, ii, p. 339.
    sub (4) *EES* I, pp. 133–40; also Kahrl, *Lincolnshire*, p. 48.
    sub (5) *REED, York*, pp. 133–4, 33–4 and 719 (translation); also Kahrl, *Lincolnshire*, pp. 80 and 87–8, and *Medieval Stage*, ii, pp. 339–40 (Beverley).

18. See *REED, York*, pp. 37 and 722–3 (translation).
19. See *Medieval Stage*, ii, p. 381.
20. See *EES* II, Pt. 2, Plate I, No. 2.
21. See *Medieval Stage*, ii, p. 380; *EES*, I, Figure 9, p. 60 and Figure 18, p. 306; also *EES* II, Pt. 1, Figure 6, pp. 50–1.
22. See *EES* II, Pt. 1, Figure 9, p. 167.
23. The most likely reason for this lies in the determination of the most zealous of Protestant Reformers to root out all traces of 'Popish plays' in the wake of the dissolution of English monasteries, chantries and guild chapels between 1536 and 1549.
24. The manuscript illustrations of the stage-settings for *Le Mystère de la Passion* at Valenciennes (1547) show that an artificial lake was set into the stage (adjacent to Limbo and Hell-Mouth) that was big enough for a ship to sail on it. (See Elie Konigson, *La Représentation d'un Mystère de la Passion à Valenciennes en 1547*, CRNS, Paris, 1969, Plates I and IV.) Since this play, which lasted fifteen days, begins with the Annunciation, the lake here represents the Sea of Galilee.
25. See *Medieval Stage*, ii, pp. 416–22; *REED, Coventry*, 'Introduction', pp. lxvi and 558; and Kahrl, *Lincolnshire*, 'Introduction', pp. xii–xxi.
26. For details, see *Medieval Stage*, ii, Appendix W, pp. 309–406.
27. See *Medieval Stage*, ii, p. 436.
28. *Macbeth*, II, 3, 15–16.
29. See Glynne Wickham, *The Medieval Theatre*, Plate 24.

'A manner of Adder is in this place,
that wings like a bird she has,
feet as an Adder, a maiden's face
her Kind I will take.'

The Chester Mystery Cycle, ed. R. M. Lumiansky and David Mills for *EETS*, 1974, p. 21 with spellings modernised from BL *Ms. Harl.* 2124.

30. Beverley, Yorks; see *Governors' Minute Book I*, Ms. BC/II/7/1, ff. 117 and 117b; also *Medieval Stage*, ii, p. 340.
31. See *REED, York*, pp. 8 and 694 (translation); see also *Medieval Stage*, ii, pp. 399–401.
32. See *REED, York*, p. 109; also *Medieval Stage*, ii, p. 401.
33. See *EES* I, p. 299; and *REED, Coventry*, p. 72.
34. See *The Digby Plays*, ed. F. J. Furnival from Bodleian Ms. Digby 1.33 for *EETS*, 1896.
35. See Chapter 4, pp. 60–62 above.

Chapter VI, pages 95–112. Renewal and Reform, 1485–1530

1. Readers must here recall that from 1574 onwards stage censorship as exercised by the Master of the Revels on the Lord Chamberlain's behalf effectively precluded the writing of any 'history play' that related directly to any member of the House of Tudor until after the death of Queen Elizabeth I. Shakespeare was thus well advised to leave the victorious Henry Tudor, Duke of Richmond, on Bosworth Field as an heroic liberator with the promise of happier and more prosperous times ahead in the closing scene of *King Richard III*.
2. See G. M. Trevelyan, *History of England*, p. 277.
3. The Venetian Ambassador in London, when writing to his masters after Henry's Coronation, said, 'There is no country in the world where there are so many thieves and robbers as in England; insomuch that few venture to go alone into the country excepting in the middle of the day, and still fewer into the towns at night, and least of all in London.' See Trevelyan, *op. cit.*, p. 278.
4. *Ibid.*, pp. 275–6 and in note 1 on p. 276.
5. See Trevelyan, *op. cit.*, pp. 266 and 271.
6. Chief among these rebellions were those led by Lambert Simnel and Perkin Warbeck, both of whom were described by their contemporaries as 'shadows'. See Trevelyan, *op. cit.*, p. 274.
7. The allusion, intended by the emblems chosen to adorn this Pageant, was to God himself who, in the *persona* of Divine Providence, had chosen Henry Tudor to restore peace and prosperity to the distressed kingdom of England.
8. See L. B. Campbell, *Scenes and Machines on the English Stage*, Cambridge University Press, 1923; and J. D. Mackie, *The Earlier Tudors*, Oxford University Press, 1952, p. 245.
9. See Mackie, *op. cit.*, pp. 174–80.
10. See *EES* I, pp. 31–8, and Alan Young, *Tudor and Jacobean Tournaments*, Sheridan House Press Inc., 1987.

11. For a detailed account of Wolsey's career, see Mackie, *op. cit.*, pp. 286–334.
12. 'Benefit of Clergy' meant that all clerks in holy orders could only be tried by Church Courts, but could then bypass the King on their way to the Vatican by direct appeal. See Keith Randell, *Henry VIII and the Reformation in England*, pp. 47–8.
13. Catherine had given Henry seven children including four sons; but of these, only the Princess Mary (born 1516) had survived for more than a few weeks. For a full account of Wolsey's negotiations with the Papacy concerning the proposed divorce, see Mackie, *op. cit.*, pp. 322–5.
14. See Chapter 4, pp. 54–6 above.
15. What these actors most resented was being bracketed with rogues, vagabonds, gypsies and other travellers, like tinkers and pedlars, in Henry VIII's Vagrancy Act of 1531 as revised in 1536. See *ES*, iv, pp. 260–1.
16. See L. B. Campbell, *op. cit.*, pp. 78–87 and 92–3.
17. See Glynne Wickham, *English Moral Interludes*, pp. 195–209; and Derek Forbes, *Lydgate's Disguising at Hertford Castle: a translation and study*, 1998.
18. Heywood's generation of young play-makers was, by then, also well acquainted with Renaissance dramatic theory relating to the 'Unities' of Time, Place and Action. See Campbell, *op. cit.*, pp. 66–70. On John Rastell's plays—*The Four Elements* (1517), *Calisto and Melebea* (1527), and I and II *Gentleness and Nobility* (1527? 1530)—see Richard Axton, *Three Rastell Plays*, D. S. Brewer, Rowman & Littlefield, 1979.
19. Edward Hall was born *c.* 1498/9. Educated at Eton College, King's College, Cambridge, and at the Inns of Court (Greys Inn), his *The Union of the Noble and Illustre Families of Lancastre and York* starts with the accession of Henry VI and ends in 1532; but it was not published until after his death in 1547. As an accomplished lawyer he probably thought that subsequent events remained too controversial to put into print under his own name, but he continued to make notes. The first edition was published in 1548. The second edition, when it appeared in 1550, was completed to include these notes by Richard Grafton (which Leland had bequeathed to him) and became known as Hall's *Chronicle*.
20. Choice of this location for the hearing was to have ironic theatrical consequences some fifty years later when this same hall was leased by Richard Farrant to be transformed into the first Blackfriars Playhouse in 1576, for use as a 'Private Theatre' and to be occupied by his own company of boy-actors (see *EES* II.2, pp. 125–9). This closed in 1584 but was sold in 1596 to James Burbage (see *EES* II.2, pp. 129–38). When it was finally recovered for use and enlargement by the Burbage/Shakespeare company in 1608 (by then the King's Men), it becomes very difficult to believe that Shakespeare and Fletcher were not prompted to write *King Henry VIII* in 1613 for performances during the winter months under the same roof and within the same walls that had sheltered Queen Catherine during the first hearing of the divorce action brought against her by Henry VIII in 1529.
21. See Keith Randell, *op. cit.*, pp. 34–48.

Chapter VII, pages 113–31. Death Sentences and Reprieves, 1530–60

1. Fisher was appointed to the See of Rochester in 1504, but he had attracted little attention until 1527 when Wolsey was urging the King to start divorce proceedings against Catherine of Aragon. By arguing then that only the Pope possessed the authority to determine whether she had any case to answer, he earned the King's anger but escaped retribution; but, when arrested for misprision and treason seven years later, he was imprisoned in the Tower of London, together with Sir Thomas More, and summarily tried and executed in the summer of 1535. See *Mackie*, pp. 326–8 and 379.

2. Born in 1485, Cromwell was self-educated as a traveller in France, Italy and the Netherlands acquiring experience as a soldier, banker and diplomat. Around 1520 he attracted Wolsey's attention and entered his service and acquired the confidence of the King, being promoted to the Privy Council in 1531, there to become the prime architect behind the Act of Supremacy and the dissolution of the monasteries. For details, see *Mackie*, pp. 351–2.

3. See *English Professional Theatre, 1530–1660*, pp. 25–30.

4. *Ibid.*, p. 21.

5. See *Mackie*, pp. 362–3.

6. See *EES* II.i, pp. 62–3 and *English Professional Theatre*, pp. 21–2.

7. See *Mackie*, pp. 414–15.

8. For details see *English Professional Theatre*, pp. 22–3.

9. For full details of this correspondence see *English Professional Theatre*, pp. 25–30.

10. *Ibid.*, pp. 30–1.

11. *Ibid.*, p. 31.

12. Henry VIII had intended to abolish the Chantries as early as 1545 but died before statutory authority could be obtained to do so. It was thus left to Lord Protector Somerset to enforce it in 1547 and to follow that up by revoking Henry's *Act for the Promotion of True Religion* and by replacing it with Edward VI's *Act of Uniformity of Service and Administration of the Sacraments*, for details of which see *EES* II.i, p. 67.

13. See *EES* II.i, pp. 69–70.

14. See *REED, York*, i, pp. 291–2, 293, 295, 303 and 307.

15. Such records as survive from Chester between 1548 and 1552 are too thin for us to be sure whether the Whitsun plays were, or were not, performed; but in 1553 they tell us that, 'Also this year the Plays were played'; see *REED, Chester*, p. 54. At Lincoln they were discreetly shifted from Corpus Christi to St. Anne's Day; see *Medieval Stage*, ii, pp. 378–9. Coventry alone seems to have ignored the existence of the Chantries Act and to have escaped with impunity; see *REED, Coventry*, pp. 177–93.

16. See *English Professional Theatre*, p. 34.

17. *Ibid.*, pp. 35–6. It was reinforced by Parliament's earlier revisions to Henry VIII's Act for the punishment of rogues and vagabonds which, for the first time, included travelling players and entertainers within its provisions.

18. See *English Professional Theatre*, p. 34.
19. For details see *Mackie*, pp. 526–9.
20. Loades, *op. cit.*, pp. 29–30.
21. *Ibid.*, see also pp. 112 and 116–17.
22. See *Tudor Church Music* by P. C. Buck and others, 10 vols., 1925–30, *sub.* Mary I.
23. See *English Professional Theatre*, p. 39.
24. What the Queen and her Council had failed to take into account was that the campaign (ignited by Sir Richard Morrison and Thomas Cromwell in the 1530s) of using what we would describe as 'agit-prop' polemical plays (i.e. calculated to stir up trouble among its audiences) would certainly be used again by confirmed Protestants, determined to prevent the reimposition of the Pope's authority over the English Church.
25. For examples, see *EES* II.i, p. 71.

Chapter VIII, pages 132–67. Death and Transfiguration, 1560–80

1. The author was Richard Mulcaster who received '40 shillings for his reward for makying the boke conteynynge and declaring the historyes set forth in and by the Cyties pageantes ... which boke was gevyen into the Queenes grace.' See CLRO *Repertory* XIV, folio 143 (4th March 1559). The text was published under the title of *The Quenes Majesties Passage through the Citie of London to Westminster the Day before her Coronation*, in 1559 and again in 1604.
2. CLRO *Repertory* ff.97–97b, 7th December 1558, specifies 'with pageantes fyne and payntynges and riche clothes of arras sylver and golde in such lyke mann(e)r and sorte as they trymd agaynst the comyng of our late Sovrangne lady Queen Mary to her Coronacon and muche better if it conveynyently may be done ...'
3. David Bergeron, *English Civic Pageantry, 1558–1642*, London, 1971; see pp. 12–22 and especially p. 16.
4. Bergeron, *op. cit.*, pp. 17–18.
5. *Ibid.*, p. 18.
6. *Ibid.*, p. 15.
7. *Ibid.*, p. 19.
8. *Ibid.*, pp. 21–2; see also *EES* I, pp. 78 and 91, and *EES* II.1, pp. 213 and 217.
9. *Ibid.*, p. 20.
10. *Ibid.*, p. 21.
11. *Ibid.*, p. 22.
12. *Ibid.*, pp. 22–3. G. M. Trevelyan also held this view when publishing the first edition of his *History of England* as long ago as 1926; see p. 327.
13. See Roy Strong, *The English Icon: Elizabethan and Jacobean portraiture*, London, 1969; and *Portraits of Elizabeth I*, Oxford, 1963.
14. See *English Professional Theatre*, pp. 50–3.
15. See J. E. Neale, *Queen Elizabeth*, London, 1934, pp. 63–4.
16. *Ibid.*, pp. 93–4.

17. *Ibid.*, pp. 107–9.
18. The first of these had to be abandoned in 1562 when the French Huguenots, following a massacre of their community at Vassy, appealed for help. It was postponed to 1563, but that meeting was likewise postponed because of an outbreak of plague in London and southern counties which had decimated Elizabeth's armed forces.

    For the meeting planned to take place at Nottingham Castle in 1564, Secretary Cecil found time to pen a scenario for a moral Mask advising the two royal cousins on how best to resolve their differences in the course of three successive nights (see *EES* III.i, pp. 267–70); but when Mary declined to accept this invitation, their meeting had yet again to be postponed.
19. Lennox was an attaindered Scot who had lived as an exile in England for some twenty years and whose son had been born there in 1545.
20. To secure their return to Scotland, Mary had first to promise to obtain Lennox's reprieve and to restore his Scottish estates and then to persuade Elizabeth to allow him and his son to leave England.
21. Riccio had accompanied the Duke of Savoy's ambassador to Scotland in 1561 as a musician. Once there, he was spotted by Mary as a bass singer and persuaded to stay. On joining her household he at once set about feathering his own nest by consoling the Queen in her loneliness and befriending the young Lord Darnley on his arrival in Edinburgh in 1565. See Neale, *op. cit.*, pp. 139–40.
22. *Ibid.*, pp. 141–2.
23. *Ibid.*, p. 156.
24. *Ibid.*, pp. 157–9.
25. *Ibid.*, pp. 160–1.
26. *Ibid.*, pp. 164–5.
27. *Ibid.*, p. 167.
28. *Ibid.*, pp. 187–9.
29. *Ibid.*, pp. 189–90.
30. *Ibid.*, pp. 191–2.
31. See *REED, York*, i, p. 352.
32. *Ibid.*, pp. 352–3.
33. *Ibid.*, p. 353.
34. *Ibid.*, p. 354.
35. See J. E. Neale, *Queen Elizabeth*, pp. 194 *et seq.*
36. *English Professional Theatre (sub* Wickham) Document 29, pp. 62–3.
37. The text that accompanied this 'riding' survives as a broadsheet in the Bodleian Library, vet A1 a5(1); it is transcribed in *REED, York*, i, pp. 359–62.
38. See *REED, York*, i, p. 378.
39. *Ibid.*, p. 390.
40. See *REED, Chester*, p. 97.
41. *Ibid.*, p. 97.
42. *Ibid.*, pp. 98 and 103–4.
43. *Ibid.*, p. 105; but see also p. 104 recording the Council's meeting in the common hall on 30th May 1575 at which a vote was taken on whether

or not to proceed. This vote is recorded there as being passed by a majority of 33 in favour and only 12 against.

44. *Ibid.*, pp. 109–10.
45. *Ibid.*, p. 112.
46. *Ibid.*, pp. 113–14.
47. See *English Professional Theatre* (*sub* Wickham) Document 33, p. 69.
48. *Ibid.* (*sub* Berry) pp. 290–4.
49. *Ibid.* (*sub* Berry) pp. 295–305.
50. On the early history of this building see *English Professional Theatre* (*sub* Berry) pp. 330–45.
51. On the playhouse at Newington Butts see *op. cit.* (*sub* Berry) pp. 320–9; and on the building of The Curtain, pp. 404–9.
52. This document survives in the Public Record Office: PRO C66/116 mem 36, and is also transcribed in *MSC* i.262. See also *English Professional Theatre* (*sub* Ingram) pp. 204–7.
53. On these companies, see Chambers, *The Elizabethan Stage*, ii, pp. 92–6, 97–9 and 134–5.
54. See Alfred Harbage and S. Schoenbaum, *Annals of English Drama, 975–1700*, London, 1964, pp. 42–7.
55. For the full text of this Act, see *English Professional Theatre* (*sub* Wickham) Document 35, pp. 73–7. For contemporary illustrations of 'public shows', see *EES* II.2, Plate XI, Nos. 12 and 13.
56. In other words, no matter whether a company claims to have had its plays licensed by the Master of the Revels, each play chosen for performance in London must again be submitted to censorship by the Lord Mayor or his deputy before clearance can be granted.
57. Licence to use any building in London for the performances of plays would only be granted on the surrender of a substantial sum of money in advance that would be confiscated in the event of any subsequent breach of it.
58. This tax undoubtedly went some distance towards neutralising the hostility of many of the priests and churchwardens, responsible for the welfare of sick and indigent parishioners, towards plays, players and the licensing of theatrical performances within the city of London; for, as the beneficiaries, the monies received from it relieved them of some of the burden of fund-raising themselves.
59. This clause was inserted to protect some of the Aldermen and Privy Councillors whose London residences were situated on the Strand and in Fleet Street facing the river, stretching from Whitehall to Blackfriars and the Tower of London.
60. The team chosen to conduct this internal inquiry was confined to the members of staff within the Revels Office itself.
61. On Lord Burghley's reforms to the Revels Office, see *English Professional Theatre* (*sub* Wickham) pp. 69–71.
62. On the building of The Rose, see *English Professional Theatre* (*sub* Berry) pp. 419–26.
63. No documented evidence exists to suggest that the builders of the first public playhouses in London had any knowledge of the Renaissance Court theatres that were being built in Italy during the 1580s for the Duke of Mantua at Sabbioneta, the Olympic Academy at

Vicenza and for the Papal Court in Rome to accord with the principles set out by the Roman engineer, Vitruvius, in his *De Architetura*, first published in 1486. See *EES* II.i, pp. 246–50.

64. For more detailed information, see notes 48 to 50 above.

65. See Glynne Wickham, *'Heavens', Machinery and Pillars in the Theatre and other Early Playhouses*, pp. 1–13, in *The First Public Playhouse: the theatre in Shoreditch*, ed. Herbert Berry, Montreal, 1979.

66. See *Henslowe's Diary*, ed. R. A. Foakes and R. T. Rickert, Cambridge University Press, 1961, Appendix 2, pp. 319–21.

67. The models for such plays as these existed in those formerly provided by the recently suppressed three- to seven-day Corpus Christi Cycles, as also by those depicting the legendary lives of Saints, Martyrs and more recent romantic 'histories' like *Cambises* (1569) and *Clyomon and Clamydes* (1570).

68. Plague reached epidemic proportions in London in 1570, 1574, 1577, 1578 and 1581, obliging the civic authorities to ban all public performances for several months. See *English Professional Theatre* (*sub* Wickham) pp. 76–7.

69. The actor Edward Alleyn, when writing to his wife from Bristol in the summer of 1593, offers us a list of those places that he expects to visit while still on tour. See *English Professional Theatre* (*sub* Ingram) Document 193, pp. 277–9.

70. These methods of play construction and theatrical representation, while familiar enough to popular audiences both in London and the provinces, earned the scorn of Sir Philip Sidney and other neo-classical dramatic theorists for their lack of respect for the unities of time, place and action. Sidney's attack on the English stage was first delivered in *The Defence of Poetry* (later reprinted as *An Apology for Poetry* in 1595) *c.* 1583. See *The Elizabethan Stage*, iv, p. 226.

71. On the image of the stage-player in Elizabethan society between 1559 and 1590 as portrayed by these pamphleteers and preachers, see *English Professional Theatre* (*sub* Ingram) pp. 158–69.

Epilogue, pages 168–87. Zenith, Eclipse and Resurrection

1. In 1589 the Lord Admiral's Men and Lord Strange's Men rashly decided to join pamphleteers in a sequence of satirical attacks on the government of the English Church known as the Marprelate Controversy (see *ES* iv, pp. 229–33). In response, the Privy Council decided to create a Licensing Commission consisting of the Archbishop of Canterbury, the Lord Mayor of London and the Master of the Revels. For the letters of appointment and the subsequent disintegration of this Commission, see *English Professional Theatre* (*sub* Wickham) pp. 96–8.

In 1597 the Earl of Pembroke's Men were deemed to have offended Russian and Polish dignitaries on trade missions to London by inserting unauthorised lines into a play called *The Isle of Dogs* at the Swan Theatre. Orders were then issued by the Privy Council for the immediate arrest of the co-authors, Ben Jonson and Thomas Nashe, together with the offending actors. Orders were also given to demolish or deface all public playhouses and to ban all performances for the next three months, but these orders were not implemented. For details see *English Professional Theatre (sub* Wickham) pp. 100–3, and *(sub* Ingram) pp. 211–16.

2. The Lord Chamberlain's company was transferred into the King's service, becoming the King's Men, on 19th May 1603. The Patent affecting this change is transcribed in *ES*, ii, pp. 208–9.

By Christmas 1603/4, the Earl of Worcester's company had become Queen Anne's and the Lord Admiral's company Prince Henry's Men. For their Patents, see *ES*, ii, pp. 229–30 and 187–8 respectively.

On the boy companies, known as the Children of the Chapel and Queen's Revels, and the Children of the King's Revels, see *ES*, ii, pp. 29 and 64–8.

3. See *EES* II.1, Notes to Illustrations, p. 382; see also *EES* I, pp. 83 and 107–8.

4. See *ES*, ii, pp. 242–3 and 246–7.

5. *Ibid.*, pp. 214 and 229–31; see also *English Professional Theatre (sub* Wickham) pp. 126–7.

6. New Place was reputedly the second largest house in Stratford-upon-Avon when built by Sir Hugh Clopton *c*. 1490. It had fallen into serious disrepair when bought by William Shakespeare a century later on 4th May 1597 (together with its two barns and two gardens) for £60. Renovation began in 1598 and was presumably completed within the next five to ten years.

7. See *English Professional Theatre (sub* Wickham) pp. 140–3.

8. *Ibid.*, pp. 143–4.

9. *Ibid. (sub* Wickham) p. 146, and *(sub* Ingram) pp. 255–8.

10. This quotation is taken verbatim from the Company's Patent as first issued on 27th March 1611. See *ES*, ii, p. 247.

11. See *English Professional Theatre (sub* Wickham) p. 135, especially note 2.

12. *Ibid.*, p. 119.

13. *Ibid.*, pp. 131–2.

14. See 'Theatre in Europe: a documentary history', in *Restoration and Georgian England, 1660–1788*, ed. David Thomas and Arnold Hare, Cambridge University Press, 1989.

15. On the contracts awarded by Charles II to Thomas Killigrew and Sir William Davenant to assemble two companies of players and to build two playhouses in London, see David Thomas *(op. cit.* in note 14 above) pp. 11–13.

16. It was still in Tate's version that Charles Lamb first saw this play.

17. Published in two volumes by Oxford University Press, this book provided its readers not only with a reliable scholarly account of the growth and development of English drama of the Middle Ages, including early humanist influences at the close of the fifteenth century, but a wide variety of authoritative illustrative appendices.

18. At this same time, Ronald Watkins, as an English teacher at Harrow School, started to embark on his influential attempts to follow William Poel's example in directing Shakespeare's plays on a stage

resembling Poel's well-publicised reconstruction of the first Globe. For his subsequent reflections on these pioneering experiments with boy actors, see Ronald Watkins and Jeremy Lemmon, *In Shakespeare's Playhouse: the poet's method*, David & Charles, 1974.

19. This received its first performance in Paris on 7th May 1933.

20. The aim of this series (abbreviated to *REED*), has been to locate, transcribe and publish systematically all surviving documentary evidence (external to the texts of plays) of dramatic, ceremonial and minstrel activity—city by city, or county by county—throughout Great Britain before 1642. These records are presented without commentary but in chronological order, to provide the raw material from which the theatrical and musical history of each city or county can be derived. In these respects they follow the pattern established by the Committee of the Malone Society in those of its annual publications described as *Collections* and devoted to the dramatic records surviving from Kent, Lincolnshire and other places.

21. In England, the first of these 'open stages' was designed and built for the Questors Theatre Company at Ealing in west London, and for the newly established Drama Department at Bristol University. Both opened in 1951 to be followed shortly after by the Crucible Theatre in Sheffield, the Nuffield Theatre at Southampton and the Festival Theatre at Chichester.

NOTES TO ILLUSTRATIONS

FRONTISPIECE

Founded in 1131, Tintern was the first Cistercian monastery to be established in Wales. A colony of 'White Monks' was imported in May of that year by Walter fitz Richard of Clare—the Anglo-Norman Lord of Chepstow—from Aumone, near Chartres.

Established on the west bank of the River Wye midway between Chepstow and Monmouth, this brotherhood grew rapidly through the twelfth and thirteenth centuries from the acquisition of fishing rights, and from gifts, purchases and endowments, enabling a start to be made on building the Abbey Church (depicted here) in 1269.

Partly to complete it and partly to pay for its upkeep, the monks began leasing some of their estates in return for annual rental fees. By the start of the sixteenth century this practice had accelerated into the granting of licences to set up shops, market stalls and taverns on land adjoining the Abbey itself.

Following the passing of the Act of Supremacy in 1534, the Abbey thus presented the King's Commissioners with a tempting prize when they assessed its wealth during their visitation in the spring of 1536.

It was finally surrendered into the King's hands by the Abbot, Richard Wyche, on 3rd September that same year with virtually no resistance. In return the Abbot himself was promised a pension of £23. The twelve choir monks likewise received £8.8s. each; and a total of thirty-five monastic servants were awarded £16.5s.1d. The principal beneficiary, however, was Henry Somerset, Earl of Worcester, who acquired most of the Abbey's estates in Wales. Gold and silver plate weighing 13.3 kilograms was confiscated into the King's treasury: glass, timber and other chattels were sold off locally at auction. Lead from the roof and the Abbey's bells were stripped off and melted down by the King's plumbers between 1541 and 1546, leaving it open to the elements to become one of those many 'Bare, ruined choirs where late the sweet birds sang', lamented by Shakespeare in line 3 of Sonnet no. 72.

PLATE 1. No. 1

Aerial view of the Colosseum, Rome, as it is today. The Colosseum, or Flavian Amphitheatre, was the creation of the Flavian dynasty of Roman Emperors. Begun by its founder, Vespasian, in 72 AD, it was opened by his elder son Titus in 80 AD, but left to his younger brother, Domitian, who succeeded him in 81 AD, to complete c. 85 AD. Titus recorded his father's and his own achievements by depicting the new amphitheatre—the largest ever built—on his coinage.

When finished, it contained four tiers of seating that could accommodate between 45,000 and 50,000 spectators. These were surmounted by a *velarium* (a huge retractable awning operated on ropes) to protect audiences against excessive heat and heavy rain.

While this aspect of Roman architecture and engineering achievement has earned the admiration and respect of posterity, the spectacles offered in it were such as to brand this building with a reputation for unparalleled cruelty and barbarity in the treatment accorded both to wild animals and human beings slaughtered in it for the entertainment of the Roman proletariat and nobility alike.

The mainstay of these entertainments were the regular gladiatorial combats (both male and female), and the *ludi venationes*, or baiting of exotic wild beasts. The most offensive of these spectacles, however, was the wanton disposal of convicts and subversive dissidents (including Christians) as defenceless fodder for hungry lions, tigers, elephants, bulls and bears imported from North Africa and the Eastern Empire.

Combats between female gladiators were banned by Imperial Decree in 200 AD; but all other games and sports customarily held in this amphitheatre continued for another 200 years until abolished by Honorius in 405 AD—five years before the sack of Rome itself by Alaric, King of the Goths, in 410 AD.

PLATE 1. No. 2

The Martyrdom of St. Ignatius in the Flavian Amphitheatre, c. 110 AD. Ignatius was a Syrian Christian who was appointed as the second Bishop of Antioch, *c.* 69 AD. He was arrested there and condemned to death during the Emperor Trajan's persecution.

On his journey to Rome he wrote his seven Epistles addressed to Christian communities in Asia Minor which were later translated into Latin and some Oriental languages. Having described himself and his evangelistic activities as 'the wheat of Christ', he was fed to lions in the Flavian Amphitheatre on his arrival in Rome (*c.* 110 AD) as depicted in this beautiful illustrated service book of the Eastern Church—or Menologium—of Basil II.

PLATES II and III. Nos. 3 and 4

Mosaic floor in the Imperial Villa at Piazza Armerina, Sicily. Thought to have been built over earlier foundations and enlarged for use as a summer residence for the Emperor Diocletian during the third century AD, this palatial and magnificently decorated villa contains an astonishingly varied and well-preserved array of mosaic floors and frescoed walls.

The floor in the 'Hall of the Ten Maidens' depicted here is divided into two registers, the upper of which is shown in Plate II and the lower in Plate III.

The girls, clothed only in garments that we would describe as 'bikinis', are represented in both registers competing in a variety of athletic games associated with the Circus. Those in the upper register illustrate several games: putting the shot, throwing the discus and sprinting. Those in the lower register depict some form of ball-game on the right-hand side of the mosaic and, on the left, the winners of the chariot races awaiting the presentation of their victors' palms and laurel crowns.

PLATE IV. No. 5.

The north aisle of Syracuse Cathedral, Sicily. The outer wall of the Cathedral still incorporates the Doric columns of the original Greek Temple of Athena that once stood on this site. The spaces between these columns can be seen here to have been filled in with stone work, and thus made strong enough to support the superstructure that now rises above it.

During the Arab occupation of the island, the seventh-century Cathedral was translated into a Mosque; but, following the Norman conquest, it reverted again to Christian use in the tenth century.

In the course of the sixteenth and seventeenth centuries it acquired the additions and modifications to the superstructure in the Baroque style which distinguish it today.

PLATE V. No. 6.

Coptic Cross superimposed upon a column in the Temple of Isis at Philae in Egypt. Philae was the largest of the three islands comprising the south end of the First Cataract on the Nile, south of Aswan. Regarded as sacred to the goddess Isis, the Temple built on it early in the Ptolemaic era was dedicated to her.

Following the conversion of the Emperor Constantine to Christianity and the establishment of Byzantium (Constaninople) as his capital, Hellenistic temples in the Eastern Empire began to be rededicated to Christian Saints and Martyrs to serve as churches for Christian use. During the fifth and sixth centuries AD, temples in Egypt and Nubia passed similarly into the hands of the Abyssinian (or Coptic) Church. That at Philae passed out of the control of the priests of Isis and into those of the Copts during the reign of Justinian in 535 AD: and it was then, or shortly after, that the Coptic Crosses were engraved over the Egyptian hieroglyphs on the columns of the hypostyle and on the altar in the Sanctuary.

With the construction of the first, or 'Old', Dam in 1898, the water level rose by nearly twenty feet to submerge the foundations of this Temple, making visits to it impossible except in August and September when the lock-gates were opened.

Following Colonel Nasser's decision, however, to build the High, or 'New', Dam it was recognised by archaeologists that the Temple would have to be dismantled and rebuilt on another island that was both large enough and high enough above the water level to contain it in safety.

This ambition was brilliantly achieved between 1972 and 1980, thus enabling visitors today to see both the original Temple and its Coptic crosses virtually throughout the whole year.

PLATE VI. No. 7

Ikon of St. Alban, Protomartyr of Britain; now in the possession of The Brotherhood of St. Seraphim of Savor, Bungay, Suffolk. Alban was a pagan British soldier who became a Christian convert while extending hospitality and refuge from persecution at his home in Verulanium to an ordained priest called Amphilubus. When Roman soldiers searched his house they found him dressed in a priest's cloak. He was arrested, tried and, on failing to recant, was condemned, beheaded and buried.

The early historians, Gildas and then Bede, both dated Alban's martyrdom to 305 AD under the Emperor Diocletian; but modern scholars have since chosen to backdate this to the persecutions initiated by Decius in 254, or even to 209 under Septimus Severus.

A church was built on the site of his execution, and an Abbey was there dedicated in his name in 793 which was later to become known as St. Alban's Cathedral.

PLATE VI. No. 8

Christ's miraculous translation of water into wine at the marriage feast at Cana in Galilee. This illustration to a medieval Armenian manuscript of St. John's Gospel illustrates Chapter 2, verses 6–11, showing the pouring of the 'two or three firkins' of water out of the first of the six stone water pots into one that was previously empty, but subsequently found to contain vintage wine.

This manuscript can now be seen in St. Deiniol's Residential Library, Hawarden, North Wales.

PLATE VII. No. 9

'The Green Man'. The 'Wild Man', 'Wodewose' or 'Green Man' is a recurrent figure in English medieval folklore, literature and church carvings, outliving pagan times as a favourite emblem of fertility and survival closely associated with ever-green trees and shrubs: most notably with holly, laurel, bay and ivy.

He has been envisaged here by the stone-mason responsible for carving this roof-boss in Warmington Church, Cambridgeshire, with a broad smile on his face encircled by a halo of oak-leaves.

He can still also be seen in the wood carvings that form the pew ends and misericords in many Christian churches dating from Saxon and Norman times and the later Middle Ages. See also Plates I, No. 1, and XXII, No. 32, in Volume I of *EES*.

PLATE VIII. No. 10

'Death and a Woman', by Hans Baldung Grien (1484/5–1545). Painted in 1517, this startling portrait now resides in the Offentliche Kunstmuseum in Basel, Switzerland.

Having draped his victim in a shroud, the skeletal figure of death is nursing her head in his right hand while delivering his fatal kiss to her lips. Looming behind them both is the dark entrance to a cavern with a tombstone adjacent to it.

PLATE VIII. No. 11

The Tudor Guildhall, Much Wenlock, Shropshire. Following the dissolution of the Priory, this was built in 1540 as a free-standing Court

House above the medieval stone prison. The richly panelled Council Chamber at the northern end was completed in 1577.

PLATE IX. No. 12

The replica of John Cabot's Matthew leaving Bristol on her maiden voyage to Newfoundland, 1997. Built in Bristol to celebrate the five hundredth anniversary of Cabot's original voyage in 1497, she sailed on 11th May and, after experiencing stormy seas in mid-Atlantic, arrived off the coast of Newfoundland six weeks later, sailing into the port of St. John's on 24th June.

PLATE X. No. 13

Cardinal Thomas Wolsey by an unknown artist, c. 1520. Wolsey, reputedly, was the son of a wealthy butcher and born in Ipswich (?) 1475. He was there thought bright enough to be sent to Magdalen College, Oxford, where he graduated M.A. in 1490 and was later elected a Fellow in 1497. He seems, however, to have thought that a career in the Church offered swifter and more lucrative prospects of promotion to positions of power than were likely to be his in academic life; a view he soon proved to be correct.

Following his institution as Rector of Limington in Somerset in 1500, he became Chaplain to the Archbishop of Canterbury a year later: then to Sir Richard Nafan (or Naphant), the King's Deputy in Calais in 1503: and on Nafan's death in 1507, Chaplain to King Henry VII and a Privy Councillor in 1509.

By 1509 he had been elevated to the Deanery at Lincoln, and in 1514 became Archbishop of York. Created Cardinal by Pope Leo X in that same year, he was presented with his Cardinal's hat in Westminster Abbey on 15th November 1514, and then became Lord Chancellor.

With that achieved, he swiftly secured the confidence of King Henry VIII who delegated most of his own concerns with political affairs both at home and abroad into his hands for the next fifteen years. When exposed and accused of corruption and treason, he was stripped of his many Offices, arrested and disgraced in 1529. He died on 30th November 1530.

PLATE XI. No. 14

The Chapter House in the Priory at Much Wenlock, Shropshire. This spaciously proportioned Norman building, reconstructed as it appeared before the dissolution of the Priory in 1538, served as its administrative, disciplinary and business centre.

Daily meetings were held in it at ten o'clock each morning under the chairmanship of the Prior, at which all monks residing in the Priory were required to be present. Each day's meeting began with the reading of a chapter from the rule of St. Benedict from whence this building acquired its name. Access to it was provided from the adjoining cloisters, and seating was on long stone benches jutting out from the surrounding walls.

The doorway (shown here on the left of the lectern and the Prior's chair) was cut after the closure of the monastery, when the Chapter House was turned into a dairy.

PLATE XI. No. 15

The ruins of the south wall of the Priory as they are today. It was these ruins that enabled David Urmiston to make his reconstruction of the Chapter House, prior to Henry VIII's dissolution of this Priory, depicted in Plate XI, No. 14, above.

For a similar building of approximately the same date and dimensions that has survived intact, readers are recommended to visit what was formerly the Augustinian Abbey Church that, after the Reformation, became Bristol Cathedral.

PLATE XII. No. 16

Elizabeth I's passage through the City of London 14th January 1559, before her Coronation: reproduced from B.L. Ms. Egerton, 3320. The royal procession set out from the Tower of London at 2.00 p.m., proceeding to Frenchurch Street and then into Gracechurch Street moving west through Cheapside to St. Paul's, and so to Temple Bar and Westminster.

Her open litter was trimmed with cloth of gold, and was reported by the Venetian Ambassador to have been preceded by an escort of 1,000 mounted guards.

Her Master of the Horse, Robert Dudley, and members of her Privy Council guarded the litter itself as the procession wound its way through the City, stopping from time to time to view the Pageants prepared for her and to listen to the speeches. Behind wooden barriers, cheering merchants and members of the City's Livery Companies, lined the route to welcome her.

PLATE XIII. No. 17 and 18

C. Walter Hodges' reconstruction of the Rose theatre, Southwark. The first of these diagrammatic sketches (No. 17) reveals the interior of Philip Henslowe's Rose playhouse as seen by its first patrons from 1587 to 1591, without a protective roof, or 'Heavens', above the stage and pillars to support it. Note the battlemented representation of the sky behind it.

The second sketch (No. 18) depicts the interior, as seen from the same viewpoint, after the enlargement of the auditorium in its northern sector, and the alterations to the stage including the addition of the hut, 'Heavens', supporting pillars and traps (with accompanying machinery) to facilitate ascents and descents both through the stage-floor itself, and through the 'Heavens' above it. This work was carried out between 1591 and 1593 while the playhouse was closed by order of the Privy Council when an outbreak of plague assumed epidemic proportions throughout the City and its adjacent suburbs.

When archaeologists at the Museum of London were given the chance in 1989 to excavate the site of the Rose, they succeeded in exposing both the foundations of Henslowe's original building of 1587, and those of his subsequent alterations made in and after 1591.

It was in the light of these discoveries that in 1991 C. Walter Hodges made his own reconstruction of the Rose as represented in these two sketches.

See also Glynne Wickham, 'Heavens, Machinery and Pillars in the Theatre and other early Playhouses', in *The First Public Playhouse: the theatre in Shoreditch*, ed. Herbert Berry, McGill-Queen's University Press, 1979, pp. 1–15.

PLATE XIV. No. 19

William Poel's reconstruction of the first Globe Playhouse, 1897. This drawing, made nine years after the discovery of Arend van Buchel's copy of Johanes de Witt's sketch of the interior of the Swan playhouse (drawn during a visit to London in 1596) in the Library of the University of Utrecht. (See *EES*, II 1, Plate VIII, No. 11.) Poel's drawing is now in the possession of Bristol University's Theatre Collection. It is reproduced here by courtesy of the Keeper.

For full details, see Martin White, 'William Poel's Globe', in *Theatre Notebook*, Vol. LIII, No. 3, 1999, pp. 146–62.

PLATE XV. No. 20

The stage and auditorium of the Vieux Colombier, Paris. This photograph was taken shortly after the completion of the renovations undertaken by Jacques Copeau in preparation for its occupancy by his *Companie des Quinze* in 1919.

PLATE XVI. Nos. 21 and 22

The Drama Studio, converted from a bombed squash court in the Wills Memorial Building, University of Bristol, 1951. Its designer, Richard Southern (seen here on the left of No. 21) explains the several types of theatre that could be set up within this small but versatile building— arena, Elizabethan and picture-frame—to its first stage-manager, (John Lavender); a lecturer in Drama (Glynne Wickham); the Bursar (Colonel C. M. Singer), and the Chairman of the Consultative Committee on Drama (Professor D. G. James). Southern had also made provision for its use as a Roman Theatre on a much reduced scale.

No. 22 shows an audience taking their seats before the start of one of the first productions in this new Studio Theatre as set up in the arena style in 1951.

(Photographs by courtesy of the Keeper of the Theatre Collection.)

BIBLIOGRAPHY

ANDERSON, M. D. *Drama and Imagery in English Medieval Churches*, Cambridge University Press, 1963.
AXTON, R. *European Drama of the Early Middle Ages*, Hutchinson, 1974.

BEADLE, R. *The Cambridge Companion to Medieval English Theatre*, Cambridge University Press, 1994.
BERGERON, D. M. *English Civic Pageantry, 1558–1642*, Edward Arnold, 1971.
BERRY, H. *The First Public Playhouse: the theatre in Shoreditch*, Montreal, 1979.
BUCER, M. *De Regno Christi*, 1550; ed. with Philip Melanchthon, *Loci communes theologici* by Wilhelm Pauck, London, 1969.
BUCK, P. C. and others. *Tudor Church Music*, 10 vols. Oxford University Press, 1922–9.
BUTTERWORTH, P. *Theatre of Fire: special effects in early English and Scottish theatre*, Society for Theatre Research, London, 1998.

CAMPBELL, L. B. *Scenes and Machines on the English Stage*, Cambridge University Press, 1923.
CHAMBERS, Sir Edmund. *The Mediaeval Stage*, 2 vols., Oxford University Press, 1904.
—— *The Elizabethan Stage*, 4 vols., Oxford University Press, 1924.
CLOPPER, L. M. See *sub Records of Early English Drama, Chester*.
COHEN, Gustave. *Histoire de la mise en scène dans le théâtre religieux français*, Paris, 1906.

ERASMUS, D. *The Praise of Folly*, trans. and ed. with explanatory notes by J. Copner, London, 1878.

FOAKES, R. A. and RICKERT, R. T. *Henslowe's Diary*, Cambridge University Press, 1961.
FRANK, G. *Medieval French Drama*, Oxford University Press, 1954.
—— See also *sub* Plays, RUTEBEUF.

GARDINER, Father H. C. *Mysteries' End*, New Haven, Conn., 1946; reprinted, 1967.
GOLDWELL, H. *A Description of the Siege of the Fortress of Perfect Beauty*, London, 1581; reprinted by J. Nichols in *The Progresses and Public Processions of Queen Elizabeth*, 2nd edn., 1823.

HALL, E. *The Union of the Noble and Illustre Families of Lancastre and York*, 1548; 2nd edn., *Hall's Chronicle*, 1550.
HARBAGE, A. and SCHOENBAUM, S. *Annals of English Drama, 975–1700*, London, 1964.

BIBLIOGRAPHY

INGRAM, R. W. See *sub Records of Early English Drama, Coventry.*

JOHNSON, A. F. See *sub Records of Early English Drama, York.*

KAHRL, S. J. *Plays and Players in Lincolnshire, 1300–1585*, ed. for Malone Society Collections VIII, 1969 (1974).
KOLVE, V. A. *The Play Called Corpus Christi*, Stanford University Press, 1966.
KONIGSON, E. *La Répresentation d'un Mystère de la Passion a Valenciennes en 1547*, CRNS, Paris, 1969.

LOADES, D. *Revolution in Religion: the English Reformation, 1530–1570*, University of Wales Press, 1992.
LUMIANSKY, R. M. and MILLS, D. *The Chester Mystery Cycle*, ed. for EETS, Oxford University Press, 1974.

MACKIE, J. D. *The Earlier Tudors*, Oxford University Press, 1952.
MORE, Sir Thomas. *Utopia*, Latin Text, Louvain, 1516; trans. R. Robinson 1551.
MULCASTER, R. *The Quenes Majesties Passage through the Citie of London to Westminster the Day before her Coronation*, London, 1559, reprinted 1604.
MUNGO, C. 'Justinian and Theophilus: the origins of iconoclasm', in *The Dark Ages*, ed. David Talbot Rice, Thames & Hudson, 1965.

NEALE, J. E. *Queen Elizabeth*, Jonathan Cape, London, 1934.
NICOLL, A. *Masks, Mimes and Miracles*, London, 1931.
NORRIS, E. *The Ancient Cornish Drama*, 2 vols., Oxford University Press, 1859.

OWST, G. R. *Literature and Pulpit in Medieval England*, Cambridge University Press, 1933.

PETIT DE JULLEVILLE, L. *Histoire du théâtre en France: les mystères*, Paris, 1880.
PINDER WILSON, R. H. 'Islam and the Tide of Arab Conquest', in *The Dark Ages*, ed. David Talbot Rice, Thames & Hudson, 1965.

RANDELL, K. *Henry VIII and the English Reformation*, Hodder & Stoughton, 1993.
RECORDS OF EARLY ENGLISH DRAMA, University of Toronto Press.
—— *Chester*, ed. Lawrence M. Clopper, 1979.
—— *Coventry*, ed. R. W. Ingram, 1981.
—— *Herefordshire and Worcestershire*, ed. David N. Zausener, 1990.
—— *Shropshire*, 2 vols., ed. J. Alan B. Somerset, 1994.
—— *York*, 2. vols., ed. Alexandra F. Johnston and Margaret Rogerson, 1979.
RICE, D. T. *The Dark Ages*, Thame & Hudson, 1965.

SALTER, F. M. *Medieval Dram in Chester*, University of Toronto Press, 1955.

BIBLIOGRAPHY

SIDNEY, Sir Philip. *The Defence of Poetry, c.* 1583: printed 1595 as *An Apology for Poetry.*

SOMERSET, J. A. B. See *sub* Records of *Early English Drama, Shropshire.*

SOUTHERN, R. *The Medieval Theatre in the Round,* 1957.

STICCA, S. *The Latin Passion Play: its origins and development,* New York, 1970.

STRONG, R. *Portraits of Elizabeth I,* Oxford, 1963.

—— *The English Icon, Elizabethan and Jacobean Portraiture,* London, 1969.

THOMAS, D. and HARE, A. *Restoration and Georgian England,* ed. for *Theatre in Europe: a documentary history,* Cambridge University Press, 1989.

TREVELYAN, G. M. *History of England,* Longmans, 1st edn., 1926; new impression, 1948.

VITRUVIOUS. *De Architectum,* 1486.

WATKINS, R. and LEMMON, J. *In Shakespeare's Playhouse: the poet's method,* David & Charles, 1974.

WHITE, M. 'William Poelt's Globe', in *Theatre Notebook,* Vol. LIII, No. 3, 1999, pp. 146–62.

WICKHAM, G. *A History of the Theatre,* Phaidon Press, 2nd edn., 1991; reprinted 1993, 1994 and 1996.

—— *Early English Stages,* Vol. I, Routledge & Kegan Paul, 1959; reprinted 1963.

Vol. II (Pt. 1) Routledge & Kegan Paul, 1963.

Vol. II (Pt. 2) Routledge & Kegan Paul, 1972.

Vol. III, Routledge & Kegan Paul, 1981.

Vol. I to III reprinted by Routledge, 2002.

Vol. IV, Routledge, 2002.

—— *English Moral Interludes,* ed. for J. M. Dent, Ltd, 1976.

—— *English Professional Theatre, 1530–1660,* ed. with William Ingram and Herbert Berry for *Theatre in Europe: a documentary history,* Cambridge University Press, 2001.

—— *'Heavens', Machinery and Pillars in the Theatre and other Early Playhouses.* See Berry, H., *The First Public Playhouse.*

—— *The Medieval Theatre,* 3rd edn., Cambridge University Press, 1987.

YOUNG, A. *Tudor and Jacobean Tournaments,* Sheridan House Press, Inc., 1987.

ZAUSENER, D. N. See *sub* Records of *Early English Drama.*

PLAYS CITED IN THE TEXT

ANONYMOUS. *The Castle of Perseverance, c.* 1405–20; printed 1904.
ANONYMOUS. *Ludus Danielis* (The Play of Daniel), ed. Noah Greenburg with music, Oxford University Press, 1959.
ANONYMOUS. *Ludus de Anti Christo* (The Play of Anti Christ), ed. J. Wright for the Pontifical Institute of Medieval Studies, Toronto, 1967.
ANONYMOUS. The Digby Plays of *St. Mary Magdalene* and *Saint Paul.* See *EES* III, List of Plays, pp. 325 and 326.
ANONYMOUS. *Everyman.* See *EES* III, List of Plays, p. 126.
ANONYMOUS. *Mankind.* See *EES* III, List of Plays, p. 330.
ANONYMOUS. *The Spanish Contract,* 1614; now lost.
ANONYMOUS. *Wisdom.* See *EES* III, List of Plays, p. 334.

BALE, J. I & II Kyng Johan, 1536; printed 1838, see also *EES* III, p. 329.

CALDERON de la Barca, P. *The Great Theatre of the World,* (El Gran Teatro del Mondo), *c.* 1645.

DRYDEN, J. *All for Love or The World Well Lost* (adapted from Shakespeare's *Antony and Cleopatra,* 1677; printed 1678).

FORBES, D. *Lydgate's Disguising at Hertford Castle: a translation and study,* Hertford Historical Society, 1998.
FURNIVAL, F. J. *The Digby Plays,* ed. for EETS from Bodleian Ms. Digby i. 33.

HADTON, Dominus (Father). *The Life of St. Meriasek, Bishop and Confessor,* 1504; printed 1872.
HEYWOOD, J. *The Pardoner and the Friar, the Curate, Neighbour Pratte,* 1519; printed 1533.
—— *Johan Johan the Husband, Tib his wife and Sir John the Priest,* 1520; printed 1533.
—— *The Four PP's,* 1520; 1st edn., n.d. ?1545.
HEYWOOD, J. *The Play of the Weather,* 1528; printed 1533. For modern editions, see *EES* III, List of Plays, pp. 326, 328, 331 and 332.

JONSON, B. *The Alchemist,* 1610; printed 1612.
—— *Bartholomew Fair,* 1614; printed 1631.
—— *Cataline, his Conspiracy,* 1611; printed 1611.
—— *Epicoene, or the Silent Woman,* 1609; printed 1616.
JONSON, B. and NASHE, T. *The Isle of Dogs,* 1597; text suppressed.
JONSON, B. with DEKKER, T. *The Magnificient Entertainment* (Coronation Entry into London for King James I), 1604/5; printed 1604/5.

PLAYS CITED IN THE TEXT

JONSON, B. *The Masque of Blackness*, 1604/5, printed *c.* 1608.
—— *Volpone*, 1606; printed 1607.
KIRCHMAYER, T. *Tragoedia nova Pammachius*, Basel, 1541. Trans. John Bale as *Pammachius*, *c.* 1544/5, now lost.

LYNDSAY, Sir David. *A Satire of the Three Estates.* 1540; printed 1931; 1954.

MARLOWE, C. *Dr. Faustus*, 1588/9; printed 1604.
—— *I and II Tamburlaine the Great*, 1587 and 1588; printed 1590 and 1591.
MEDWALL, H. *Fulgens and Lucres, I and II*, 1497, 1st edn. J. Raste, *c.* 1515: ed. Glynne Wickham, *English Moral Interludes*, J. M. Dent, 1976. For other editions see *EES* III, p. 326.
—— *I & II Nature*, 1496; printed *c.* 1530–4.

NORTON, T. and SACKVILLE, T. *Gorboduc, or Ferrex and Porrex*, 1562; printed 1565.

PRESTON, T. *Cambises*, 1561; printed *c.* 1569.
—— (?) *Clyomon & Clamydes*, 1570; printed 1599.

RUTEBUEF, *Le Mystère de Théophile*, (*c.* 1276), ed. Grace Frank, Paris, 1925; 2nd edn., 1949.

SHAKESPEARE, W. *As You Like It*, 1598–1600; printed 1623.
—— *Hamlet*, 1599–1601; printed 1603.
—— *King Henry IV*, Parts I & II, 1597; printed 1598 (Pt. I) and 1600 (Pt. II).
—— *King Henry VIII*, 1613; printed 1623.
—— *King Richard* II, 1594/5; printed 1597.
—— *Macbeth*, 1606; printed 1623.
—— *A Midsummer Night's Dream*, 1594–8; printed 1600.
—— *Othello*, 1604; printed 1623.
—— *Twelfth Night*, 1600–2; printed 1623.
SKELTON, J. *Magnificence*, 1515; printed *c.* 1530. See *EES* III, List of Plays, p. 330.
—— *Nigromansir* (The Necromancer), *c.* 1504; lost.
STEVENSON, W. (?) *Gammer Gurton's Needle*, 1553; printed 1575.

WHETSTONE, G. *I and II Promos and Cassandra*, 1578; printed 1578.

INDEX

Aachen (Aix-la-Chapelle) 20

Abbeys: iconoclasm by Protestant Reformers 118–19; staging of plays attached to Calendar Festivals 47; Thomas Cromwell's assault on 116

Abelard, Peter 46

Académie Française 176

Account rolls and books: records of entertainments and performers 44, 50, 60–2, 89–92, 173–4; scholarly research in early nineteenth century 177, *see also* Household order and account books

Acrobats *see* Tumblers

Act for the Advancement of True Religion (1543) 7, 119–20, 122, 124, 129

Act for the Punishment of Vagabonds (1572) 147

Act for the Uniformity of Service (1549) 124, 129, 137

Act of Supremacy (1535) 115, 117, 124, 126, 138

Acting: acceptance as part of celebration 42; acceptance as universal pursuit 4; medieval beliefs about 174; problem of legitimacy 3, 174; Protestant extremists' demand for abolition of 155; relicensing of in 1660 174, 187; support of by Martin Bucer 127–8; threatened due to Reformation 42

Acting companies: Elizabeth I's players 138; from schools 39; licensing of 161, 162–3, 170, 172, 174–5; maintained by the Court and nobility 4, 12, 60–3, 64, 109–10, 123; needed for Mystery Plays 27; performing in Elizabethan playhouses 159–60; rise of professionalism 12, 62–3, 109–10, 123, 154, 163, 169; Royal Households of James I 170, 171; withdrawal of rights of squirearchy to maintain 147, *see also* Actors; Travelling players

Actor: vocabulary of the word 44–5

Actors: achievement of professional status 163, 185; anonymity in Middle Ages 56–7, 58, 65–6, 68; in Benedictine Mass ceremonies 23; change in social status 60, 63–4; continuation of style forged within Corpus Christi Cycles 135; Corpus Christi plays 8, 56, 58, 78, 90–1; effect of restrictive measures in mid-sixteenth century 126, 127–8, 168–9; expansion of repertoire of plays in fourteenth century 68–9; extending of horizons to secular world 24; impact of invention of printing 63–4; legacy of medieval theatrical methods 167; legacy received from medieval and early Tudor drama 177–8; licensing by Church 67; Morality Plays and Moral Interludes 59, 85–6, 87, 88; official and ecclesiastical opponents 61, 172, 173–4; parodying of in *A Midsummer Night's Dream* 163–7; performing in Elizabethan playhouses 160–1; persecution under Mary I 131; of plays and Enterludes in reign of Henry VIII 123; protection by monastic foundations 115; in Protestant polemical plays 119; publication of records in nineteenth century 177; recruited from household servants 12, 58, 60, 84, 88, 93; restriction of in Elizabethan era

215

INDEX

25; replacement of with *Book of Common Prayer* 124; restoration by Mary I 128–9, *see also* Liturgy

Master of the Revels 123, 138, 155, 156, 157, 158–9, 162, 172, 173

Matthew, Gospel of: Beatitudes 134; in Benedictine Easter Sunday Mass 21–2, 45

Maunday Thursday 54

Maxstoke Priory 62

May-Day 40, 62

Mayors: authorisation to arrest actors in James I's reign 172, 173; duties as authorised by Elizabeth I 138; and 'the Mayor's play' 162

Mecca 17

Medieval drama: achievement and legacy of play-makers 76–7, 161, 177–8; final eclipse of traditions of 167, 174, 175; monasteries as giving birth to 152; revival of interest in eighteenth and nineteenth centuries 167; sources of information on performances 89–92, *see also* Middle Ages

Medina 17

Medwall, Henry 35, 99–100, 110

Mendicant friars 26, 35, 53–4, 68

Mercers' Livery Company 59

The Merchant of Venice (Shakespeare) 176

Merchants: aiding of professional acting companies 152; founding of new schools 100

Meriasek, St. 85

The Merry Wives of Windsor (Shakespeare) 32

Meyerhold, Vsevolod 183

Middle Ages: achievements in nurturing dramatic art 43; understanding of 'acting' and 'playing' 63; understanding of Easter Mass 65, *see also* Medieval drama

Middle class: emergence of 52; rise in Tudor England 99, 184–5

Middlesex 159

Middleton, Thomas 185

Midlands: popular agitation against Mary I 130

A Midsummer Night's Dream (Shakespeare) 36, 163–7, 176

Milan: auditoria 10

Miletus, Abbot 16

Mimes 48, 49, 94; Graeco-Roman 13, 14, 49

Mimesis: survival of ancient Greek spirit of 19–20

Mind Will and Understanding see Wisdom

Minstrels: in thirteenth-century troupes 49

Minute Books: information about medieval performances 89–92

Miracle Cycles *see* Mystery (or Miracle) Cycles

Moisewitch, Tanya 182

Monastic foundations: birth of religious drama in medieval era 152; corrals in Iberian Peninsular 11; dissolution of 6, 7, 118, 124, 129; elaboration of liturgies 20–1; growth and influence 16; itinerant and mendicant communities 26, 53, 68; Latin words describing players 44; libraries 16, 51, 53, 74, 80, 118; play-makers 47; practice of amateur acting 4; refectories as performance spaces 29; under threat following Act of Supremacy 1534 115–16

Monastic Orders 28, *see also* Benedictines; Dominicans; Franciscans

Monck, Nugent: attempt to stage Passion Plays in 1901 179

Monks: as actors of plays and Enterludes 123

Moothalls 30, 31, 36, 37, 162, 173

Moral Interludes 29, 32, 35, 58–9, 60, 84–8, 93, 99, 110, 138; twentieth-century revivals 167, 179, 183

Morality Plays 29, 34, 58, 63, 84, 85–8, 92–3; style of continued throughout Elizabethan

229

INDEX

Tegerensee (Bavaria) 51
The Tempest (Shakespeare) 176
Terence 16, 29, 51, 80, 110–11
Tertullian 14
Tewkesbury Abbey 179
The Theater (Shoreditch) 42, 134, 153, 163
Theatre critics 177, 178, 183
Theatre-goers: late nineteenth century 178; pilloried in sixteenth-century satires 185, *see also* Audiences
Theatres: Cornish Cycle of Mystery Plays 81–2, **82**; erected for Corpus Christi performances 80; fifth-century closure of Roman establishments 19, 49; Hellenistic 13; seen as abomination by Christian fathers 53, *see also* Playhouses
Theatrical performance: acceptance of as part of celebration 42; achievements of Middle Ages 43; broadening horizons in Elizabethan era 152; celebration of Church Calendar Festivals 3–4; consequences of creation of Feast of Corpus Christi 69–70; continuation of style of Corpus Christi Cycles 135; denial of to provinces for twenty years 175; Elizabeth I's measures to control 137, 168–9; ending of by Charles I's Parliament 174; extensions in Courts of Henry VII and VIII 109; foundations of secular drama 27–8; Graeco-Roman populist culture 14; Guildhall regulation of (1574) 156–8; gulf between neo-classical and traditional tastes 169–70; late nineteenth- and twentieth-century experiments 178–80; opportunities in banquet halls 35; problem of legitimacy with Reformation 3, 17, 42; rapid growth in fifteenth century 84; rapid growth in medieval London 72; restriction by royal Proclamations 121–3, 125–6,

127–8, 129–30, 137–8; role of Church and town halls 37, 38; threatened due to Reformation 42; transfiguration into professional and commercialised forms 159–60, 168–9; twentieth-century revolution 183; under threat at time of Elizabeth I's accession 131
Theatrical representation: affected by social changes Henry VII's reign 98; different methods of presenting Corpus Christi plays 80–4; effect of emergence of middle class 52; effects of Vatican reforms 68–9; emblematic nature of medieval plays 77–8, 174; erosion in sixteenth and seventeenth centuries 94; final eclipse of medieval traditions 175; iconography of Corpus Christi plays 75; medieval understanding of 63, 167; rebirth in liturgical ceremonial 23, 24, 25, 27; twentieth-century restoring of early principles 180–1; visual iconography used in Elizabethan playhouses 159–60, 161
Les Théophileans (society) 181
Thomas à Becket *see* Becket, St. Thomas à
Thomskrew, Robert (Alderman) 91
Thordon (Suffolk) 117
Tilney, Edmund (Master of the Revels) 158–9, 168
Tiltyards 33, 34–5, 36, 59
Tiring house: in Elizabethan playhouses 160
Tokyo: Japanese 'Globe' Theatre 182
Toronto, University of 182
Torrigiano, Pietro 100
Toto del Nunziato, Antonio 100
Tournaments 33, 34, 36, 41, 59, 103
Town halls 30, 31, 37–8, 56, 71, 93, 94, 173
Townley manuscript 76
Towns: civic pageantry for festive occasions 38–9; growth in

237

INDEX

Christi plays 73, 76; revival of Corpus Christi plays in recent times 167, 180
Wales 101, 130
Walpole, Horace 177
Wambus, Francis 172–3
Wanamaker, Sam: reconstruction of second Globe Theatre 178–9
Wareham, William (Archbishop of Canterbury) 107, 114
Wars of the Roses 64, 84, 97, 101
Warwick, Earl of 155
Warwickshire 140, see also Coventry; Maxstoke Priory
Wassail 40, 62
Wedekind, Frank 181
Westminster: Caxton's printing press 63; removal of Court of Richard II from 57; sparing of monastery from dissolution 118
Westminster Abbey 98
Whetstone, George: *Promos and Cassandra* 161
Whitehall Palace 34–5, 175
Whitsuntide (Pentecost) 3, 24, 67, 68; Corpus Christi Cycle in Chester 6, 57, 71, 73, 114; stopping of Chester plays 149–51
William of Nassyngton 50
William of Wykeham (Bishop of Wincester) 50
Wilson, Robert 155
Winchester: Benedictine community 21
Winchester College 50, 62, 116
Windsor Castle: Royal Chapel 154
Wisdom (Mind Will and Understanding) 35, 84
Witt, Johannes de 178

Wolsey, Thomas 107–8, 110, 111, 112, 113, 119, 184
Worcester: reception of Henry VII during provincial Progress 98
Wordsworth, William 177
Worship: as dramatic performance in Mass ceremonies 23–4; *laissez-faire* stance of Elizabeth I towards 138
Wrestling: in Moral Interludes 99
Writers: extending horizons to secular world 24, see also Playwrights and Playwriting
Wycliffe, John 94

Yeomen of the Guard 98
York: censoring of religious drama in Elizabethan era 148–9, 152; Corpus Christi plays 8, 47, 57, 69–70, 71, 72, 73, 76, 78, 91, 119, 131; establishment of Ecclesiastical Commission 138; Mystery Plays 38; persecution of papists ordered by Henry VIII 6, 117–18; play dramatising life of St. Dionysys 59; reception of Henry VII during provincial Progress 98, 101; replacement of Corpus Christi Cycle by Creed play 145–6; restricting of Corpus Christi Cycle following Chantries Act 125; revival of Mystery Plays by Browne and Eliot 180; rioting following suppression of plays 6; staging of Corpus Christi plays in recent times 167, 180; on touring circuit of Elizabethan players 162
Yule 40, 62, 148

239